Lecture Notes in Computer Science   11521

Commenced Publication in 1973
Founding and Former Series Editors:
Gerhard Goos, Juris Hartmanis, and Jan van Leeuwen

More information about this series at http://www.springer.com/series/7410

James Joshi · Surya Nepal · ·
Qi Zhang · Liang-Jie Zhang (Eds.)

Blockchain – ICBC 2019

Second International Conference
Held as Part of the Services Conference Federation, SCF 2019
San Diego, CA, USA, June 25–30, 2019
Proceedings

 Springer

Editors
James Joshi (iD)
University of Pittsburgh
Pittsburgh, PA, USA

Surya Nepal
CSIRO Data61
Sydney, NSW, Australia

Qi Zhang
IBM Research – Thomas J. Watson
Research Center
Yorktown Heights, NY, USA

Liang-Jie Zhang (iD)
Kingdee International Software
Group Co., Ltd.
Shenzhen, China

ISSN 0302-9743   ISSN 1611-3349   (electronic)
Lecture Notes in Computer Science
ISBN 978-3-030-23403-4   ISBN 978-3-030-23404-1   (eBook)
https://doi.org/10.1007/978-3-030-23404-1

LNCS Sublibrary: SL4 – Security and Cryptology

This Springer imprint is published by the registered company Springer Nature Switzerland AG
The registered company address is: Gewerbestrasse 11, 6330 Cham, Switzerland

Preface

The 2019 International Conference on Blockchain (ICBC) aimed to provide an international forum for researchers and industry practitioners alike to exchange the latest fundamental advances in the state-of-the-art technologies and best practices of blockchain, as well as emerging standards and research topics that would define the future of blockchain.

ICBC 2019 was part of the Services Conference Federation (SCF). SCF 2019 had the following ten collocated service-oriented sister conferences: 2019 International Conference on Web Services (ICWS 2019), 2019 International Conference on Cloud Computing (CLOUD 2019), 2019 International Conference on Services Computing (SCC 2019), 2019 International Congress on Big Data (BigData 2019), 2019 International Conference on AI & Mobile Services (AIMS 2019), 2019 World Congress on Services (SERVICES 2019), 2019 International Congress on Internet of Things (ICIOT 2019), 2019 International Conference on Cognitive Computing (ICCC 2019), 2019 International Conference on Edge Computing (EDGE 2019), and 2019 International Conference on Blockchain (ICBC 2019). As the founding member of SCF, the First International Conference on Web Services (ICWS) was held in June 2003 in Las Vegas, USA. The First International Conference on Web Services – Europe 2003 (ICWS-Europe 2003) was held in Germany in October 2003. ICWS-Europe 2003 was an extended event of the 2003 International Conference on Web Services (ICWS 2003) in Europe. In 2004, ICWS-Europe was changed to the European Conference on Web Services (ECOWS), which was held in Erfurt, Germany. To celebrate its 16th birthday, SCF 2018 was held successfully in Seattle, USA.

This volume presents the accepted papers for the 2019 International Conference on Blockchain (ICBC 2019), held in San Diego, USA, during June 25–30, 2019. All topics regarding blockchain technologies, platforms, solutions and business models align with the theme of ICBC. Topics of interest include, but are not limited to, new blockchain architecture, platform constructions, blockchain development and blockchain services technologies as well as standards, and blockchain services innovation lifecycle including enterprise modeling, business consulting, solution creation, services orchestration, services optimization, services management, services marketing, business process integration and management.

We accepted 15 papers, including 13 full papers and two short papers. Each was reviewed and selected by at least three independent members of the ICBC 2019 International Program Committee. We are pleased to thank the authors, whose submissions and participation made this conference possible. We also want to express our thanks to the Program Committee members, for their dedication in helping to organize the conference and in reviewing the submissions. We would like to thank Prof. Bhavani Thuraisingham and Prof. Jeffrey Tsai, who provided continuous support for this conference. We look forward to your great contributions as a volunteer, author, and conference participant for the fast-growing worldwide services innovations community.

May 2019

James Joshi
Surya Nepal
Qi Zhang
Liang-Jie Zhang

Organization

General Chairs

Bhavani Thuraisingham   The University of Texas at Dallas, USA
Jeffrey Tsai   Asia University

Program Co-chairs

James Joshi   University of Pittsburgh, USA
Surya Nepal   CSIRO Data61, Australia
Qi Zhang   IBM Thomas J. Watson Research Center, USA

Services Conference Federation (SCF 2019)

SCF 2019 General Chairs

Calton Pu   Georgia Tech, USA
Wu Chou   Essenlix Corporation, USA
Ali Arsanjani   8x8 Cloud Communications, USA

SCF 2019 Program Chair

Liang-Jie Zhang   Kingdee International Software Group Co., Ltd., China

SCF 2019 Finance Chair

Min Luo   Services Society, USA

SCF 2019 Industry Exhibit and International Affairs Chair

Zhixiong Chen   Mercy College, USA

SCF 2019 Operations Committee

Huan Chen   Kingdee International Software Group Co., Ltd., China
Jing Zeng   Kingdee International Software Group Co., Ltd., China
Liping Deng   Kingdee International Software Group Co., Ltd., China
Yishuang Ning   Tsinghua University, China
Sheng He   Tsinghua University, China

SCF 2019 Steering Committee

Calton Pu (Co-chair)   Georgia Tech, USA
Liang-Jie Zhang (Co-chair)   Kingdee International Software Group Co., Ltd., China

ICBC 2019 Program Committee

Ladjel Bellatreche	LISI/ENSMA University of Poitiers, France
Bo Cheng	Beijing University of Posts and Telecommunications, China
Roberto Di Pietro	Hamad Bin Khalifa University, Qatar
Praveen Jayachandran	IBM India, India
Nagarajan Kandasamy	Drexel University, USA
Qinghua Lu	CSIRO, Australia
Reza M. Parizi	Kennesaw State University, USA
Catalin Meirosu	Ericsson, Sweden
Vallipuram Muthukkumarasamy	Griffith University, Australia
Roberto Natella	Federico II University of Naples, Italy
Petr Novotny	IBM Thomas J. Watson Research Center, USA
Jiuyun Xu	China University of Petroleum, China
Xiwei Xu	CSIRO Data61 and UNSW, Australia
Lina Yao	University of New South Wales, Australia
Rui Zhang	Institute of Information Engineering, Chinese Academy of Sciences, China
Salman Baset	Columbia University, USA
Luca Cagliero	Politecnico di Torino, USA
Salil Kanhere	UNSW Sydney, Australia
Rudrapatna Shyamasundar	Indian Institute of Technology Bombay, India
Carol Fung	Virginia Commonwealth University, USA
Bhaskar Krishnamachari	University of Southern California, USA
Albert Lam	The University of Hong Kong, SAR China
Damian Andrew Tamburri	Politenico di Milano, Italy
Andreas Veneris	University of Toronto, Canada
Jiayu Zhou	ASU, USA
Huan Chen	Kingdee International Software Group Co., Ltd., China
Shiping Chen	CSIRO, Australia
Gowri Ramachandran	University of Southern California, USA
Ernesto Pimentel	University of Malaga, Spain
Paci Federica Maria	University of Southampton, UK

Contents

Blockchain: An Empirical Investigation of Its Scope for Improvement

Evgeniia Filippova[1(✉)], Arno Scharl[2], and Pavel Filippov[3]

[1] Interdisciplinary Research Institute for Cryptoeconomics,
WU Vienna University of Economics and Business, Welthandelsplatz 1,
1210 Vienna, Austria
evgeniia.filippova@wu.ac.at
[2] Department of New Media Technology, MODUL University Vienna,
Am Kahlenberg 1, 1190 Vienna, Austria
[3] Technical University Vienna, Karlsplatz 13, 1040 Vienna, Austria

Abstract. General Purpose Technologies, or GPTs are defined in the economic literature as the key technologies that shape the economy. Despite the large conceptual literature base on Blockchain potential to revolutionize the current economic system, there is a lack of empirical research on its economic nature and the course of technological development. The paper at hand covers this research gap by providing the quantitative approach aimed at understanding the evolutionary path of Blockchain and its scope for improvement – an acknowledged feature of a GPT - in line with the industrial dynamics and GPT literature. The longitudinal analysis of Blockchain-related patents from PATSTAT and their rule-based classification both from technological and application perspectives is complemented by the study of Blockchain media landscape to provide insights into the social context in which it emerges. The increasing amount of patents addressing essential technical issues, such as security, scalability, and usability contribute to wider adoption of the technology, whereas the positive sentiment in the media associated with Blockchain creates beneficial social context for its development. The empirical results advance the claim that Blockchain does show a positive scope for improvement peculiar to the GPTs in the making and, therefore, deserves attention as a technology that will define macroeconomic dynamics in a long term.

Keywords: Blockchain · General Purpose Technologies · Web intelligence

1 Introduction

Key technologies that determine macroeconomic dynamics in long-term and cause major changes in economic, social and political structures are defined as General Purpose Technologies, or GPTs, in the economic literature [2]. Along with transforming GPTs of the past, such as electricity, steam engine [9], information and communication technology [5], and nanotechnology [25, 36] to name the few, Blockchain is often addressed as a game-changing technology with potential to reshape the economy [13].

© Springer Nature Switzerland AG 2019
J. Joshi et al. (Eds.): ICBC 2019, LNCS 11521, pp. 1–17, 2019.
https://doi.org/10.1007/978-3-030-23404-1_1

Despite the large number of conceptual studies dedicated to disruptive potential of Blockchain, there is still a lack of empirical research on its economic nature and the course of technological development [16]. The paper at hand covers this research gap by providing, to the best of the authors' knowledge, the first empirical investigation of scope of Blockchain-related inventions and their evolution over the time in line with industrial dynamics and GPT literature. Novel to the GPT literature, examination of Blockchain-related inventions is complemented with the study of Blockchain media landscape that provides useful insights into the public discourse around the technology and enables to understand social context in which Blockchain develops [11].

The results of the analysis provide not only insights about course of technological development of Blockchain over the past, but also reveal the economic nature of this technology and its potential impact in the subsequent years, and are, therefore, of relevance for a wide range of readers, including researchers, policy makers, potential investors and practitioners from the industry. Methodological approach that combines patent data with media analytics extends existing literature on technological assessment and can be lately used by scholars for evaluation of other emerging technologies.

The paper is structured as follows. Section 2 introduces the GPT concept and its defining features, provides an overview of technological development of Blockchain and its potential applications across industrial fields, and lists current challenges and hurdles to adoption from the literature. The importance of public discourse around technology and its role for further technological development are also explained in the second section. Data for empirical investigation and employed methods are subjects of Sect. 3 and Sect. 4 accordingly. Section 5 provides overview of development of Blockchain-related inventions over time and visualizes public discourse about this technology. Section 6 concludes and suggests possible directions for the further research.

2   Theoretical Background

2.1   General Purpose Technologies

General Purpose Technologies, or GPTs, is a term used in economic literature to define disruptive technologies that cause long-lasting effects on macroeconomic dynamics and determine the course of economic development [2]. [9] provide the list of 24 GPTs over the history, including electricity, steam engine, railways, information and communication technology, and biotechnology that induced substantial changes in economic and societal structures. Despite various origins and heterogeneous technological nature, GPTs share three defining characteristics: pervasiveness, innovation spawning effects, and scope for improvement [2, 36]. Pervasiveness refers to applicability of a technology to a large number of industries and is commonly measured by a generality index of related inventions [5]. GPTs are sometimes called 'enabling mechanisms' to generate innovation in the downstream application sectors, or cause innovation spawning effects [2]. Scope for improvement, a third necessary feature of a GPT that is in focus of the present paper, has a two-fold definition in the literature. Many scholars observe that "GPTs are improved continuously at every level of the value creation chain" [25], therefore a permanent technological development is regarded a valid indicator for scope for improvement. Other economists point out, that GPTs offer significant benefits to their users and provide solutions to complex technological issues that remained unsolved within the existing technologies [20].

At a conceptual level, a technology's scope for improvement can be identified by generalization of its technological features, while its empirical measurement is based on various approaches. Some authors analyse application sectors of a technology in order to capture its benefits. For example, [20] assesses economic impacts of biotechnology in its four major application areas – pharmaceuticals, agriculture, food and chemical industry. [21] provide descriptive evidence for price decrease and quality increase in various sectors caused by adoption of nanotechnology. Other scholars find patterns of scope for improvement of a technology in related patent data. [25] examines patent filings in nanotechnology and analyse the development of average number of forward citations per patent application. [5] analyse patterns in patenting activity within application sectors of a GPT. The major limitation of these approaches consists in their applicability only to mature technologies, due to a long time lag needed to enable analysis of economic activity within the downstream application sectors. In order to analyse scope for improvement of Blockchain already at its early stage, we suggest complementing patent data with the news articles to provide insights not only about long-term technological development of Blockchain, but also about social context and public discourse around this technology.

2.2 Blockchain Technology

Blockchain, widely known as an underlying technology of Bitcoin [15], expanded its scope beyond cryptocurrencies and found applications in a variety of industrial sectors over the last years [13]. Although the description of Blockchain first appeared in the White Paper of Nakamoto in 2008, its technological pillars – public key cryptography, game theory and distributed computation – have been a subject of active scientific research over the past decades [13, 18]. Game theory explores and mathematically models the behavior of rational decision makers under different conditions. Incentive models from game theory are included into Blockchain protocols through a so-called consensus mechanism. Consensus mechanism is the crucial aspect of Blockchain platform, since it enables decentralized nodes to agree on the state of a ledger without trusting each other and without having a trusted third party [1]. Bitcoin Blockchain is based on the proof-of-work consensus algorithm, however, a range of alternative consensus mechanisms have been developed over the years [18]. For example, proof-of-stake (PoS) consensus is an alternative mechanism, which pseudo-randomly selects a node to validate a creation of a new block, based on the respective stake in the Blockchain. Other consensus models include proof-of-elapsed time, modifications of Byzantine Fault Tolerance Algorithm, Paxos, RAFT and others [1]. Public key cryptography, and its elements such as digital signatures, ring signatures, homomorphic encryption, private and public keys, enables privacy and transparency at one time for Blockchain users [13].

Taken separately, concepts of cryptography, software engineering, and game theory existed long before the Bitcoin, but the combination of them resulted in an innovative technology with a disruptive potential [18]. Typical for the emerging technologies, Blockchain did undergo a substantial development, or scope for improvement in GPT terms, over the last decade. The first aspect of this technological evolution of Blockchain consists in development efforts to overcome its challenges, such as scalability, wasted resources, usability, and others [12, 24]. The second aspect – consistent with the evolutionary theory of technological change [17] – is adaptation of the technology to new application domains beyond cryptocurrencies. Both aspects of continual technological development of Blockchain, being the focus of the present paper, deserve a more detailed description.

Technical Challenges of Blockchain. [24] summarized technical challenges of Blockchain – throughput, latency, size and bandwidth, security, wasted resources, and usability – that were used by several scholars to map existing research and identify promising directions for the further investigation of the technology [12, 35]. There is a wide range of studies that consider some of these technical problems of Blockchain separately. Throughput, or transaction processing rate, of centralized systems is much better than of Blockchain [34]. Logically connected issues, namely size and bandwidth, as well as latency, or time when transactions are considered to be committed, also pose hurdles to adoption especially of public Blockchains [35]. Security is a broad term which refers to the possibility of 51% attack [34], data malleability issues, and authentication problems in cryptocurrency transactions [35]. Wasted resources, an issue that arises particularly due to the proof-of-work consensus mechanism, attracted a lot of attention in the last years, and numerous efforts have been made to make Blockchain more sustainable (see [1] for overview). However, the high power consumption remains a serious matter for Blockchain systems and requires further research efforts [23]. The lack of Blockchain usability is another issue to be improved – development of user-friendly interfaces, visual analytics of data and increase of developer's support should facilitate the acceptance of the technology [23]. Being not a part of the list of technical challenges of Blockchain provided by [24], privacy leakage is another important technical challenge of Blockchain to consider [37].

Table 1. Overview of technical challenges of Blockchain

Challenge	Short description	Reference
Throughput	Relatively low number of transaction inclusions per second	[24]
Latency	Long time until transaction is committed	[35]
Size and bandwidth	Data storage challenges and limited throughput	[12]
Security	51% attack; data malleability; authentication issues	[35]
Privacy	Privacy leakage, lack of anonymity	[37]
Usability	Limited developer and end-user support	[23]
Wasted resources	High energy intensity	[23]

Table 1 summarizes technical challenges of Blockchain that provide the basis for the further empirical investigation of related inventions.

Possible Applications of Blockchain. According to the evolutionary theory of technological change [17], the second aspect of technological development consists in adaptation of a certain technology to the new uses, therefore, it is important to provide a short summary of application areas of Blockchain technology in the discourse of its scope for improvement. The application domains of Blockchain, along with its technical challenges, provide framework for later empirical examination.

Blockchain, being initially an underlying technology of Bitcoin, received increasing attention from other industries over the last years due to the number of its functional features, such as decentralization, persistency, and enabling transactions between actors that do not trust each other without involvement of the third party, and others [13]. Below we summarize some of the Blockchain applications within various domains examined by the large body of literature.

Cryptocurrencies are the first and the most widely known application scenario of Blockchain. [18] revised 460 commercially attractive usages of the technology and grouped them into 17 classes: cryptocurrencies account for 26,5% of total number of Blockchain applications, and financial transactions – for 21%. In fact, Blockchain has a substantial impact on financial services, including payments and money transfer, investments, prediction markets, donations, and others. Blockchain-based solutions also exist in supply chain tracking, energy management and distribution, healthcare, digital identity, internet of things, certificate issuance and verification digital content distribution systems), and e-voting [18]. Blockchain-based tokenization is another promising application that might be beneficial for a variety of industries [7].

2.3 Public Discourse About Blockchain

There is an extensive literature base regarding the social shaping of a technology [31]. According to this concept, "the technology is affected at a fundamental level by the social context in which it develops" [11]. A number of studies explore various social factors that shape the course of technology development and its subsequent adoption [6]. Media landscape and news articles constitute an integral part of the social context in which a technology emerges, therefore, their detailed analysis is used by scholars for predicting technological trends [8]. Social media, and in particular Twitter, remains the most widely used source for exploring users' perceptions of a certain technology [32], whereas news articles map public discourse in the media around a technology and shed light on social context in which technology evolves. News articles provide insights on sentiment and concepts associated with a particular technology, identify opinion leaders and entities that have impact on media, and show the geographical distribution of news coverage [19].

Blockchain, its disruptive nature, and a range of potential applications have been extensively covered in the media over the last years [26], while leading experts from industry and policy makers expressed their opinions regarding this technology. Such a large news coverage represents a fruitful source for exploring public discourse around the technology and defines a social context in which Blockchain develops. Several studies recently focused on examination of Blockchain-related media analytics. [10] examine Blockchain-related Twitter posts over the year posted by media, IT, financial and consulting companies. [6] provides semantic network analysis of tweets regarding Blockchain and cryptocurrencies. Some studies are restrained to Bitcoin coverage in social media. [22] investigate, whether Bitcoin-related tweets can predict its trading volume and volatility, whereas [27] employs Google Trends to analyse interrelation between volumes of Bitcoin trade and its attention in the media. All of these studies are limited to either Twitter analysis or focus solely on cryptocurrencies and Bitcoin and, therefore, do not provide insights on the social context in which Blockchain emerges. A part of empirical analysis of the present paper investigates Blockchain-related news articles and uncovers the recent public discourse around the technology.

3   Data

3.1   Blockchain-Related Patents

Consistent with the other GPT-related studies [5, 25, 36], the primary data source for quantitative assessment of scope for improvement of Blockchain are related patent applications. Despite the general shortcomings of patent data, such as non-patentability of certain inventions, strong dependency on policy and relatively late appearance in the innovation cycle, patents are largely used by scholars to assess technological development [8], identify radical innovations with substantial impact on the economy [36], and uncover potential GPTs [25].

The original code for Bitcoin and underlying technology is open-source, however, Blockchain-related inventions are patent eligible and relate to the field of computer implemented inventions [4]. According to the statistics of the European Patent Office (EPO), Blockchain patent filings mostly represent improvements over an existing technology (scalability and security solutions, privacy enhancing methods, etc.) or refer to adaptation of technology to a specific applications (payment processing, healthcare, Blockchain-based identity, etc.). The growing interest towards Blockchain over the last decade resulted in the exponential growth in related patent applications, from 6 distinct patent families in 2012 to 1,285 in 2017. The source of the Blockchain-related patents is PATSTAT Online, Autumn 2018 Edition – a patent statistical relational database that contains raw patent data from more than 80 patent offices worldwide and is widely used by scholars for mapping technological development [3]. The patents are retrieved from PATSTAT and further analyzed using MySQL queries. Due to the early stages of Blockchain there is still no unified international patent classification (IPC) codes assigned to this technology, which makes identification of the Blockchain patents a challenging task. Other scholars used keyword search in both patent title and abstract to retrieve patents related to emerging technology. However, a keyword 'Blockchain' and its modifications ('Block chain' or 'Block-chain') have other meanings unrelated to Blockchain technology, such as bar-link chain in machinery, copolymer chain in chemistry, and cipher block chain in software engineering. Therefore, in order to retrieve only those patents that are actually related to Blockchain technology and overcome usual shortcomings of the keyword search approach [33], a search strategy for Blockchain patents based on both keywords and IPC codes was developed and verified by the domain experts from the EPO. Table 2 provides summary of the employed search strategy.

Table 2. Search strategy of Blockchain-related patent applications

Only keywords	Keywords and IPC4 classes	Keywords and IPC subclasses
Cryptocurrenc (y/ies) Smart contract Bitcoin Distributed ledger Ethereum Consensus mechanism	Blockchain/Block_chain & G05B, G05D; G06F, G06K, G06N, G06Q; G07B, G07C, G07D, G07F, G07G; G08G; G09C; G10L; G16H; H01B; H04B, H04L, H04M, H04N, H04W	Proof-of-work, digital currenc (y/ies) Hash tree Merkle tree Merkle root Counterparty & G06Q20/065, G06Q20/0655, G06Q20/0658, G06Q20/4016; H04L9/0643, H04L9/3236, H04L9/3239, H04L9/3242, H04L9/3247, H04L9/3252, H04L9/3257, H04L2209/30, H04L2209/38, H04L2209/56

A screening of retrieved patents based on their abstracts and exclusion of applications in languages other than English yielded the sample of 2,073 distinct Blockchain-related patent families filed between 2008 (publication of the Bitcoin white paper) and 2017. Due to insignificant number of Blockchain patented inventions from 2008 to 2013, the patents filed between 2014 and 2017 (total of 2,061) have been considered for the further analysis.

3.2 Blockchain-Related News Articles

In order to explore the media landscape and public discourse around Blockchain, we used a Web crawler to collect news media coverage in four different languages: English, French, German and Spanish. This resulted in a corpus of more than 9.6 million Web documents between August 2018 and January 2019. Using the set of regular expressions shown in Table 3, the advanced search of the webLyzard visual analytics dashboard [29] helped to identify a total of 19,286 Blockchain-related documents (from 01.08.18 to 31.01.19) that have been taken for the further investigation.

Table 3. Search strategy of Blockchain-related news articles

Block(-|)?chain Blockchain technology Bitcoin Ethereum	Distributed ledgers? Cryptocurrenc(y|ies) Consensus mechanisms? proof-of-work	Proof-of-stake block chain technology crypto(-|)?monnaies?

4 Method

4.1 Rule-Based Text Classification of Blockchain-Related Patents

Extensive body of literature on technology management considers two aspects of technological development of emerging technologies – R&D aspect, or research activities to overcome major technical challenges, and application aspect that refers to adaptation of the technology to new application domains [8, 17, 20]. Such a distinction between R&D and application aspects of technological development underlies an empirical analysis in order to map evolution of Blockchain-related inventions.

Table 4. Framework for rule-based text classification of Blockchain patents

Category	Subcategory	Keywords (examples)
R&D aspect	Throughput	Transaction inclusion; lightweight; updating period; etc.
	Latency	Side chains; transaction completion; operation efficiency; etc.
	Size and bandwidth	Blockchain size; data storage; etc.
	Security	Auditability; visibility; transparency; mitigating risk; prevent hacking; etc.
	Privacy	Confidentiality; personal information; etc.
	Usability	User interface; user experience; customized; etc.
	Wasted resources	Power consumption; quantity of electricity; resource waste; etc.
Application aspect	Cryptocurrency transactions	Cryptocurrency transaction; bitcoin transfer; cryptocurrency payment; etc.
	Finance	Trading; prediction markets; settlement; asset management; etc.
	Identity	Blockchain-based identity; KYC; etc.
	Internet of things	IoT; internet-connected devices; etc.
	Supply chain	Supply chain; logistics; verification of goods; etc.
	Digital content distribution	Digital content; permission of content; etc.
	Healthcare	Healthcare; medical records; etc.
	Certificate issuance and verification	Certificate authentication; certificate authority; education certificates; etc.
	Energy distribution	Energy management; photovoltaic power transaction; etc.
	Tokenization	Tokens; tokenization of assets; etc.
	E-voting	Voting; voting data; etc.
Others		Patents that do not related to any of previous categories

To classify Blockchain inventions in R&D and application aspects we use text classification of patents based on their title and abstract. Text classification, also known as text categorization, or topic spotting is widely used by scholars for various purposes, including a deep analysis of a technological field [33]. There are three types of text classification systems: rule-based, machine learning based, and hybrid. Due to the ease of implementation, a large number of R&D and application subcategories and a relatively small sample size (2,061 patents), we chose a rule-based classification system based on manually designed set of rules for subsequent automation. Table 4 summarizes subcategories and examples of related keywords used for classification of Blockchain-related inventions. The identification of the relevant subcategories is based on comprehensive literature review presented in the theoretical background of the paper, whereas keywords were defined empirically by screening a subset of patents. Some patents, depending on core of the invention, relate to more than one subcategory.

4.2 Factual and Affective Knowledge Extraction from Web Content

Automated techniques to extract factual and affective knowledge transform unstructured collections of crawled Web content into structured repositories of actionable knowledge. Such knowledge extraction techniques help to shed light on various types of context information including lexical context – specific entities or sentiment terms that precede or follow a statement [28]; geospatial context– the geospatial references contained in a document [19]; relational context – frequency distribution of named entities in the content repository, and co-occurrence patterns among these entities.

Factual Knowledge. The webLyzard Web intelligence platform includes a named entity recognition and resolution component called *Recognyze* [30] that draws upon structured external linked data sources such as DBpedia.org and Wikidata.org to identify and disambiguate named entities (organizations, persons and locations). The system assigns confidence values and aligns references in a document with the corresponding items of the linked data sources – e.g. the DBpedia entry for the CEO of JPMorgan Chase Jamie Dimon (dbpedia.org/page/Jamie_Dimon). The result is a continuously evolving knowledge graph that helps to understand better communication networks and the dynamic relations among their actors.

Affective Knowledge. The second category includes sentiment and other emotions expressed in a document, which are captured and evaluated by opinion mining algorithms. Such algorithms typically are based on machine learning, lexical methods, or a combination of both [30]. Lexical methods rely on sentiment lexicons, which contain known sentiment terms and their respective sentiment value. The ratio of positive and negative terms found in the vicinity of a target term is used as an indicator of overall polarity. Overall accuracy is improved by considering linguistic features such as negations and intensifiers, and by creating a contextualized version of the sentiment lexicon to disambiguate terms and consider specifics of the domain under consideration. Such a contextualized lexicon contains additional information on possible polarity shifts when a term co-occurs with a specific set of other concepts.

Visualisation of Extracted Knowledge. The various dashboard components, such as trend charts, word tree, and a geographic map, combine factual and affective knowledge to uncover the social context in which a technology emerges. The colorcoding within the diagrams reflects normalized document sentiment, ranging from green (positive) to grey (neutral) and red (negative). Sentiment is shown with variable saturation, depending on the degree of polarity – vivid colors indicate emotional articles or postings, and lower saturation a more factual online coverage.

5   Results

5.1   Scope for Improvement of Blockchain

The number of Blockchain-related patent families remained insignificant in the first five years following the publication of Bitcoin White Paper in 2008 [15]. In the subsequent years, the amount of Blockchain inventions showed exponential growth, from 52 patent families registered in 2014 to 1,285 registered in 2017. In such a way, to ensure a sufficient sample size we considered in our analysis Blockchain patents filed between 2014 and 2017. Applications from 2018 are not taken into account due to their incomplete presence in the current version of PATSTAT. Figure 1 shows evolution of the total number of Blockchain-related patent families between 2014 and 2017 – according to [17] and [25], such a fast growth of patented inventions serves as an indicator for scope for improvement of a technology.

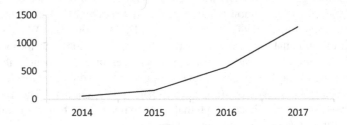

Fig. 1. Number of Blockchain-related patent families (2014–2017)

The closer look at the Blockchain patents showed that inventions that aim at overcoming main technical challenges of Blockchain, such as security, latency and others, from 2016 are getting patented more than applications of the technology in a particular domain (see Fig. 2). On the one side, this trend testifies the relatively early development stage of the technology [13]. On the other side, the fact that technical issues of Blockchain are increasingly addressed within the related inventions is beneficial not only for the course of technology development, but has positive impact on the subsequent adoption of Blockchain by various industries [17].

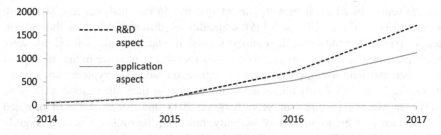

Fig. 2. R&D and application-related Blockchain patents in absolute numbers (2014–2017)

R&D Aspect of Blockchain Patents. What are the technical issues of Blockchain that are addressed in related patents? Which of them are addressed more than the others? How does it evolve over time? The answers to these questions are important to understand the current focus of technological development and predict technology's scope for improvement in the subsequent years.

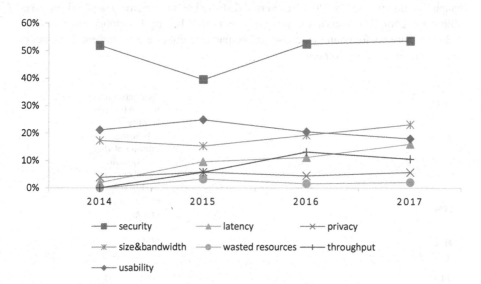

Fig. 3. Relative numbers of Blockchain patents that address R&D aspect (2014–2017)

Following the overall growing trend of Blockchain patents, the absolute number of inventions that relate to all seven technical challenges of Blockchain (see Table 1) does constantly grow between 2014 and 2017. Figure 3 represents how the relative number of patents that address each of these challenges developed over the last four years. Security is the most often addressed technical challenge. Inventions that propose novel solutions to ensure data reliability, prevent Blockchain attacks and malicious behaviour, and ensure safety of transactions are classified under security aspect which still remains one of the most crucial factors for a wider adoption of Blockchain [37]. Scalability is another necessary challenge to overcome in order to ensure competitiveness of Blockchain with current systems. In our analysis, consistent with the approaches of [12, 24], and [35] scalability is differentiated into throughput, latency, size and bandwidth. Inventions addressing latency and throughput were underrepresented in 2014, however, their number started to increase in the subsequent years. Size and bandwidth, particularly in connection with the cryptocurrency trans-actions, was more frequently addressed in the beginning than other elements of scal-ability. On average for the four years between 2014 and 2017, 21.1% of patented solutions aim at overcoming lack of usability, however, their relative number slightly declines (21.15% in 2014 versus 17.98% in 2017). Evident from the Fig. 3, wasted resources, though being often addressed in the literature [23], remains still heavily underrepresented in the patent data. Other scholars came to the similar conclusion with the analysis of other Blockchain-related data sources [35].

Application Aspect of Blockchain Patents. After having analysed the R&D aspect of Blockchain-related patents, we additionally examined their application aspect in order to get a complete picture of evolution of the technology in the last years. Blockchain is patented mainly in the eleven application areas, including cryptocurrency transactions, financial infrastructure, healthcare, energy distribution management and others (see Table 4 for complete overview). Several patents that belong to application domains other than these, as for example, construction management or e-government, have been grouped under category 'others'.

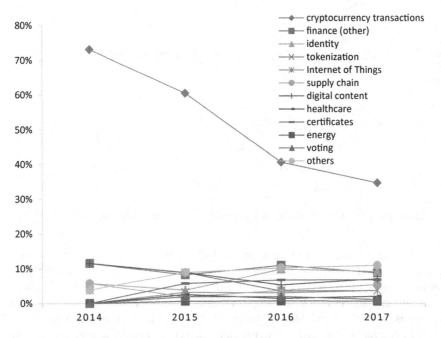

Fig. 4. Relative numbers of Blockchain patents that address application aspect (2014–2017)

As clearly evident from the Fig. 4, inventions related to cryptocurrency transactions prevail, however, their relative number decreases. If 73.08% of all Blockchain-related patents filed in 2014 belonged to cryptocurrency transactions, in 2017 their amount accounts for 34.71%. Applications of Blockchain in various domains of finance, on average, equal to 10% of the total patent filings. In such a way, there is a clear empirical evidence that financial industry is being more than others disrupted by Blockchain [13]. In 2014, applications of Blockchain in only six application areas, such as identity, tokenization, supply chain, digital content distribution in addition to cryptocurrencies and other areas of finance, have been patented. In the next years, their number doubled, and other domains, such as healthcare, issuance and verification of certificates, voting, and others have been added to possible usages of Blockchain. Such an expanding to various domains is an evidence not only for continuous technological evolution, but is also a sign of pervasiveness peculiar to General Purpose Technologies [9].

Overall, a deep examination of the R&D and application aspects of Blockchain-related patent data advances the claim that Blockchain does undergo a continual technological development and, therefore, shows a positive scope for improvement typical for the GPTs in the making [2]. The increasing amount of patents related to fundamental challenges of Blockchain at its early stages contributes to subsequent adoption of the technology, and the growing number of application areas where Blockchain is already applied testifies its pervasive character already now. The next paragraphs, dedicated to related media landscape, complement examination of technical evolution of Blockchain with analysis of the social context in which it evolves.

5.2 Visualizing the Public Discourse About Blockchain

A sentiment analysis of the Blockchain-related news media coverage in four languages (English, French, German and Spanish) between August 2018 and January 2019 showed the overall positive sentiment in the media regarding Blockchain: 69% of news are positive, 24% - negative and 7% are neutral. The trend chart shown in the Fig. 5 compares sentiment across sources in different languages. As evident from the graph, the most positive are French media, followed by Spanish and German media. The sentiment of the English media is substantially lower. In fact, the closer look at the news articles in English language reveals less positive social context: while half of the media is positive, 41% is negative, and 9% - neutral.

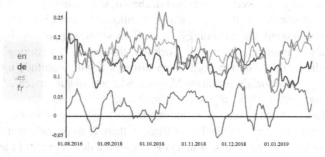

Fig. 5. Sentiment of the English, German, Spanish and French media coverage in Blockchain domain between August 2018 and January 2019

Another trend clearly seen in the Fig. 5 is a strong correlation between the sentiment in the media and cryptocurrency price fluctuations: for example, the rapid fall of Bitcoin price in late November 2018 is reflected in sentiment decrease across news in all four languages.

The word tree visualization of lexical context (see Fig. 6) facilitates the rapid exploration of search results and conveys a better understanding of how language is being used surrounding a Blockchain topic. Based on the popular keyword-in-context technique [28], the specific implementation of the word tree metaphor adopts a symmetrical approach [14]. The root of the tree is the search term – 'Blockchain'. The left and right parts of the tree display all sentence parts that occur before or after the search term (prefix vs. suffix tree).

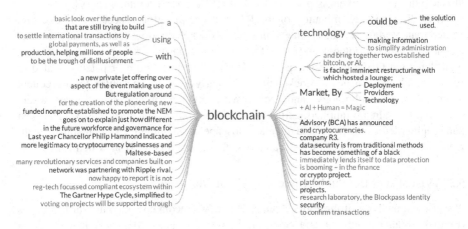

Fig. 6. Word tree representation of search results for the query "Blockchain" in English-language media between August 2018 and January 2019

The atomistic character of the word tree complements aggregated term visualizations such as the tag cloud and keyword graph shown in the Fig. 7. As evident from both the word tree and the tag cloud, the words related to Blockchain with a positive attitude refer to some of it promising application areas, such as finance, global payments and identity, as well as mention technological convergence with artificial intelligence and internet of things. Negative mentions are associated with cryptocurrencies, a hype around the technology, as well as security issues mainly related to cryptocurrency transactions – words such as 'hacking', 'laundering' and 'price volatility' indicate this. The keyword graph displays negative attitude towards ICOs, cryptocurrency, Venezuela's president Maduro, whereas words 'token', 'digital', and 'trading', among others, have a positive connotation.

To conclude, though several news exhibit rather a negative connotation in relation to cryptocurrencies and price volatility of Bitcoin, there is an overall positive sentiment of Blockchain itself in the media, which is fostering the development of technology at the relatively early stages [11].

adoption ai asset atm bank banking bitprime
bloomberg btc bubble cannabis capital cash cent
change cloud coin company compliance computer
computing currency cyber cybersecurity
digital dollar dominance ecosystem enterprise
exchange facebook finance financial fund global
google hacking ibm ico identity index industry
innovation institutional internet investment investor
iot iranian laundering maduro market mining
money network nvidia payment percent platform
price ransom regulation regulatory ripple scam sec
securities software startup tech token trading
transaction value venezuela venture ventures virtual
volatility wallet whatsapp xrp

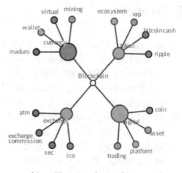

a) Tag cloud   b) Keyword graph

Fig. 7. Tag cloud and keyword graph for the query "Blockchain" in English-language media between August 2018 and January 2019

6 Conclusions and Outlook

The present study goes beyond a conceptual investigation of Blockchain's potential and suggests an empirical approach aimed at understanding the evolutionary path of Blockchain development in line with industrial dynamics and GPT-related literature. The results of the study advance the claim that Blockchain does already possess a scope for improvement – a wide acknowledged feature of the GPT [2, 9]. In such a way, Blockchain deserves attention as an emerging GPT that, along with the other GPTs, will define the long-term macroeconomic dynamics in the subsequent years [2, 25, 36].

The results of the paper are of relevance for a wide range of readers, including scholars, policy makers and experts from the industry. The insights on what technical issues exactly are addressed in Blockchain-related patents, and how does it develop over time provide a solid empirical base for understanding the R&D efforts in the field. Therefore, the results can be used by policy makers for policy adaptation, by practitioners - for evaluation of applicability of technology in the subsequent years, and by scholars – as a starting point for the further analysis of technology. Moreover, other scholars investigating the technological evolution of Blockchain in the future can employ a framework that we developed for the rule-based text classification of Blockchain-related patents. The examination of the media landscape around Blockchain technology represents a novel to the GPT literature extension of the method and provides insights on social shaping of the technology – an important component of its evolution [11].

The study opens numerous possibilities for the further interdisciplinary research in the field. These include empirical measurement of effects of Blockchain on various macroeconomic indicators, usage of the complementary data sources for investigation of Blockchain's scope for improvement, and a consideration of the longer time period for the sentiment analysis of media landscape.

References

1. Baliga, A.: Understanding blockchain consensus models. Persistent (2017)
2. Bresnahan, T., Trajtenberg, M.: General purpose technologies 'Engines of growth'? J. Econom. **65**(1), 83–108 (1995)
3. De Rassenfosse, G., Dernis, H., Boedt, G.: An introduction to the Patstat database with example queries. Aust. Econ. Rev. **47**(3), 395–408 (2014)
4. DiNizo Jr, A.: From alice to bob: the patent eligibility of blockchain in a post-CLS bank world. J. Law Technol. Internet **9**(1), 1–2 (2018)
5. Hall, B., Trajtenberg, M.: Uncovering GPTs with patent data, No. w10901. National Bureau of Economic Research (2004)
6. Hong, Y.: How the discussion on a contested technology in Twitter changes: semantic network analysis of tweets about cryptocurrency and blockchain technology (2018)
7. Kamboj, D., Yang, T.: An exploratory analysis of blockchain: applications, security, and related issues. In: Proceedings of the International Conference on Scientific Computing (CSC), pp. 67–73. The Steering Committee of the World Congress in Computer Science, Computer Engineering and Applied Computing (2018)
8. Li, X., Xie, Q., Jiang, J., Zhou, Y., Huang, L.: Identifying and monitoring the development trends of emerging technologies using patent analysis and Twitter data mining: the case of perovskite solar cell technology. Technol. Forecasting Soc. Change (2018). https://doi.org/10.1016/j.techfore.2018.06.004
9. Lipsey, G., Carlaw, I., Bekar, C.: Economic Transformations: General Purpose Technologies and Long-Term Economic Growth. OUP, Oxford (2005)
10. Lynn, T., Rosati, P., Fox, G.: Legitimizing# Blockchain: an empirical analysis of firm level social media messaging on Twitter. In: 26th European Conference on Information Systems (2018)
11. MacKenzie, D., Wajcman, J.: The Social Shaping of Technology. Open University Press, Buckingham (1999)
12. Mendling, J., et al.: Blockchains for business process management-challenges and opportunities. ACM Trans. Manag. Inf. Syst. (TMIS) **9**(1), 4 (2018)
13. Mougayar, W.: The Business Blockchain: Promise, Practice, and Application of the Next Internet Technology. Wiley, Hoboken (2016)
14. Muralidharan, A., Hearst, M., Fan, C.: WordSeer: a knowledge synthesis environment for textual data. Paper Presented at the 22nd ACM International Conference Information and Knowledge Management (CIKM-2013), San Francisco, USA (2013)
15. Nakamoto, S.: Bitcoin: a peer-to-peer electronic cash system (2008)
16. Risius, M., Spohrer, K.: A blockchain research framework. Bus. Inf. Syst. Eng. **59**(6), 385–409 (2017)
17. Rotolo, D., Hicks, D., Martin, B.: What is an emerging technology? Res. Policy **44**(10), 1827–1843 (2015)
18. Salviotti, G., De Rossi, L., Abbatemarco, N.: A structured framework to assess the business application landscape of blockchain technologies. In: Proceedings of the 51st Hawaii International Conference on System Sciences (2018)
19. Scharl, A., Tochtermann, K.: The Geospatial Web - How Geo-Browsers, Social Software and the Web 2.0 are Shaping the Network Society. Springer, London (2007). https://doi.org/10.1007/978-1-84628-827-2
20. Shea, C.M.: Future management research directions in nanotechnology: a case study. J. Eng. Tech. Manag. **22**(3), 185–200 (2005)
21. Shea, C., Grinde, R., Elmslie, B.: Nanotechnology as general-purpose technology: empirical evidence and implications. Technol. Anal. Strateg. Manag. **23**(2), 175–192 (2011)

22. Shen, D., Urquhart, A., Wang, P.: Does Twitter predict Bitcoin? Econ. Lett. **174**, 118–122 (2019)
23. Sikorski, J., Haughton, J., Kraft, M.: Blockchain technology in the chemical industry: machine-to-machine electricity market. Appl. Energy **195**, 234–246 (2017)
24. Swan, M.: Blockchain: Blueprint for a New Economy. O'Reilly Media, Inc., Sebastopol (2015)
25. Teichert, N.: Innovation in General Purpose Technologies: How Knowledge Gains when It Is Shared. KIT Scientific Publishing, Karlsruhe (2012)
26. Umeh, J.: Blockchain double bubble or double trouble? ITNOW **58**(1), 58–61 (2016)
27. Urquhart, A.: What causes the attention of Bitcoin? Econ. Lett. **166**, 40–44 (2018)
28. Wattenberg, M., Viégas, F.: The word tree, an interactive visual concordance. IEEE Trans. Vis. Comput. Graph. **14**(6), 1221–1228 (2008)
29. WebLyzard. http://www.weblyzard.com/. Accessed 17 Feb 2018
30. Weichselbraun, A., Streiff, D., Scharl, A.: Consolidating heterogeneous enterprise data for named entity linking and web intelligence. Int. J. Artif. Intell. Tools **24**(2), 1540008 (2015)
31. Williams, R., Edge, D.: The social shaping of technology. Res. Policy **25**(6), 865–899 (1996)
32. Williams, S., Terras, M., Warwick, C.: What do people study when they study Twitter? Classifying Twitter related academic papers. J. Doc. **69**(3), 384–410 (2013)
33. Xie, Z., Miyazaki, K.: Evaluating the effectiveness of keyword search strategy for patent identification. World Patent Inf. **35**(1), 20–30 (2013)
34. Xu, X., et al.: A taxonomy of blockchain-based systems for architecture design. In: 2017 IEEE International Conference on Software Architecture (ICSA), pp. 243–252. IEEE (2017)
35. Yli-Huumo, J., Ko, D., Choi, S., Park, S., Smolander, K.: Where is current research on blockchain technology?—a systematic review. PLoS ONE **11**(10), e0163477 (2016)
36. Youtie, J., Iacopetta, M., Graham, S.: Assessing the nature of nanotechnology: can we uncover an emerging general purpose technology? J. Technol. Transf. **33**(3), 315–329 (2008)
37. Zheng, Z., Xie, S., Dai, H.N., Chen, X., Wang, H.: Blockchain challenges and opportunities: a survey. Int. J. Web Grid Serv. **14**(4), 352–375 (2018)

Establishing Standards for Consensus on Blockchains

Derek Sorensen[(✉)] [ID]

Pyrofex Corporation, 4692 North 300 West Suite 100, Provo, UT 84604, USA
derek@pyrofex.net

Abstract. We survey six popular blockchain consensus algorithms, showing that the blockchain community does not have well-established theoretical foundations. We consolidate and unify these foundational notions, establishing high quality standards and exploring the comparative relationship between foundations used on these different algorithms. The framework established here is meant to be used by academic and industrial blockchain researchers as a foundation for the theory of consensus.

Keywords: Blockchain · Consensus algorithm · Nakamoto consensus · Byzantine fault tolerant · Network model · Adversarial model · Safety · Liveness · Finality

1 Introduction

Blockchain technology, as an academic discipline, is very much in its development phases. New journals, such as *Ledger* and *International Journal of Blockchains and Cryptocurrencies*, have emerged to make a space for academics to discuss the economic, legal, social, mathematical, and computer scientific implications of these technologies. To an academic mathematician entering the field, it is immediately obvious that blockchain-related consensus algorithms are in urgent need of both formalization and standardization. Since most blockchain consensus algorithms come out of industry, these almost never make it through a peer-review process. Instead, they appear on company websites, as white papers, or simply on the ArXiv.

We see important drawbacks from this phenomenon. The first is that blockchain scientists in general do not communicate with each other. While it can, admittedly, be difficult to have research-sensitive conversations because of economic interests, this phenomenon inhibits the field from achieving unity because observations, definitions, techniques, and results end up being rediscovered by each respective party. Not only does this waste time, but each party introduces nuances, and thus more confusion. The second, perhaps a symptom of the first, is that most blockchain consensus algorithms use their own seemingly *ad hoc* definitions of consensus, safety, liveness, finality, and their own, nuanced network assumptions. At times these call distinct notions by the same

© Springer Nature Switzerland AG 2019
J. Joshi et al. (Eds.): ICBC 2019, LNCS 11521, pp. 18–33, 2019.
https://doi.org/10.1007/978-3-030-23404-1_2

name, or equivalent notions by distinct names. For a scientist trying to compare blockchain consensus algorithms, this lack of standardization and communication causes undue confusion and wastes significant amounts of time in comparing author's ideas regarding these more basic notions in addition to the algorithms.

This paper seeks to fulfill two purposes. The first is to compare and contrast the definitions, models, and network assumptions from several popular blockchain consensus algorithms. We show how the notions relate and differ to give motivation for our standardization and insights as to why comparison is so difficult and nearly always unfruitful. The second is to standardize these definitions and notions, relating them back to the foundations of classical, pre-Nakamoto literature on consensus. Our purpose here is not to give a survey of consensus, nor to give readers a sense of existing consensus algorithms. Rather, our purpose is to inform researchers who are either selecting a consensus algorithm for a new blockchain or building a consensus algorithm of their own, what high-quality foundations look like and why they must take them seriously.

In this paper, we explore six fundamental notions underlying consensus on a blockchain, which are: Byzantine agreement, network assumptions, the adversarial model, finality, safety, and liveness. For each of these notions, we demonstrate the lack of unity and the ensuing problems with the following consensus algorithms: Nakamoto's consensus algorithm [14] run on BTC and ETH, PBFT [4], Gosig [11], Best of Both Worlds (BoBW) [12], Ouroboros [10], and Honey Badger BFT [13]. Realizing that we could not survey every popular consensus algorithm, we chose to only survey from those that have published papers and that claim to have proofs of both safety and liveness in the face of a Byzantine adversary. Thus we neglect some popular algorithms such as Raft [6], which explicitly only treats crash faults, and Tangaroa [5], which lacks a proofs altogether. As part of this analysis we also propose standard definitions sufficiently general to apply to any consensus algorithm on a blockchain or blockdag.

2   Related Work

There have been several efforts to give summaries, descriptions, or taxonomies on different aspects of blockchain technology. While these are, in general, very useful, each has their own goals, and none of these work exclusively within the mathematical foundations of consensus like we do here.

For example, [15, 21, 22] give surveys of consensus algorithms as they exist within the blockchain world. These introduce concepts such as proof of work or proof of stake, and give examples. We assume that our reader is familiar with consensus algorithms used within industry. Instead of giving a survey of the algorithms themselves, we survey their theoretical foundations.

Similarly, [18–20] give surveys of consensus algorithms but do so from a practical perspective, describing the technology itself or its performance metrics. For example, [18] focuses on and analyzes the Stellar Consensus Protocol and the Linux Foundation's hyperledger product; [20] focuses on the issue of scaling, contrasting proof-of-work algorithms with BFT replication; and [19] gives an introduction to the technology surrounding Bitcoin, including concepts such as double spending, transaction malleability (finality), mining, bonding/unbonding, traffic analysis, and so on. The features of different consensus algorithms mentioned in these articles, while important, do not strongly relate to the topic that we treat of consistency in mathematical models, foundations, and assumptions.

In [23], the authors propose a taxonomy with which one can understand and compare consensus algorithms. In some ways, the purpose of this paper is similar to ours. The standards we establish are meant to facilitate comparison. However, we do so from the standpoint of fundamental, mathematical assumptions, while [23] does so from a feature-oriented perspective. Furthermore, we seek to *set* mathematical standards that blockchain scientists will adopt so that the consensus algorithms produced within industry can be rationally compared to one another. These standards do not yet exist, and without them it is extremely difficult to perform any meaningful, mathematical comparison.

Perhaps the article closest in purpose and content to ours is [3], which explores blockchain consensus algorithms "in the wild". The authors briefly touch on definitions and assumptions related to safety, though they do not mention in rigorous detail the other key concepts that we cover such as network assumptions, adversarial model, liveness, and finality. Furthermore, the definition given for safety does not apply to consensus on blockdags such as [1,2,7,17]. While they do criticize some consensus algorithms, such as Tangaroa [5], as lacking in theoretical fondations, the authors neither propose standards nor thoroughly explore the essential foundations of consensus.

The mathematical standards we propose tie consensus algorithms that have emerged for the specific purpose of the blockchain to classical consensus algorithms made for general distributed systems. In the process, we uniquely give a survey of mathematical foundations to show the need for such standards to exist. Our principal contribution is to propose standards that ground blockchain consensus firmly in solid mathematical theory, making it more feasible to compare consensus algorithms in terms of their network and adversarial models, finality properties, and conditions for safety and liveness.

3   Byzantine Agreement

Every consensus algorithm for a practical blockchain tries to achieve *Byzantine agreement*, which is to achieve safety, liveness, and finality under some specified network assumptions and a given adversarial model. Byzantine agreement is the core problem to be solved, and so should have a standard, constant definition that we can all draw from. Surprisingly, only two of the algorithms we surveyed explicitly stated a definition of Byzantine agreement, and those definitions that were explicitly stated differed in nontrivial ways. The remaining algorithms neglected to mention the problem in any formal way. We find this perplexing, as one cannot know if a problem has been solved if there is no good definition to begin with.

To illustrate our point, consider those two algorithms, BoBW [12] and Honey Badger BFT [13], that actually stated definitions of Byzantine agreement. The former, in Definition 3.1, defines Byzantine agreement to be a distributed protocol Π that satisfies *validity*, *consistency*, and *p-termination*. The latter, in Appendix C, requires *agreement*, *termination*, and *validity*. In these definitions, BoBW's consistency corresponds to Honey Bader's agreement, but both definitions of termination and validity differ. Honey Badger's definition of termination corresponds to a quasi-combination of BoBW's validity and p-termination, without reference to any probability p. The notion of validity as defined in Honey Badger isn't even found in BoBW's definitions.

The importance of having a clear objective in research cannot be understated. We cannot achieve a goal we do not set. Even more troubling than inconsistent definitions is no definition at all. Not only does this betray a lack of rigorous thinking, but it can be actively deceptive. Since there was no rigorous problem definition to begin with, these papers usually declare their algorithms to be satisfactory if they meet some benchmark of safety and liveness that the authors place, seemingly arbitrarily. From these kinds of arguments, it is never clear if a given algorithm actually satisfies its purpose, since there was no concrete purpose to begin with.

We reiterate that the problem of achieving Byzantine agreement on a blockchain is simply to achieve safety, liveness, and finality under specified network assumptions and a adversarial model. These five mentioned components, then, must necessarily be standard notions if we are to claim to be after the same problem.

In all of the definitions that follow, we follow convention and use N to refer to the total number of members of consensus, and f to be the number of Byzantine nodes, those nodes whose behavior can be arbitrary. As these notions do not apply to Nakamoto consensus [14], where appropriate we specify the analogous notions specific to that case. We call members of consensus *validators*.

4   Network Assumptions

We prefer a minimalist approach to network assumptions. While it is impossible to guarantee consensus on a fully asynchronous network, it is possible to achieve consensus under some mild assumptions [8]. The weakest of these, which we see as the gold standard, is *intermittent synchrony*. A network is intermittently synchronous, or Δ-intermittently synchronous, if any interval of time can be extended to one during which the average message delay is at most Δ (for a more technical definition, see the Appendix of [13]).

Of the consensus algorithms we review in this paper, only Honey Badger has proofs based on intermittent synchrony. The rest assume variants or special cases of a slightly stronger assumption called *partial synchrony*. A network is partially synchronous if there exists some finite time bound Δ before which all messages get delivered. Researchers should be careful not to require knowledge, or even an estimate, of Δ at any point in the consensus algorithm. Most commonly, safety is achievable in complete asynchrony; it is usually liveness that requires intermittent or partial synchrony. Partial synchrony is strictly stronger than intermittent synchrony [13], though as we remark at the end of this section, in practice the difference between the two is insignificant.

Many of the algorithms we compare make this partial synchrony assumption, some opting for a variation that says partial synchrony holds after some time t, often called the *Global Stabilization Time*. Most, however, make other subtle assumptions about the network that are difficult to compare with each other. For example, for safety Gosig assumes partial synchrony but also requires that any adaptive attacks on validators take effect only after a delay of time Δ. For liveness, it assumes partially synchronized clocks, meaning that any two validator's local clocks only differ by some fixed number [11, §3.2]. In contrast, in addition to assuming partial synchrony, Best of Both Worlds (BoBW) assumes that validators are in *lock step*, which means that they proceed in rounds of fixed time and any two validators are always within some fixed bound of each other in consensus. This may seem stronger than Gosig's partially synchronized clocks assumption, but as the authors of BoBW point out, one can achieve lockstep synchrony with partial synchrony and partially synchronized clocks, which they call *bounded drift* [12, p. 7].

Thus, aside from BoBW assuming that validators proceed through consensus in rounds of fixed length and Gosig assuming that adaptive attacks take effect after a delay, BoBW and Gosig carry the same network assumptions but present them with different terminology and in entirely different ways. For a researcher seeking to read and compare these algorithms, it is not easy to tell that they rest on almost identical network assumptions. Even with this insight in place, because of these additional, nuanced assumptions that BoBW and Gosig, respectively, make, it is yet unclear how to compare the algorithms because of a differing network model. In particular, it is unclear that either of these assumptions is easy to satisfy in practice, or even that one is stronger or less desireable than the other.

PBFT also assumes partial synchrony, but uses entirely different language than BoBW and Gosig to do it. Rather than assuming a bounded delay, the authors define partial synchrony to be that $delay(t)$, the time a message sent at time t is delivered to its recipient, cannot grow faster than t indefinitely [4, §3]. In other words, there is an upper bound Δ on the delay between a message being sent and it being received. Of the algorithms we surveyed, PBFT is the only one to make the partial synchrony assumption and nothing else. Still, it is difficult to compare its network model with others if such a fundamental notion is defined in this uncommon way.

Finally, Ouroboros' assumptions are simply incomparable to the others. It assumes a form of lockstep, without using any standard terminology, which appears to be strictly stronger than that of BoBW, as it says that any difference in validator's local clocks is insignificant in comparison to the length of computational steps in the algorithm. It also assumes, again without standard terminology, a very strong form of synchrony, which is that any message is received within the length of a computational step in the algorithm. Recognizing how practically infeasible this is, Ouroboros is manifestly inferior to the others because these assumptions sharply curb the speed at which the network can execute the algorithm.

As the authors of Honey Badger point out, intermittent synchrony more accurately models the real world and is evidently superior to partial synchrony [13, §3]. We take the position that any researcher building a consensus algorithm should do so assuming only intermittent synchrony. While inferior, we also recognize that partial synchrony, in either form of the definition, still works in practice. If the algorithm requires assumptions additional to partial synchrony, the authors should provide evidence that they are readily satisfiable in practice for any network or algorithm. They should also try to quantify any resulting effects of these assumptions on network speed or algorithm performance. In order to make fruitful comparisons between consensus algorithms, authors should be explicit on any network assumptions that do not fall in either of these categories, including restrictions on hardware, requirements such as bandwidth or computation power, and so on.

Remark 1. The authors of Honey Badger mention that those consensus algorithms that require partial, as opposed to intermittent, synchrony often rely on the upper bound Δ in such a way that an intermittently synchronous network could starve the system. The example they give is a network that exhibits longer and longer periods of asynchrony, with corresponding longer and longer periods of synchrony. In the case of PBFT, this can starve the system, while Honey Badger would still make progress. However, for practical purposes this network would also starve Honey Badger if, for example, the network delays go on for more than a day, or a week, or a year.

The conclusion from their analysis is that an algorithm that performs well on an intermittently synchronous network can perform better in general than one that uses the partial synchrony assumption to deal with faults via timeouts. It is yet unclear how these algorithms that use the partial synchrony assumption for something other than timeouts compare in performance to those that can use intermittent synchrony. Since, in practice, messages still need to arrive in a reasonable time frame for any algorithm to be live, we do not see a meaningful difference between these intermittent and partial synchrony (Fig. 1).

5   Adversarial Model

In general we see it as essential that researchers assume the strongest adversarial model possible, so as to give the most accurate picture of an algorithm's strength. This includes assumptions about the proportion of malicious agents and their behavior.

The standard is to assume that some number less than $\frac{N}{3}$ of validators are Byzantine. Their behavior can be arbitrary, including intentionally malicious activity, collusion, or inactivity. If the protocol uses cryptographic tools, there should be clear assumptions about what a malicious validator can and cannot do. In this case it is reasonable to assume that Byzantine validators can't forge

Standard Network Assumption	Intermittent synchrony, or Δ-intermittent synchrony, that one can always find an interval of time during which the average message delay is at most Δ.		
Algorithm	**Network Assumptions**	**Special Case of Standard?**	**How It Differs From The Standard**
Nakamoto	No network assumptions.		
PBFT	Assumes partial synchrony, using a unique definition, asserting that the function $delay(t)$ does not grow faster than t indefinitely.	Yes.	Using the function $delay(t)$ is not standard, but turns out to be a special case of partial synchrony. For a proof, see Proposition 4 in the Appendix.
Gosig	Assumes for safety partial synchrony and that adaptive attacks take effect only after a delay of time Δ. For liveness, also assumes partially synchronized clocks.	Yes.	In addition to partial synchrony, assumes a delay of time Δ in adaptive attacks, as well as partially synchronized clocks.
BoBW	Assumes partial synchrony as well as lock step synchrony.	Yes.	Assumes that validators proceed in rounds of fixed time, and that any two validator are always within some fixed bound of each other in consensus. The latter assumption is equivalent to partially synchronized clocks.
Ouroboros	Assumes, with nonstandard terminology, a form of lock step. From the definition it is unclear how that compares with other definitions of lock step. Also assumes a strong form of synchrony.	Yes.	Strengthens partial synchrony to strong synchrony. Also assumes a form of lock step synchrony.
Honey Badger	Assumes Δ-intermittent synchrony.	Yes.	This is the standard, of which partial synchrony is a special case.

Fig. 1. Network assumptions display little to no unity across different algorithms and are thus inherently difficult, if not impossible, to effectively compare with each other. In this table, we compare each to the standard network assumption. As indicated, our recommended standard assumption is weaker than each of those that had explicit assumptions, and strictly so than all but Honey Badger's. This means that each of the network assumptions we analyzed are a special case of the standard, Δ-intermittent synchrony.

signatures or invert hash functions. It is, however, perfectly possible that all the Byzantine nodes collude, even controlling the network to slow consensus, but not to violate network assumptions. For this reason, again, network assumptions must be as light as possible.

Researchers proposing a new consensus algorithm should assume the maximum number of Byzantine validators, $\lfloor \frac{N-1}{3} \rfloor$. These malicious nodes should be assumed to be both colluding and controlling the network, where adversaries can delay messages, duplicate them, or deliver them out of order. Any restrictions on the adversary should be explicitly stated. These include restrictions on which messages the network can drop, what a Byzantine node may or may not know, and even assumptions relating to cryptographic techniques such as hashes or signatures. For example, PBFT states,

> We do assume that the adversary cannot delay correct nodes indefinitely. We also assume that the adversary (and the faulty nodes it controls) are computationally bound so that (with very high probability) it is unable to subvert the cryptographic techniques mentioned above. [4, §2]

BoBW is similarly high quality, in that it assumes a fully adaptive, knowledgeable adversary that can know the entire internal states of all other Byzantine validators. As part of their network assumptions, the authors state,

> The adversary has full control over the network: It has the power to delay messages arbitrarily up to Δ time steps. It can reorder messages, and it can make some messages arrive multiple times at its intended recipient. [12, §3]

Nakamoto's adversarial model is simple, stating that "the system is secure as long as honest nodes collectively control more CPU power than any cooperating group of attacker nodes." [14, §1]. Assumptions related to the hash function, *etc.*, are implicit in the fact that CPU power is the metric of adversarial power.

Honey Badger, on the other hand, only explicitly states that "the [message] delivery schedule is entirely determined by the adversary, but every message sent between correct nodes must eventually be delivered" [13, §4.1]. It reasons about the adversary throughout the paper, but rather than giving a specific model of adversarial behavior beforehand, one discovers the assumed adversarial abilities as the adversary appears in arguments.

There is, for the most part, unity in the blockchain literature about the behavior of Byzantine validators. We advocate explicit, technical definitions of possible Byzantine behavior in order to provide as much rigor as possible. In general, Byzantine behavior should be assumed to be *truly arbitrary* unless the algorithm explicitly states limitations. Any limitations imposed should be clearly stated, though we stress that limitations on Byzantine behavior make comparative analysis difficult at best.

6   Finality

The highest quality consensus algorithms for the blockchain must have both a precise measure of finality and a point at which a block or transaction can be declared final such that, under the network and adversarial assumptions, it is impossible (not just improbable) to be rewritten. Of course, this notion of finality must depend on the assumptions about the network and adversarial model being satisfied. Researchers should also explore any inherent limitations on latency and throughput that the finality conditions in their algorithms impose.

Perhaps unsurprisingly, most algorithms do not mention finality explicitly, but many do exhibit good finality properties. In particular, blockchains built on a consensus algorithm based on rounds of message passing, including most of those we survey here, have an inherent notion of finality because the network decides on one block at a time. Thus once a block has passed through consensus, it becomes final.

For these algorithms, finality on a chain is straightforward, but finality on, for example, a DAG, would be less straightforward and should come with proofs. Other situations which complicate finality are those, like that of Nakamoto's algorithm, that can only give a probability of finality that approaches 1 as time goes on. For both of these kinds of algorithms, researchers should devote the time to give a thorough exposition on their algorithm's finality properties.

The kind of probabilistic finality in Nakamoto's consensus algorithm seems inherent to unpermissioned chains, since one can never fully know the entire set of participants. Understandably, then, of the existing chains, only the permissioned chains give exact statements on finality. Considering the nontrivial security breaches in these unpermissioned chains, most recently ETC [9], we are partial to permissioned chains principally because of their finality properties. Despite having a proof of safety, if a consensus algorithm cannot give definitive finality it can, in practice, not always be safe if the heuristic used to declare a block "safe" is not always reliable.

In the following sections we treat safety and liveness using a notion of exact finality. This, of course, precludes straightforward compatibility with Nakamoto-style proof-of-work consensus. As we mention in Sect. 8, the definitions we give can still be used with probabilistic finality with some minor modifications.

7   Safety

Safety is the first of the two core results that any consensus algorithm absolutely must have. It inherently relies on the notions we have established above, namely network assumptions, adversarial model, and finality. As it is trivial to write an algorithm that is live but not safe, namely that in which each validator produces and finalizes its own blocks only, a consensus algorithm without a proof of safety is pragmatically worthless. In the definition and discussion that follows we refer to blocks as the subject of consensus; however, safety can be equivalently proved on transactions and smart contracts.

Definition 2. *A consensus algorithm is safe if and only if:*

1. Every finalized block is valid, and

2. *For any pair of honest validators v and v' and blocks b and b', if v considers b to be final and v' considers b' to be final, then b and b' do not conflict.*

This definition requires the notions of *validity* and *conflicts* between blocks, both of which should be explicitly defined. For a traditional blockchain, a block is valid if it is constructed correctly according to protocol. Most neglect to mention validity because it is implicit in the adversarial model. That is, since an adversary cannot forge signatures, it is easy to reliably identify a block's sender. The same is true of transactions from clients. As long as the block structure can be easily verified to be correct by looking at the contents, one generally need not prove validity. However, a good researcher will carefully consider the network and adversarial models to ensure that there are no issues of validity, supplying a proof if validity is not self-evident. For an excellent example of a definition of block validity, see Blockmania [7, §2].

Again, on a traditional blockchain, two blocks conflict if they have the same block height and are not equal. In other words, an algorithm is safe if it cannot fork. Most of the algorithms we surveyed capture the essence of safety as we define it here, but the definitions are not equivalent. Definitions of safety tend to come in two camps. The first is that if one honest validator commits a block, then all other honest validators will eventually do the same (see Ouroboros and Honey Badger). The second is that if any two honest validators compare their chains, their blocks at any given height will be identical (see Nakamoto consensus, PBFT, Gosig, and BoBW). While the first implies the second, the second does not imply the first, as the first has a sort of "totality" property (see Proposition 5 in the Appendix for a proof). We opt for the second of these two definitions for safety, as such a totality property decidedly relates to liveness, rather than safety (Fig. 2).

Since it's easy to determine if two blocks conflict on a chain by checking block height, we might be tempted to define property (2) of Definition 2 as if honest validators v and v' each consider b and b' to be final, then either b and b' are at different block heights or they are equal. However, this excludes consensus algorithms that build a block*dag* as opposed to a blockchain, such as [1], [2], [7], and [17]. In this case, a block's height is defined to be one more than the maximum height of its parents, so equality at a given block height is not a sufficient notion to describe conflicts, since there can be many blocks at a any height.

Thus on a blockdag one must clearly define what it means for two blocks to conflict. In Casanova, for example, the authors clearly define the notion of a *conflict domain*, and two blocks conflict if and only if they belong to the same conflict domain [2]. In contrast, in Blockmania the notion of a block conflict is intimately related to the notion of block validity [7, §2], and in Prism conflicts relate to the idea of consistency [1, p. 36], but neither give explicit definitions. For researchers building a consensus algorithm for a blockdag, we recommend clearly defining the notion of block conflicts in order to produce high quality, rigorous proofs.

Algorithm	Terminology for Safety	Translated
Nakamoto	Negligible probability of forking or of a block being overwritten.	No forking.
PBFT	Impossibility of forking.	No forking.
Gosig	Validity and consistency.	If two honest players committed blocks at height n, the blocks are equal.
BoBW	Validity and consistency	If two honest players committed blocks at height n, the blocks are equal.
Ouroboros	Persistence.	If an honest player commits a block, all honest players eventually will.
Honey Badger	Agreement and total order.	If an honest player commits a block, all honest players eventually will, and if two honest players committed blocks at height n, the blocks are equal.

Fig. 2. Modulo the mention of validity, each of the algorithms we surveyed defined safety as the property that forking is impossible, honest players have the same blocks at the same heights, or that any output from an honest player would eventually be output by all honest players. While these definitions are not actually equivalent, coupled with liveness properties they are (see Proposition 5 in the Appendix). Aside from that, the only inconsistency in definitions was a mention of validity, which did not always happen.

8   Liveness

Liveness is the second core result of any consensus protocol. As it is trivial to produce a safe algorithm that is not live, where validators simply do nothing, an algorithm with all the above properties clearly defined, including safety, is worth almost nothing until one can prove liveness. Liveness, like safety, depends on network assumptions, the adversarial model, and finality. It is crucial to clearly understand each of these as they relate to a consensus algorithm in order to give a proof of liveness.

Definition 3. *A consensus algorithm is live if and only if for every honest validator v and finite time t:*

1. *For any block b generated by v, there exists some time $t' > t$ where v will have finalized b, and*
2. *There is some time $t'' \geq t'$ where every other honest validator will have also finalized b.*

Both of the properties of liveness are important. The first says that correct blocks can make it through to finalization, while the second block says they do so transitively, *i.e.* once they have been finalized by one honest node, they will

Algorithm	Definition of Liveness	Translated
Nakamoto	Honestly generated transactions eventually finalize.	Honestly generated transactions eventually finalize.
Ouroboros	Honestly generated transactions eventually finalize.	Honestly generated transactions eventually finalize.
Honey Badger	Censorship resilience.	Honestly generated transactions eventually finalize (if they're input to $N - f$ correct nodes).
PBFT	Clients eventually receive correct replies to their requests.	The network responds correctly to transactions.
BoBW	Honest parties eventually terminate with some output.	Honest parties eventually terminate with some output.
Gosig	Starting from any point in time, there is a finite waiting period before any given honest player will commit a valid block.	Honest parties eventually terminate with some (valid) output.

Fig. 3. Definitions of liveness come in two principal groups: that honestly generated transactions eventually finalize (or a variant of that), and that honest players eventually have an output. These two definitions are not equivalent (see Proposition 6 in the Appendix for details). The definition we supply combines the essential ideas of both groups.

eventually be finalized by all honest nodes.[1] In certain situations, such as in algorithms on a traditional blockchain, where the network decides on one block at a time and only moves forward after a decision has been made, the second requirement can be implicitly satisfied by the structure of the system. Merely requiring termination suffices in that case because we know that consensus must begin, and that correct nodes must be consistent. Therefore, if it terminates, then it must necessarily satisfy the second requirement. In these situations, liveness can be simply referred to as *termination*.

Liveness in the algorithms we surveyed falls generally into two groups. The first is that honestly generated transactions eventually finalize (see Nakamoto consensus, Ouroboros, and Honey Badger). PBFT gives a similar, but nuanced, definition, that the network responds correctly to transactions. The second is that honest parties eventually terminate with some (valid) output. Interestingly, these two are not only not equivalent, but they are independent from each other (see Proposition 6 from the Appendix). Our definition combines and refines the concepts from both groups, which is significant because of their independence. Figure 3 gives more details.

It is worth noticing that our definition relies heavily on the notion of finality, and thus lends itself to permissioned chains better than unpermissioned ones. However, if, like in the case of BTC or ETH, finality is defined by waiting a fixed number of blocks, then this definition may still apply. Indeed, the paper

---

[1] As noted in the last section, some definitions of safety incorporate the second property implicitly.

that proved Nakamoto's algorithm to be safe and live uses the strictly stronger definition of liveness given both by Ouroboros and Honey Badger [16]. That is that an honest miner (or validator) that submits blocks to the blockchain will eventually get them committed. Our definition of liveness requires a specified moment of finality, thus the existence of t' and t''. A consensus algorithm on an unpermissioned network that, like Nakamoto's algorithm, can only give probabilistic guarantees of finality can modify our definition to talk about the limit as time goes to infinity instead of specific instants t' and t'', which may not exist. While being unable to specify specific moments of finality is less than ideal, we consider this to be the standard for liveness on an unpermissioned chain.

9   Conclusion

The blockchain community, as it matures scientifically, must have firm theoretical foundations on which to build the theory of consensus on blockchains. Without standardized foundations, notation, terminology, and assumptions, it is difficult, if not impossible, to make fruitful comparisons between consensus algorithms for the blockchain. To this end, this paper surveys six popular consensus algorithms and, noting problematic inconsistencies, proposes a strong, standard, theoretical foundation on which any consensus algorithm should be able to draw. Technical rigor and standardization with regards to Byzantine consensus, network assumptions, the adversarial model, finality, safety, and liveness are necessary for confidence in the algorithms themselves. It is our hope that through these foundations we will be able to reason about and compare consensus algorithms more successfully, avoiding security problems overlooked either through casual reasoning or through problematic theoretical foundations.

Acknowledgment. Many thanks to my colleague Justin Meiners, who is always willing to dig into a good math problem.

A   Appendix

Proposition 4. *For any time t, let delay(t) equal the delay a message sent at time t takes to be received. Then requiring that delay(t) does not grow faster than t indefinitely is a special case of partial synchrony, but they are not equivalent.*

Proof. We first treat the case that time t is a real number in the interval $[0, \infty)$, where 0 is the time that the first message is sent. Thus delay(t) must be at least piecewise differentiable to have the notion of "growth". Suppose that delay(t) does not grow faster than t indefinitely. Since delay(t) is piecewise differentiable on $[0, \infty)$, it is piecewise continuous on the same interval. Let G be the set of all $t' \in [0, \infty)$ such that the derivative of delay(t) at t' is greater than 1 (in other words, delay(t) is growing faster than t at t'). By assumption, G is bounded above, and therefore has a least upper bound. Let us call that t_u. Now consider delay(t) $- t$ on the interval $[0, t_u]$. Since $[0, t_u]$ is closed and bounded, it is compact. And since $delay(t) - t$ is piecewise continuous on $[0, t_u]$, $delay(t) - t$ achieves its maximum value Δ on $[0, t_u]$. Note that no message delay ever exceeds Δ, and thus we have partial synchrony.

Going the other direction, we see that there could be cases in which $delay(t)$ could grow faster than t indefinitely but still achieve partial synchrony. In particular, we still achieve partial synchrony any time the integral from 0 to ∞ of $(\frac{d}{dt} delay(t)) - 1$ converges. In this case, we have partial synchrony where Δ is the value of the integral.

In this proof we assumed $delay(t)$ to be piecewise differentiable because it has a notion of "growth" unspecified by the authors of PBFT. This treats the case that t is a real number in the interval $[0, \infty)$. If time is treated as discrete time slots, then the proofs only involve a finite number of points, and thus are trivial. $\square$

Proposition 5. *Consider the following definitions of safety.*

1. *If any honest player commits a block, then all honest players eventually commit a block.*
2. *If two honest players have a block at height n, then their blocks are equal.*
3. *The chain will never fork.*

Then the first implies the second and third, the second and third are equivalent, and neither the second nor the third implies the first.

Proof. (1) $\implies$ (2): Suppose that honest player v_1 has block b at height n, and honest player v_2 has block b' at height n. If $b \neq b'$, then eventually v_1 will commit b' at height n, which is a contradiction since v_1 is honest.

(2) $\iff$ (3): Going forward, if the chain forks, then two honest players must have different blocks at the same height by definition. Going backward, if two honest players have different blocks at the same height, there is by definition a fork.

(2), (3) $\not\Rightarrow$ (1): Finally, if v_1 has block b at height n, and v_2's chain is not yet at height n, if v_2 doesn't commit any more blocks to the blockchain, v_1 and v_2 can satisfy definition (2) but will never satisfy definition (1). If we have liveness, then v_2 will eventually commit b at height n. Thus every honest validator will eventually commit b at height n, and we have property (1). $\square$

Proposition 6. *Consider the following definitions of liveness.*

1. *Clients eventually receive correct replies to their requests.*
2. *Honestly generated transactions eventually finalize.*
3. *(Censorship resilience) Honestly generated transactions submitted to $N - f$ correct nodes eventually finalize.*
4. *Honest nodes eventually produce output.*

Then (1) $\implies$ (2) $\implies$ (3), *but nothing else. In particular, none of these definitions are equivalent and* (4) *is independent of the rest.*

Proof. (1) $\implies$ (2): If clients eventually receive correct replies to their requests, then they will receive confirmations of honestly generated transactions. The other direction is not true, as an algorithm could satisfy (2) while not responding to incorrect transactions.

(2) $\implies$ (3): If an honestly generated transaction always finalizes, then it will in the case that it's submitted to $N - f$ correct nodes. Going the other direction, there is an equivalence only if $N - f$ correct nodes have to see and approve a transaction in order to finalize one. Since there are algorithms that don't require that, the backward direction does not work.

(4) is independent: Clients could receive correct replies to their requests, and transactions can finalize, while an honest node is partitioned away or has temporarily crashed. Coupled with some totality property, an implication would hold from any of the first three definitions to the fourth. We can't go the other way to any of the three, since honest nodes producing an output does not necessarily end in finalization, *e.g.* if the outputs are different. Furthermore, if a client submits an honest transaction to a Byzantine node, the network could ignore the message, satisfy (4), and not satisfy the first three definitions.   □

References

1. Bagaria, V., Kannan, S., Tse, D., Fanti, G., Viswanath, P.: Deconstructing the Blockchain to Approach Physical Limits (2018). https://arxiv.org/abs/1810.08092
2. Butt, K., Sorensen, D., Stay, M.: Casanova (2018). https://arxiv.org/abs/1812.02232
3. Cachin, C., Vukolić, M.: Blockchain Consensus Protocols in the Wild (2017). https://arxiv.org/pdf/1707.01873.pdf
4. Castro, M., Liskov, B.: Practical byzantine fault tolerance. In: Proceedings of the Third Symposium on Operating Systems Design and Implementation (1999). http://pmg.csail.mit.edu/papers/osdi99.pdf
5. Copeland, C., Zhong, H.: Tangaroa: a Byzantine Fault Tolerant Raft. Class project in Distributed Systems, Stanford University (2014). http://www.scs.stanford.edu/14au-cs244b/labs/projects/copeland_zhong.pdf
6. Coreos Raft. https://github.com/coreos/raft. Accessed 24 Apr 2019
7. Danezis, G., Hrycyszyn, D.: Blockmania: from Block DAGs to Consensus (2018). https://arxiv.org/abs/1809.01620
8. Fischer, M.J., Lynch, N.A., Paterson, M.S.: Impossibility of distributed consensus with one faulty process. J. Assoc. Comput. Mach. **32**(2), 374–382 (1985). https://doi.org/10.1145/3149.214121
9. Girimath, A.: Ethereum Classic [ETC]: A deep-dive into 51% attack leading to the loss of $1.1 million worth in ETCs. AmbCrypto (2019). https://ambcrypto.com/ethereum-classic-etc-a-deep-dive-into-51-attack-leading-to-the-loss-of-1-1-million-worth-etcs/
10. Kiayias, A., Russell, A., David, B., Oliynykov, R.: Ouroboros: A Provably Secure Proof-of-Stake Blockchain Protocol (2017). https://eprint.iacr.org/2016/889.pdf
11. Li, P., Wang, G., Chen, X., Xu, W.: Gosig: Scalable Byzantine Consensus on Adversarial Wide Area Network for Blockchains (2018). https://arxiv.org/pdf/1802.01315.pdf

12. Loss, J., Moran, T.: Combining Asynchronous and Synchronous Byzantine Agreement: The Best of Both Worlds. Cryptology ePrint Archive (2018). https://eprint.iacr.org/2018/235.pdf
13. Miller, A., Xia, Y., Croman, K., Shi, E., Song, D.: The Honey Badger of BFT Protocols. Cryptology ePrint Archive (2016). https://eprint.iacr.org/2016/199.pdf
14. Nakamoto, S.: Bitcoin: A Peer-to-Peer Electronic Cash System (2008). https://bitcoin.org/bitcoin.pdf
15. Nguyen, G., Kim, K.: A survey about consensus algorithms used in blockchain. J. Inf. Process Syst. 4(1), 101–128 (2018). https://doi.org/10.3745/JIPS.01.0024
16. Pass, R., Seeman, L., Shelat, A.: Analysis of the Blockchain Protocol in Asynchronous Networks (2016). https://eprint.iacr.org/2016/454.pdf
17. Popov, S.: The Tangle (2018). https://assets.ctfassets.net/r1dr6vzfxhev/2t4uxvsIqk0EUau6g2sw0g/45eae33637ca92f85dd9f4a3a218e1ec/iota1_4_3.pdf
18. Sankar, L.S., Sindhu, M., Sethumadhavan, M.: Survey of consensus protocols on blockchain applications. In: 2017 4th International Conference on Advanced Computing and Communication Systems (ICACCS), pp. 1–5, January 2017. https://doi.org/10.1109/ICACCS.2017.8014672
19. Tschorsch, F., Scheuermann, B.: Bitcoin and beyond: a technical survey on decentralized digital currencies. IEEE Commun. Surv. Tutor. 18(3), 464 (2016). https://doi.org/10.1109/COMST.2016.2535718
20. Vukolić, M.: The quest for scalable blockchain fabric: proof-of-work vs. BFT replication. In: Camenisch, J., Kesdoğan, D. (eds.) iNetSec 2015. LNCS, vol. 9591, pp. 112–125. Springer, Cham (2016). https://doi.org/10.1007/978-3-319-39028-4_9
21. Wahab, A., Memood, W.: Survey of Consensus Protocols (2018). https://arxiv.org/abs/1810.03357
22. Wang, W., et al.: A Survey on Consensus Mechanisms and Mining Strategy Management in Blockchain Networks (2018). https://arxiv.org/abs/1805.02707
23. Xu, X., et al.: A taxonomy of blockchain-based systems for architecture design. In: 2017 IEEE International Conference on Software Architecture (2017). https://doi.org/10.1109/ICSA.2017.33

An Experimental Evaluation of BFT Protocols for Blockchains

Mohammad M. Jalalzai[1,2]([⊠]), Golden Richard III[1,2], and Costas Busch[1]

[1] Department of Computer Science, Louisiana State University,
Baton Rouge, USA
{mjalal7,goldenrichard1,kbusch}@lsu.edu
[2] Center for Computation and Technology, Louisiana State University,
Baton Rouge, USA

Abstract. Byzantine Fault Tolerant (BFT) protocols have been used in blockchains due to their high performance and fast block acceptance. However, their weakness is a lack of scalability to support a large number of nodes in the network due to message demanding broadcasts. There have been recent improvements to the classic Practical Byzantine Fault Tolerant (PBFT) protocol. Evaluating the performance and reliability of the different BFT based protocols in the context of blockchains will give users a better picture of the behaviour and scalability of these protocols under different circumstances. For this purpose, we implemented and evaluated the performance of different BFT based protocols for blockchains under normal conditions as well as when byzantine failures are encountered in the network. Furthermore, we also calculated the reliability of each protocol under the desired throughput.

Keywords: Byzantine Fault Tolerant · Blockchains consensus · Experimental evaluation · Reliability

1 Introduction

Blockchains are data structures consisting of chains of blocks, with each block referencing the hash of the previous block, creating a linked list of blocks. Blocks are added to the chain after consensus, where a majority (depending on the type of consensus) of participants in the network agree on the block and its contents, which typically consists of a set of transactions. There are several different types of consensus protocols available, such as Proof-of-Work, Proof-of-Stake, and Byzantine Fault Tolerant protocols.

In Proof-of-Work (PoW)-based protocols each miner node (i.e., a block proposer) has to solve a crypto-puzzle before proposing the block. Solving this crypto-puzzle is expensive in terms of processing but the solution can be verified quickly by other nodes. This helps the network to achieve consensus in a reliable manner by avoiding Denial of Service (DoS) and Sybil attacks on the network. PoW-based consensus protocols are highly scalable in terms of the number of

© Springer Nature Switzerland AG 2019
J. Joshi et al. (Eds.): ICBC 2019, LNCS 11521, pp. 34–48, 2019.
https://doi.org/10.1007/978-3-030-23404-1_3

nodes in the network, but exhibit low throughput (number of transactions per second). Bitcoin [13] is one of the most successful examples of a PoW protocol and achieves consensus with an average time of ten minutes and throughput of 3 to 7 transactions per second. Ethereum [18] is another example of PoW which generates around 37 transactions per second but still suffers from PoW limitations [19]. According to Luu *et al.* [12] 95% of the Bitcoin network is controlled by ten mining pools, while 80% of Ethereum network mining power resides in six mining pools. As these pools are controlled by pool operators in a centralized fashion, the Bitcoin and Ethereum networks are both susceptible to 51% attacks. Furthermore the presence of forks in PoW protocols potentially allows double spending attacks. To avoid double spending it is recommended that a user/application has to wait a certain number of blocks to make sure that it is highly unlikely that the current blockchain segment will be replaced with a different one. In Bitcoin this confirmation wait time is about 60 min or six blocks of wait time [13].

In systems that use Proof-of-Stake (PoS) [2,4,16,17] protocols instead of PoW, block proposers (so called "forgers") in the network must have some stake in the network. Usually, the next forger is selected randomly proportional to their stake in the network. The forger validates transactions before proposing those transactions in a new block. Thus, the higher the stake, the higher the probability a particular node will be selected as the next forger.

Byzantine Fault Tolerant (BFT) [11] protocols are another class of consensus protocols that are used in blockchains to achieve consensus efficiently. BFT based protocols do not require solving crypto-puzzles or proving stake for participants in the network. Instead, BFT protocols generally reach consensus through exchange of multiple rounds of messages. BFT protocols can achieve consensus in the presence of less than a third Byzantine replicas and these potentially malicious nodes can behave in arbitrary ways by failing, sending arbitrary or malicious messages, or performing coordinated attacks. BFT protocols generally use a replica called a primary to validate, sort, aggregate, and propose transactions inside a block to all the replicas in the network. Upon receipt of the block, each replica verifies it based on its own history (chain of blocks) and if the block is valid, each replica communicates with other replicas based on specifics of the underlying BFT Protocol mechanism to achieve consensus. Once more than two thirds of replicas agree on the block, the block will be added to the blockchain and committed. In case the primary behaves maliciously and there is sufficient proof of maliciousness present (for example more than one third complaints against primary), a view change is triggered, which results in replacement of the primary. Two thirds majority agreement gives an important characteristic to the BFT protocols, called finality. Finality means that once a block is committed, it will never be revoked. This is in sharp contrast to PoW and PoS protocols which suffer from forking and the associated risks of transactions within a fork being revoked.

There are a variety of BFT based protocols [1,3,5,9,10,13] that address the consensus problem in different ways. Message complexity, cryptography, and latency are various parameters that effect the performance of BFT protocols. We argue that it is very important for users to know how different BFT-based protocols perform in different scenarios (e.g., error-free mode, in the presence of Byzantine nodes, etc.), when implemented in the context of blockchains.

To address this concern, we present experimental analysis of our Musch BFT protocol for Blockchains [10] against different flavours of BFT based protocols. Theoretical analysis of the Musch BFT protocol shows promising results as it reduces the message complexity to $O(f'n)$ from $O(n^2)$ (where f' is the actual number of faulty nodes, and n the total number of nodes) without affecting the critical path (number of one way message latencies from a client sending a request to the network and associated response). We have implemented the Musch BFT protocol for blockchains in Go, using more than $2.3k$ lines of code. We also implemented other flavors of BFT including PBFT [3], Bchain-3 [5] and SBFT (a Scalable Decentralized Trust Infrastructure for Blockchains) [9]. Each variant of the BFT protocols selected here uses different mechanisms to improve BFT performance and scalability. We tested each protocol on different network sizes ranging from 40 to 160 EC2 instances on the Amazon cloud.

PBFT is classic BFT and the first practical protocol for this type of consensus. It uses multiple rounds of broadcast to achieve consensus. Bchain-3 is a member of a class of protocols called chain-based BFT protocols, where participants/replicas in the network are arranged in an overlay chain structure. This gives Bchain-3 better message complexity and throughput with increased latency. SBFT and Musch are both improvements of PBFT, where both of them in normal mode avoid broadcast through message aggregation. But upon experiencing failure, SBFT falls back to the PBFT protocol, whereas Musch switches to failure mode, where failure is addressed by communicating to other replicas in the network through an increasing size of window of replicas. Initial window size is 1 (communicating with only one node to recover from failure) and increases exponentially $(1, 2, 4, 8, \ldots, (2n/3) + 1)$ until failure is addressed. In this paper, we implemented the Musch BFT protocol for the first time and analyzed and evaluated performance, along with the PBFT, Bchain-3, and SBFT protocols. Additionally, we also provide reliability measures for each protocol when the network is under attack and desired performance is constant.

Paper Outline: In Sect. 2 we present in detail the four BFT protocols that we implemented. Section 3 shows experimental evaluation of BFT based protocols for blockchains. In Sect. 4 we discuss reliability analysis of BFT protocols when network is under attack. We conclude our paper and discuss our future work in Sect. 5.

2   Byzantine Fault Tolerant Protocols

We present a brief overview of protocols under test. This includes how protocols behave in normal operation to achieve consensus and how consensus is achieved in the presence of failures. It should be noted that all of these protocols operate in a semi-synchronous environment where communication is bounded by time. At any time, the number of failures or Byzantine replicas in the network cannot exceed $f < n/3$, as a BFT protocol cannot guarantee consensus in asynchronous environment if the number of failures reaches one third [6]. Suppose that $n = 3f + 1$. The protocols we consider here use authenticated messages for communication.

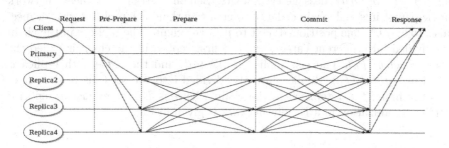

Fig. 1. PBFT communication pattern

2.1 Practical Byzantine Fault Tolerant Protocol

PBFT was the first practical Byzantine fault tolerant protocol to be proposed. It shows that it is possible to implement BFT protocols for use in practical systems, unlike the previous protocols [7,14] that were theoretically feasible but not efficient enough to be used in practice. Normal PBFT operation in the context of blockchains can be described as:

- Clients send transaction requests to the primary replica
- The primary replica is responsible for aggregating (batching), sorting, and proposing a block of transactions
- Once transactions are added to the block, the block is proposed by broadcasting
- Each replica receives the proposed block of transactions (also called the "preprepare" message) and verifies the current view (primary), the sequence number (block height), transactions, and primary signature
- Upon successful validation, each replica broadcasts a signed prepare message which includes the block sequence number, view number, hash of the transactions, and its ID
- Upon receipt of $2f$ valid prepare messages the replica broadcasts a commit message that includes view number, sequence number, transactions hash, as well as the replica's own ID
- Upon receipt of $2f + 1$ commit messages, the replica commits the block

The PBFT communication pattern is shown in Fig. 1. It can be seen that the PBFT critical path is constant (4) but it exhibits quadratic message complexity, $O(n^2)$ messages, to guarantee consensus even in the absence of failures.

2.2   Bchain-3

Bchain [5] was developed to address the quadratic message complexity of PBFT. Bchain uses two types of algorithms. Bchain-3 can tolerate $f < n/3$ failures, whereas Bchain-5 can tolerate $f < n/5$ failures. We evaluated Bchain-3, since the number of faults it can tolerate is similar to the other protocols under testing. To achieve $O(n)$ message complexity, Bchain-3 arranges replicas (network participants) in serial/chain order, in such a way that each replica forwards messages to another one positioned next to it in the chain. The replicas in the chain are divided into different categories. The first replica in the chain is called the *head/primary* (P_h). The last replica is the *tail*, and the $(2f + 1)$th replica is called *proxy tail* (P_p). Replicas are also divided into two sections in the chain. A is the first $2f + 1$ replicas in the chain where as B are the last f replicas. Replica organization in a Bchain network is given in Fig. 2.

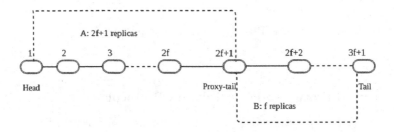

Fig. 2. Replicas are organized serially in Bchain

During normal operation the first $2f + 1$ replicas perform consensus whereas the last f replicas, simply update their chain by appending the block agreed by A replicas. The Bchain protocol transmits two types of messages: $\langle CHAIN \rangle$, that represents request/proposed block to its successor, and $\langle Ack \rangle$ which is the reply/acknowledgement of successful execution of the proposed block to predecessor (in opposite direction of $\langle CHAIN \rangle$). Bchain message pattern is shown in the Fig. 3.

The normal operation for the Bchain protocol can be described as:

- After receipt of a transaction from a client, the head/primary node assigns a sequence number to it
- After aggregating the transaction into a $\langle CHAIN \rangle$ message the primary adds the chain order and forwards the block to the next replica in the chain (its successor)
- Upon receipt of a $\langle CHAIN \rangle$ message by proxy tail, it forwards an Ack message to its predecessor toward the head replica and a reply message to the client
- Upon receipt of an Ack message, each replica in A commits the block, forwards the Ack message to its predecessor along the chain, and forwards its $\langle CHAIN \rangle$ message to replicas in B

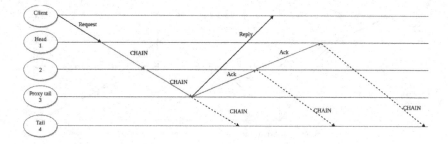

Fig. 3. Bchain communication pattern

Upon encountering failures, Bchain uses a re-chaining mechanism to recover from failure and this mechanism works as follows:

- Every replica (except head and tail) starts a timer after forwarding the $\langle CHAIN \rangle$ message to its successor. If it does not receive an *Ack* message before the timer expires, it will send two $\langle SUSPECT \rangle$ messages to the head (one directly and the other along the chain)
- If the head receives multiple $\langle SUSPECT \rangle$ messages, it will handle the closest one to the tail
- The head will begin the re-chaining mechanism, which involves moving the accused replica to the tail and moving the accuser to the end of A (proxy tail), so that it cannot accuse other replicas. In this way a malicious replica cannot falsely accuse more replicas.

2.3 Scalable Decentralized Trustable Infrastructure (SBFT)

SBFT improved PBFT's performance by using two set of collectors of size c to collect, prepare, and commit messages from replicas, thus avoiding the $n \times n$ broadcast of prepare and commit messages, while achieving $O(cn)$ message complexity during normal operation. As shown in Fig. 4, during failure-free operation, a primary collects transactions, sorts them into a block, adds a sequence number, view number, hash of the block, and broadcasts it to all replicas. Upon receipt of the block proposal/pre-prepare message, replica i verifies the validity of the block and if it is valid, i sends a prepare message containing the block hash, view number, block sequence number, and replica i's signature to a set C of collectors (the sign-share phase). Upon receipt of $3f + 1 + c$ valid signatures, the C collectors generate a signature and broadcast it to all replicas (full-commit-proof).

Once a replica receives the valid signature(meets threshold of require signatures), it executes the transactions in the block and signs the new state using signatures and sends it to E collectors. E collectors generate signatures (with threshold of $f + 1$ valid signatures) along with an execution certificate and send it to all replicas through broadcast (sign-state). E collectors also send a reply back to the client, verifying execution of the client transaction (execution-proof).

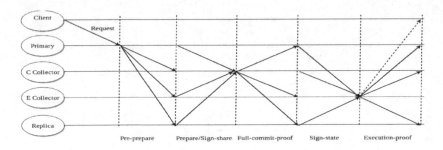

Fig. 4. SBFT communication pattern

Additionally, unlike normal BFT based protocols in which the number of Byzantine replicas are bounded by $f < n/3$, in SBFT the bound is $f < (n-2c)/3$, where $c \geq 0$. If collectors fail to respond before the timeout period, SBFT switches into fallback mode, reverting to $n \times n$ broadcast. Increasing the number of collectors c, will increase message complexity, whereas keeping the number small can cause frequent switching to fallback mode.

2.4   The Musch BFT Protocol for Blockchains

Musch uses an adaptive mechanism of a sliding window or response nodes to address failures/complaints in the network. The main contribution of the Musch BFT protocol is that it improves message complexity without sacrificing latency. For complaints against malicious replicas or primary, the protocol has a set of window nodes that respond to complaints. The window size is adaptive. Initially the window size is 1. If the complaints are not addressed by the window, then the window size doubles. Eventually, when the window size reaches $f' + 1$ then the complaints will be properly addressed, where f' is the actual number of byzantine nodes that have triggered the complaints (and $f < n/3$ is an upper bound on f', $f' \leq f$). The network broadcasts are through the window. Thus, the message complexity stays at $O(f'n + n)$. If there are no failures ($f' = 0$) the message complexity is linear, which improves on the PBFT quadratic complexity.

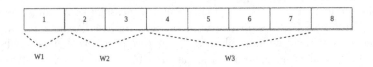

Fig. 5. Exponential increase in window size

Musch BFT uses Echo broadcast [15], to propose the block to replicas in the network. If the proposed block is valid, replicas send back a signed hash of the block to the primary. Upon receipt of $2f + 1$, agreement messages from replicas, the primary aggregates them into an aggregated signature α_p, and broadcasts it back. Collecting $2f + 1$ agreements for a proposed block means the majority of replicas have agreed on all transactions and the order of their execution. Upon receipt of an aggregated message each replica verifies the validity of the *COMMIT* message and if valid, they commit the block. If each replica has received the same block, they will agree on the hash and the order of transactions to be executed. In case replicas detect malicious activity by the primary, which might include sending invalid blocks, different blocks of transaction to different replicas, or not sending a block to more than f replicas (which will then complain about it) the primary will be replaced by changing the view.

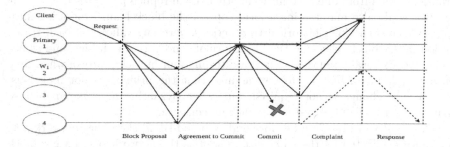

Fig. 6. Musch BFT communication pattern

If failures are encountered replicas switch to recovery mode. In normal BFT protocols if a replica does not receive a pre-prepare/block proposal or receives conflicting or malicious messages from the primary, it broadcasts its complaint ("I hate primary") message. But in case of Musch BFT, a replica will complain to a predetermined subset of replicas called window nodes. Each replica has set of node *IDs* of other nodes/replicas in the network that are arranged in ascending order. During recovery mode, a replica moves its sliding window of increasing size over the *ID* list and complains to the nodes in the window. Assuming the complaining replica is i, it will send a *COMPLAINT* message to the first window (W_1). If it does not receive a *RESPONSE* before the timeout period ends, the sliding window will double in size and move to the next window W_2 and so on, for sending *COMPLAINT* messages. If the set $\{1, 2, 3, ..., n\}$ of node IDs is arranged in ascending order, then the sequence of windows over them will be $W_1, W_2, W_3, ..., W_k$ as shown in the Fig. 5. A window W_j will have 2^{j-1} nodes/replicas, where $j \geq 1$. The Musch BFT protocol guarantees that at worst case when the window size reaches $k = \lceil \lg(f' + 1) \rceil$, at least one honest node will be in that window to provide response to replica i. The message exchange pattern of Musch BFT for Blockchains is shown in the Fig. 6.

3   Experimental Evaluation

We implemented the PBFT, Bchain-3, SBFT and Musch BFT consensus protocols for Blockchains in Go, in order to evaluate them. We tested all of the protocols on the Amazon Cloud using EC2 instances of type *t2large*. Each *t2large* instance contains two virtual CPU cores and 8 GB of memory. We evaluated these protocols on different network sizes ranging from 40, 70, 100, 130, to 160 nodes and different block sizes (5, 000, 10, 000, 15, 000 and 20, 000 transactions). Figure 7 shows latency comparisons and Fig. 8 shows throughput comparisons among the implemented protocols.

Each transaction is a simple blockchain transaction generated randomly that transfers funds from one account to another. Each replica processes messages it receives while also maintaining a local copy of the blockchain. Processing messages includes checking historical transactions, verifying validity of each transaction in the block, checking the block format, and verifying hashes and signatures. We also evaluated the latency and throughput of each protocol when they encounter failures. In this case we assume that the primary is not malicious, thus a view change is not required, but other Byzantine replicas can behave maliciously to delay the system in reaching consensus.

Our results in Figs. 7 and 8 (for window-based BFT) show that network performance is affected by the block size as well as the network size. Larger block sizes ($15k$ and $20k$) normally provide better performance when network size is small (40 and 70). Whereas with smaller block sizes ($5k$ and $10k$) the network capacity (for small network sizes) is under-utilized. Smaller block sizes provide better performance in larger networks (see Figs. 7(a), (b) and Figs. 8 (a), (b)). But in larger networks (130 and 160) larger block sizes also cause a performance bottleneck. Additionally it can be seen that the Musch protocol outperforms PBFT and Bchain for all network sizes. Furthermore, during failures in the network as shown in Figs. 9 and 10, the performance of Musch is negligibly effected. This is because even if malicious replicas try to download more blocks from window nodes, they cannot cause a bottleneck as a window node will only send a requested block once and we have implemented the window node functionality as a separate Go-routine (thread), to leverage concurrency. Thus, overall protocol performance of Musch is not affected by the Window go-routine (addressing complaints from other replicas). Since PBFT is using multiple rounds of broadcast, its performance remains stable as f number of failures cannot further degrade its performance. Bchain-3 on other hand is affected by introduction of failures in the chain. Its performance reduction during failure mainly depends on timeout values. We set the performance threshold timer Δ_1 as $\Delta_1 = 1.10\delta_1$ (as in [5]), where δ_1 is the average time taken by the network to reach consensus. During fault free operation SBFT performance matches that of Musch. But due to

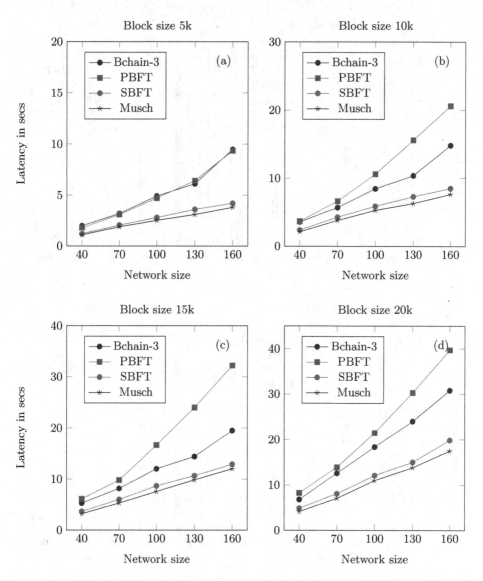

Fig. 7. Latency with block sizes 5000, 10000, 15000 and 20000

falling back to PBFT during failure, SBFT's performance degrades. SBFT has an optimized PBFT fallback protocol but timeout for failure detection (to switch from normal to fallback mode) adds additional latency to it when collectors fail.

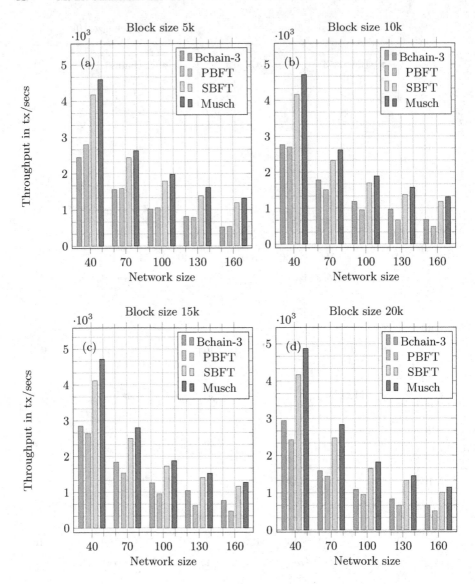

Fig. 8. Throughput with block sizes 5000, 10000, 15000 and 20000

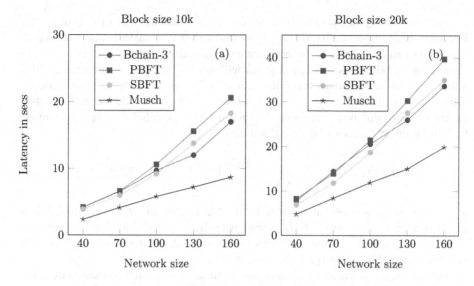

Fig. 9. Latency with failures for block sizes 10000 and 20000

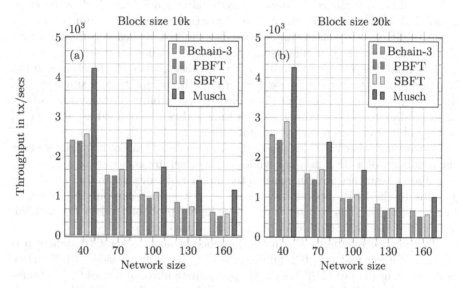

Fig. 10. Throughput with failures for block sizes 10000 and 20000

4   Reliability Analysis Under Attacks

Scalability of a blockchain protocol allows additional nodes to be accommodated and improves decentralization. Seen another way, the ability to add more replicas to the network provides a chance for more parties to be part of the consensus process. Gartner [8], has cautioned against using BFT-based protocols in contexts where Byzantine failures are equated with resilience against malicious attackers.

He argues that Byzantine failure in security is a measurement of reliability [8]. From the FLP impossibility result [6], we know that consensus is impossible if at least one third of replicas in the network are Byzantine ($f \geq n/3$). In practice, we cannot be certain that this assumption will hold. Therefore, Gartner, provides a methodology to estimate the reliability of a Byzantine fault tolerant network (failure assumptions hold in practice), while the network might be under attack by attackers of different strengths. In such a case, the reliability of a Byzantine fault tolerant system can be quantified as:

$$R_C(f, n, t) = \sum_{i=n-f}^{n-C(t)} \binom{n - C(t)}{i} R_{(t)}^i (1 - R_{(t)})^{n-C(t)-i} \tag{1}$$

where n is total number of replicas in the BFT network, $f < n/3$, and t is a measure of time. Moreover, $C(t)$ defines attacker classes which can be parameterized based on some value p, which is the amount of time for an attacker to take full control of one replica in the network.

For example, a linear class attacker with $p > 0$ is an attacker that compromises each server separately one after another. Such a model assumes replicas uses diverse versions of operating systems and are controlled by different entities. A linear class of attacker can be written as: $C(t) = \min(\lfloor t \cdot p \rfloor, n)$. Logarithmic class attackers can compromise the first replica and then compromising other replicas gets increasingly difficult and follows a logarithmic curve: $C(t) = \min(\lfloor \log_p t \rfloor, n)$. In similar fashion, other classes of attackers like the constant time attacker can be defined. $R_{(t)}$ is the reliability of a single system during a given time t. It can also be called the probability of the system behaving according to expectation at a given time and can be defined as: $R_{(t)} = e^{\lambda \cdot t}$, where failure rate λ is assumed constant for all $t \geq 0$.

By keeping other variables constant (except n and f) in Eq. 1, we can see that the reliability of a BFT network while under attack by an adversary of power p shows more resilience with increase in the number of faults it can tolerate (larger f). Due to the FLP impossibility result [6], $f < n/3$, f can only be increased by increasing n. Thus, greater n will gives higher probability that $f < n/3$ will hold in practice, in the presence of malicious attackers.

To compare reliability R_C in the presence of an attacker $C(t)$, where p is attacker's power and $p = 0.2$, failure rate $\lambda = 10^{-3}$, we considered 1.7k tx/sec as desired throughput (D_t). We chose approximate maximum sizes for n_B (number of replicas in Bchain-3 network), n_P (number of replicas in PBFT network), n_S (number of replicas in SBFT network) and n_E (number of replicas in Musch network) that can achieve our desired throughput (with a block size of 10k) from results presented in Fig. 10(a). Thus, for D_t to be equal or more than 1.7k, $n_B = 40$, $n_P = 40$, $n_S = 70$ and $n_E = 100$. Similarly, $f_B = 13$, $f_P = 13$, $f_S = 22$ and $f_W = 32$ (maximum number of failures for each protocol) was chosen for each protocol. As shown in Fig. 11, due to its high scalability, the reliability of the Musch protocol shows more resistance to powerful attackers. Then, it is followed by SBFT. On the other hand, both PBFT and Bchain-3 show identical weaker reliability, and by time $t = 70$ they are both compromised and have lost their redundancy.

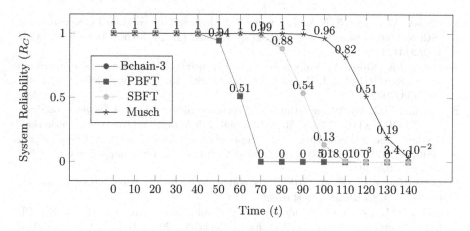

Fig. 11. System reliability in the presence of attacker $C(t)$

5 Conclusion and Future Work

In this paper we presented performance and reliability evaluations for several different BFT protocols in the context of blockchains. We also showed how performance of these protocols is affected when failures are introduced in the network. Additionally, we also calculated the reliability of each protocol, when the network is under attack and showed that a scalable protocol can tolerate more faults and hence offer more resilience to the attacks. Our future work will move focus on developing efficient asynchronous BFT protocols for blockchains and evaluating their performance.

References

1. Buchman, E.: Tendermint: byzantine fault tolerance in the age of blockchains (2016).   http://atrium.lib.uoguelph.ca/xmlui/bitstream/handle/10214/9769/Buchman_Ethan_201606_MAsc.pdf. Accessed 06 Feb 2017
2. Buterin, V., Griffith, V.: Casper the friendly finality gadget (2017). arXiv:1710.09437. Accessed 06 Nov 2017
3. Castro, M., Liskov, B.: Practical byzantine fault tolerance. In: Proceedings of the Third Symposium on Operating Systems Design and Implementation, OSDI 1999, Berkeley, USA, pp. 173–186. USENIX Association (1999). http://dl.acm.org/citation.cfm?id=296806.296824
4. Pike, D., Nosker, P., Boehm, D., Grishm, D., Woods, S., Marston, J.: Proof-of-stake-time (2015). https://www.vericoin.info/downloads/VeriCoinPoSTWhitePaper10May2015.pdf. Accessed 12 Mar 2019
5. Duan, S., Meling, H., Peisert, S., Zhang, H.: BChain: byzantine replication with high throughput and embedded reconfiguration. In: Aguilera, M.K., Querzoni, L., Shapiro, M. (eds.) OPODIS 2014. LNCS, vol. 8878, pp. 91–106. Springer, Cham (2014). https://doi.org/10.1007/978-3-319-14472-6_7

6. Fischer, M.J., Lynch, N.A., Paterson, M.S.: Impossibility of distributed consensus with one faulty process. J. ACM **32**(2), 374–382 (1985). https://doi.org/10.1145/3149.214121

7. Garay, J.A., Moses, Y.: Fully polynomial byzantine agreement for $n>3t$ processors in $t+1$ rounds. SIAM J. Comput. **27**(1), 247–290 (1998). https://doi.org/10.1137/S0097539794265232

8. Gärtner, F.C.: Byzantine failures and security: arbitrary is not (always) random. In: INFORMATIK 2003 - Mit Sicherheit Informatik, Schwerpunkt "Sicherheit - Schutz und Zuverlässigkeit", 29 September–2 Oktober 2003 in Frankfurt am Main, pp. 127–138 (2003). http://subs.emis.de/LNI/Proceedings/Proceedings36/article1040.html

9. Golan-Gueta, G., et al.: SBFT: a scalable decentralized trust infrastructure for blockchains. CoRR abs/1804.01626 (2018)

10. Jalalzai, M., Busch, C.: Window based BFT blockchain consensus. In: 2018 IEEE International Conference on Blockchain (Blockchain 2018), Halifax, Canada (2018)

11. Lamport, L., Shostak, R., Pease, M.: The byzantine generals problem. ACM Trans. Program. Lang. Syst. **4**(3), 382–401 (1982). https://doi.org/10.1145/357172.357176

12. Luu, L., Velner, Y., Teutsch, J., Saxena, P.: Smartpool: practical decentralized pooled mining. In: 26th USENIX Security Symposium (USENIX Security 2017), Vancouver, pp. 1409–1426. USENIX Association (2017). https://www.usenix.org/conference/usenixsecurity17/technical-sessions/presentation/luu

13. Nakamoto, S.: Bitcoin: a peer-to-peer electronic cash system. http://bitcoin.org/bitcoin.pdf

14. Canneti, R., Rabin, T.: Optimal synchronous byzantine agreement. Technical report (1992)

15. Reiter, M.K.: Secure agreement protocols: reliable and atomic group multicast in rampart. In: Proceedings of the 2nd ACM Conference on Computer and Communications Security, CCS 1994, New York, USA, pp. 68–80. ACM (1994)

16. King, S., Nadal, S.: PPCoin: peer-to-peer crypto-currency with proof-of-stake (2012). https://peercoin.net/whitepapers/peercoin-paper.pdf. Accessed 12 Mar 2019

17. Vasin, P.: Blackcoin's proof-of-stake protocol v2. https://blackcoin.org/blackcoin-pos-protocol-v2-whitepaper.pdf. Accessed 12 Mar 2019

18. Wood, D.G.: Ethereum: a secure decentralised generalised transaction ledger (2017). https://ethereum.github.io/yellowpaper/paper.pdf

19. Wüst, K.: Security of blockchain technologies (2016). http://e-collection.library.ethz.ch/eserv/eth:49632/eth-49632-01.pdf. Accessed 08 Feb 2019

Layered Consensus Mechanism in Consortium Blockchain for Enterprise Services

Sheng He[1,2,3,4(✉)], Yishuang Ning[1,2,3,4], Huan Chen[3,4], Chunxiao Xing[1,2], and Liang-Jie Zhang[3,4]

[1] Research Institute of Information Technology,
Beijing National Research Center for Information Science and Technology,
Beijing 100084, China
heshengpku@gmail.com
[2] Department of Computer Science and Technology Institute of Internet Industry,
Tsinghua University, Beijing 100084, China
[3] National Engineering Research Center for Supporting Software of Enterprise
Internet Services, Shenzhen 518057, China
[4] Kingdee Research, Kingdee International Software Group, Shenzhen 518057, China

Abstract. The concept of blockchain born out of Bitcoin in just a decade ago has greatly attracted the attentions of industry and academia. The third generation of blockchain is believed to be able to support a large number of commercial and social applications with security, scalability, speed and developer friendly. To maintain a distributed ledger in many independent peer nodes without central authority, the consensus mechanism is the key protocol to construct a blockchain system with multiple technologies. However compared to the well-studied consensus protocols in public blockchain, the customized consensus mechanism is still lack of research for the consortium blockchain in both industry and academia, especially in the enterprise scenarios of applications and services. The layered consensus mechanism in the consortium blockchain is discussed after considering and combining the common characteristics of enterprise applications and services. Based on the famous Service-Oriented Architecture (SOA), the new layered and service-oriented consensus mechanism should be more practical to apply the blockchain technology to much diversified enterprise services with decentralization and extensibility in the principle of enterprise-level security.

Keywords: Consensus mechanism · Consortium blockchain ·
Enterprise services · Layered architecture ·
Service-Oriented Architecture (SOA)

1 Introduction

The concept of blockchain born out of Bitcoin [1] in just a decade ago has greatly attracted the attentions of industry and academia. The first generation of

© Springer Nature Switzerland AG 2019
J. Joshi et al. (Eds.): ICBC 2019, LNCS 11521, pp. 49–64, 2019.
https://doi.org/10.1007/978-3-030-23404-1_4

blockchain, like Bitcoin and Litecoin [2], is the mode known as public blockchain, in which anyone can join or exit the network freely and easily without any constraint. The second generation of blockchain has aroused great interest in business applications of enterprises since 2015 [3]. The important feature of smart contract [4] allows the performance of credible transactions without the third parties. Since the transactions are trackable and irreversible in the blockchain, massive businesses are expected to improve security and reduce transaction costs with the unique power of smart contract. So the third generation of blockchain, which is actually not well-defined yet, is believed to be able to support a large number of commercial and social applications with security, scalability, speed and developer friendly [5].

To maintain a distributed ledger in many independent peer nodes without central authority, the consensus mechanism is the key protocol to construct a blockchain system with multiple technologies like peer-to-peer (P2P) network, distributed database, and necessary cryptography methods. With certain authentication, authority and supervision, the consortium blockchain is considered more suitable for the complex enterprise applications. However the currently well-known consensus protocols, like Proof of Work (PoW) [6] and Proof of Stake (PoS) [7], are more applicable to the public blockchains. Instead, the consortium blockchains currently in the stage of scenario exploration have just used some traditional consistency algorithms as the consensus mechanism, which are usually based on some assumptions e.g. centralized controlling. So the customized consensus mechanism is still lack of research for the consortium blockchain in both industry and academia, especially in the enterprise scenarios of applications and services where the features of boundary, organization, certification and connection for business should be carefully considered.

In this paper, we are going to discuss the consensus mechanism in the enterprise scenario of consortium blockchain with a layered architecture, based on the famous Service-Oriented Architecture (SOA) [8] for enterprise application architecture. The paper is structured as following. Section 2 introduces some common consensus protocols in public blockchain and some traditional consistency algorithms in current consortium blockchain. Section 3 discusses the layered architecture for the consensus mechanism in the enterprise scenario of consortium blockchain. Section 4 applies the new layered and service-oriented consensus mechanism to enterprise services and provides an overview of some potential enterprise applications and services which shows the benefit of the layered consensus architecture with the ability of decentralization and extensibility. The summary is concluded in Sect. 5.

2   Status of Consensus Mechanism

As we all known, the consensus mechanism is the key protocol to maintain a distributed ledger in many independent peer nodes without central authority [9]. For a practical blockchain, the consensus algorithm should be able to achieve the Byzantine agreement [10]. That means in a given potential adversarial model, the system could be safety, aliveness, and finality under some specified network assumptions. That is, nodes and users are independent, and they may have no trusted relationship, especially within the possibility of malicious attackers. This section provides a useful context and will facilitate subsequent research after discussing the development of consensus mechanism. Inspirations are also discussed from some new built-up consensus mechanisms and blockchain exploratory applications in enterprises.

2.1   Consensus Protocols in Public Blockchain

The concept of consensus mechanism just comes from the domain of public blockchain. The public blockchain, which is also called *permissionless blockchain*, records the transactions which anyone can be a user to invoke transactions or be a recorder to maintain a node with the ledger. The principle in public blockchain is anyone can participant in the consensus process where a "final" valid state should be determined.

Table 1. A summary of the consensus protocol in the current top 10 cryptocurrencies by market cap. (Apr 8, 2019. Market Cap data from CoinMarketCap https:// coinmarketcap.com/)

Name	Market cap in billion USD	Protocols	Comments
Bitcoin	93.7	PoW	
Ethereum	19.4	PoW	Expected turning to PoS
Ripple	15.3	XCP	Based on a trusted validation
Bitcoin cash	5.7	PoW	A fork coin from bitcoin
Litecoin	5.7	PoW	
EOS	5.0	DPoS	
Binance coin	2.6	-	A token on ethereum
Stellar	2.6	SCP	
Cardano	2.3	PoS	
Tether	2.1	-	A security token offering

Table 1 gives a summary of the consensus protocol in the current top 10 blockchain by market cap, where XCP means XRP Consensus Protocol and SCP means Stellar Consensus Protocol. The most famous consensus protocol is obviously Proof of Work i.e. PoW. In theory, PoW exactly uses a random process which is determined by the node's computing power in a probabilistic competition. So before a valid proof is generated, a lot of trials and errors are required on average since the random process is in a low probability. As the most successful consensus mechanism, PoW is however unsuitable for the enterprise services due to its high latency, high power cost, low extensibility, and other original deficiencies.

On the other hand, PoS aims to reduce the waste of PoW [11] but arises the "noting-at-stake" and other problems. The founders of Cardano claimed they presented "Ouroboros" which is the first secure PoS protocol with mathematically proven [12]. However any protocol Proof of X is still a random process because of the freedom of nodes, where X means some computing work, stake or other things. That means a "valid" transaction just after a round of consensus process is transient in strickly speaking and it needs times or more rounds to be finally persistent or even on the contrary to be moved out because of a soft fork. The rollback of a successful transaction is generally unacceptable in enterprise services, so the consensus protocols adjusted to the public blockchain are typically not suitable for the consortium blockchains.

2.2   Consistency Algorithms in Consortium Blockchain

The consortium blockchain is also known as *permissioned blockchain*, where the blockchain can only be operated by a number of permitted members in a given business context which forms a consortium. Permissioned blockchains will identify the nodes how to control and update the shared ledger, and also often have methods to control who can issue transactions.

Table 2. Summary of the consensus protocols in some common technology platforms for consortium blockchain.

Platform name	Consensus protocols	CFT/BFT
Hyperledger fabric	Kafka	CFT
Hyperledger fabric	PBFT	BFT
Tendermint	Tendermint	BFT
R3 corda	Raft	CFT
R3 corda	BFT-SMaRt	BFT
Sawtooth lake	PoET	CFT
Quorum	Raft	CFT

The consortium blockchains are currently still in the stage of scenario exploration. As Table 2 shown, the consortium blockchains usually adopt some traditional consistency algorithms as the consensus mechanism like Raft [13] and PBFT [14]. However the traditional consistency algorithms usually assume a centralized control where most of the protocols only considered the crash fault tolerant (CFT) [15] e.g. Raft. CFT guarantees a transaction to be atomic broadcast, that is each transaction has *broadcast* and *deliver* events which can be invoked multiple times. So the transaction will be broadcasted to the connected nodes in the network and always kept as a "unit" even if the transaction contains multiple statements, whether succeeds or fails finally.

More recently, the Byzantine fault tolerant (BFT) protocols are developed, where nodes can come to consistency even though some malicious nodes may act as an adversary to subvert the common goal of reaching agreement. In the eventual-synchrony model, the most prominent protocol is PBFT (Practical Byzantine Fault-Tolerance). It can be understood as an extension of the Paxos family [16] and also uses a progression of views, especially a unique leader is needed within every view. In a PBFT system, $f < n/3$ Byzantine nodes can be tolerated with n nodes in an optimal situation, where f is the number of Byzantine nodes and n is the total number of system nodes. Many research works have analyzed and improved aspects of BFT and made it more robust in prototypes [17].

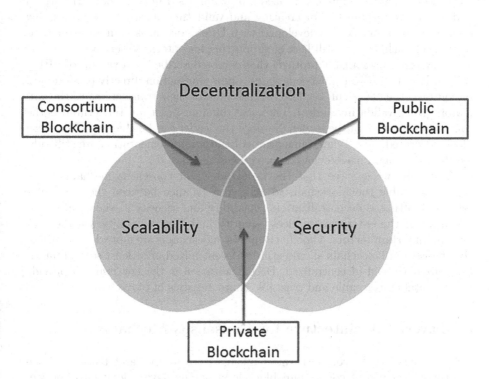

Fig. 1. The triangular relationship for blockchains. It was proved that it is impossible to satisfy all these three characteristics at the same time, but a balance should be tried to reach. For consortium blockchain, decentralization and scalability are obbligato and an enterprise-level security is still needed for the practical enterprise services

However, the traditional consistency algorithms are designed for distributed system based on some assumptions e.g. centralization. Even though the PBFT and its extensions solve the Byzantine problem, the traditional BFT algorithms need a unique leader in a round of consensus process. In the case of normal operations, the leader of BFT is typically unchanged and so it may be attacked easily.

On the other hand, in the case of abnormal operations, the consensus of transaction or the election of the new leader will cost a lot of time and seriously affect the performance of continuous services. Therefore, using a traditional consistency algorithm may damage some essential and important features of blockchain.

2.3 Inspirations of Consensus Mechanism in Consortium Blockchain

Delegated Proof of Stake (DPoS) [18] is a consensus algorithm first implemented by BitShares and then well-known EOS. It is designed as an implementation of technologies based on democracy. DPoS uses voting and election process to protect blockchain from centralization and malicious usage. Compared to PoW, DPoS seems however more centralized. For examples, EOS only have 21 witness nodes who are responsible for creating and validating blocks. For a governable point of view, a blockchain developed with DPoS consensus is more like a consortium blockchain, but still lack of supporting for enterprise services.

Tendermint uses a BFT protocol that can be described as a variant of PBFT [19]. In PBFT protocol, the client sends a new transaction directly to all nodes. In contrast, the clients in Tendermint disseminate their transactions to the validators (some validating nodes). The most different point for Tendermint is the continuous rotation of the leader. Namely, the leader can be changed after every block generated. The Tendermint protocol and its implementation are still subject to a thorough, peer-reviewed correctness analysis.

Generally, we can see that the development of consensus mechanism are trying to enable the blockchain to achieve a balance between the triangular relationship that is decentralization, scalability and security as shown in Fig. 1. For most of the enterprise services, security and also scalability are the self-evident important factors. Though the public blockchains are more decentralized, the consortium blockchain should still be decentralized or at least so said multi-centralized instead of centralized. Decentralization is the key issue to provide the immutable, traceable and trustable characteristics of blockchain.

3   Layered Architecture for Consensus Mechanism

Before discussing the consensus mechanism with a layered architecture for the enterprise scenario of consortium blockchain, let us have a look into Service-Oriented Architecture (SOA) to understand the common characteristics of enterprise applications and services. Our goal is to implement a new layered and service-oriented consensus mechanism to meet the serious requirements for enterprise services with decentralization, diversity, extensibility, scalability, and enterprise-level security.

SOA is an architectural pattern in computer software design in which application components provide services to other components via a network protocol. The principles of service-orientation are independent of any product, vendor or technology. SOA has some key principles, for examples, the services can provide a standardized service contract which describes what the service is about, and the services should be loose coupling that is less dependency on each other. SOA is able to make it easier for enterprise services over various networks to work with each other.

Based on the SOA principles, we deconstruct the consensus mechanism to three loose coupling layers. These are the layers of sequential consensus, consequential consensus, and eventual consensus which are able to construct a service-oriented consensus mechanism architecture in a consortium blockchain for the enterprise services.

3.1 Sequential Consensus

Transaction ordering is the orderly arrangement of transactions collected by the entire blockchain nodes. The purpose of transaction ordering in blockchain is to ensure that all the nodes ultimately execute the same transaction order, which is called sequential consensus. For typical distributed system, the sequential consensus means the eventual consensus can exactly be reached, since all distributed nodes are centrally controlled or trusted. That is, each node executes the transaction in the same order and they can get a same result since the nodes are honest. However this is not always true in the blockchain system, where there may exist aggressive node who will provide a different result even though the order is the same. The sequential consensus is commonly not specified in the public blockchain, because the transaction order is exactly achieved synchronously when the block is packaged.

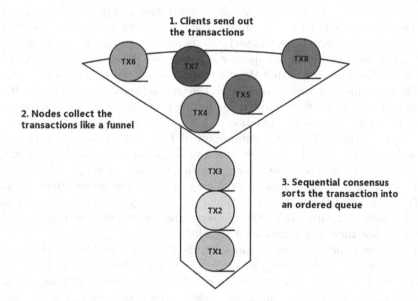

Fig. 2. The sequential consensus acts like a funnel to sort the collected transactions into an ordered queue

However ordering and blocking can be done in two separate steps in the consortium blockchain. The nodes can use a traditional consistency algorithm to achieve the sequential consensus like Raft, even though it is a not BFT algorithm. It is an important fact that the transaction is not needed to be executed and the nodes don't need the detail or result of transaction but only a transaction id at the process of sequential consensus. The transaction id should be an address of context e.g. a hash value which can verify the detail of transaction. The sequential consensus mechanism can provide a channel of ordered transaction consistently if more than 50% nodes (or stake holders) are working and honest.

In addition to addressing the order how the transactions are executed, the sequential consensus can also solve the issue of transaction missing in network broadcast from client to server. So the sequential consensus layer provides a high-performance, scalable and QoS guarantee service. It just acts like a funnel which can sort the huge amount of transactions into an ordered queue as shown in Fig. 2 so that the subsequent blockchain services can process with an ordered label.

3.2 Consequential Consensus

The consequential consensus means the distributed nodes can confirm a final consistency on the transaction results. We can understand it as the verification of the computed transaction results. For most of transactions, the executions can be totally independent. That means for two transaction, e.g. TX1 and TX2, the final result will keep the same even if the executing order is swapped, i.e. changing TX2 to execute before TX1 does not matter. So these independent transactions can be executed parallelly and improve the node's throughput and reduce the response time. However some transactions are dependent, that is one transaction can only be executed after the another is completed. These transactions will be executed serially to ensure that the distributed nodes can get the same results.

The consequential consensus confirms the transaction computing results from the distributed nodes. For a limited computing time, the nodes must show their computing result for each transaction. For examples, in a system of four nodes, node A, B, C shows they get a same result of TX1 then the consequential consensus is already reached no matter with node D giving a same or different result or even no response. Therefore, the consequential consensus is a process in which the minority will be subordinate to the majority after the nodes broadcast and verify the result of the transaction. When the majority of results reaches a certain threshold, e.g. larger than 50% or even higher for security, the consequential consensus is achieved or otherwise it is failed.

The consequential consensus can solve the Byzantine problem in the decentralized nodes. For most enterprise services, the transaction only involves a subset of the whole nodes. The computing results can be confirmed to achieve the consequential consensus by the major nodes in the subset instead of the entire blockchain network. This will greatly reduce the communications via P2P network and improve the performance and scalability of the blockchain network.

3.3   Eventual Consensus

The block in blockchain ledger is a method to save and solidify the transactions. So within a period, a block is packaged by a node with a set of transactions and the new block will be connected into a chain structure or DAG (Directed Acyclic Graph) structure to form the blockchain ledger. That is also how the name of *blockchain* comes from. A block is just a checkpoint of the distributed system for the sequence and results of transactions.

The eventual consensus or called the block consensus should determine or confirm which node can and will package the new block. The block will be finally saved into the ledger by each blockchain node after a verification process. So the eventual consensus is actually the sequential consensus of blocks. For PoW, it is just a random process determined by nodes' computing power. For PBFT, the sequence of block is determined by the three-stage process for a proposal to confirm. So for scalability, PoW is $O(n)$ for communications while PBFT is $O(n^2)$, where n is the number of blockchain node.

An important problem to be solved in block consensus is to avoid some nodes take advantage of the block generation to prevent some effective transactions from being written to the blockchain. So each node should have the opportunity to generate the block and also can validate the blocks generated by the other nodes. A deterministic block sequence is therefore not a good choice in the blockchain, so a random process in block consensus will be more secure and effective to achieve the eventual consensus of blockchain transactions.

3.4   A Practical Layered Consensus Mechanism

For the consensus mechanism PoW in the public blockchain, the layers are equivalent to sorting transactions at first and then packing out a block to broadcast and validate. That is called mining process which can achieve the block consensus, sequential consensus and consequential consensus at a same time while the new block has been verified by other nodes. In this mechanism where the sequence of blocks is determined at first, the node who signs the new block will also determine the sequence of transactions and the nodes can only check the consequential consensus after the new block is generated and broadcasted. The soft bifurcation and the attack of computing power cannot be avoided in a competitive environment of blockchain nodes Because of the uncertainty of block, the eventual consensus is not deterministic.

However, the sequence of consensus layers is not always like the above in consortium blockchain. For an instance, in a PBFT consensus mechanism, the consequential consensus and sequential consensus can be usually achieved at first and finally the eventual consensus. So the issue of soft bifurcation can be avoided but again it leads to the issue of scalability since the communication of network is $O(n^2)$.

Our idea is to divide the consensus mechanism into three layers of different services. As shown in Fig. 3, the blockchain system can complete the consensus process in the sequence of (1) transaction ordering to achieve sequential

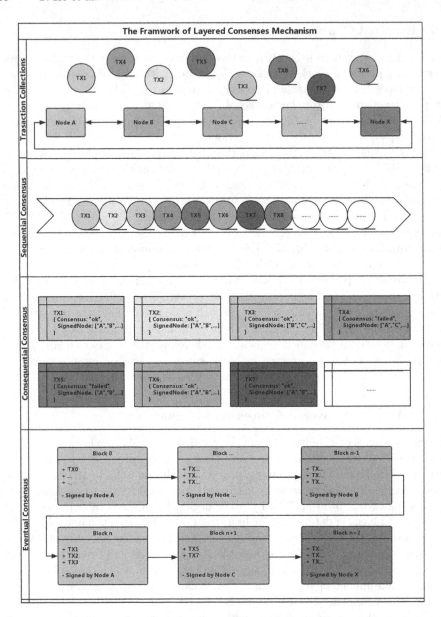

Fig. 3. The framework of new layered consensus mechanism. The first process is the transaction collections where the blockchain nodes collect the service invocations individually in the struct of transaction (TX) from clients. To obtain a consistent result in the independent nodes, the transactions go through a high-efficiency ordering queue to achieve the sequential consensus. Then, the nodes compute the results of these transactions synchronously or even asynchronously if possible and achieve the consequential consensus to accept or reject the transaction concordantly. Finally after the eventual consensus, a node will generate the block which will contain multiple successful transactions and the blockchain system will save the block to the respective ledger where the records will be consistent, trackable and irreversible.

consensus, (2) results verification to achieve consequential consensus and finally (3) the block consensus process to determine which node to package block and to achieve the eventual consensus. The whole process can be divided into two relatively independent steps. The first one is a process of transaction ordering → sequential consensus → result verification → consequential consensus in the dimension of transactions. The second one is block consensus that is eventual consensus in the dimension of blocks.

After the consensus mechanism is divided into the three layers of loose coupling services, different consistency algorithms can be adopted for sequential consensus, consequential consensus and eventual block consensus respectively. Sequential consensus does not care about the execution results of transactions, so CFT algorithms like Kafka clusters or even a centralized service can be used to collect as many transactions as possible and improve the throughput and performance. So the sequential consensus mainly solves the availability issue in a distributed system. The consequential consensus ensures the ultimate consistency of the data and generally addresses Byzantine problems. So BFT algorithms such as PBFT can be used in the subset of relevant nodes which are required to verify the transaction. Therefore, the consequential consensus mainly solves the consistency issue. Block consensus or eventual consensus ensures the availability of the blockchain system, that is, there are always some nodes to provide the blockchain services. The random consensus algorithm can be used to avoid network attacks like DDoS. So the eventual consensus mainly solves the partition fault tolerance. This loose coupling and layered consensus mechanism will help the blockchain services to reach a better balance of decentralization, scalability and security in the enterprise scenarios.

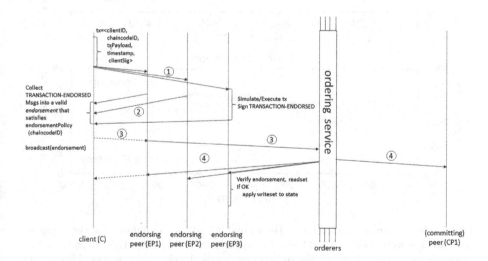

Fig. 4. Illustration of one possible transaction flow (common-case path) in the original architecture of Hyperledger Fabric. From the *architecture reference* of Hyperledger Fabric tutorials https://hyperledger-fabric.readthedocs.io/en/release-1.4/

4   Enterprise Services and Applications

When applying the new layered and service-oriented consensus mechanism to the architecture of a blockchain framework, it shows a positive and exciting achievement e.g. for the optimization of Hyperledger Fabric. We also gives some examples of enterprise services to show the benefit and great power of the layered consensus architecture with the ability of decentralization and extensibility.

4.1   Optimization of Hyperledger Fabric Framework

Hyperledger Fabric is a blockchain framework implementation and one of the Hyperledger projects hosted by The Linux Foundation[1]. A common transaction flow is shown in Fig. 4 for the original architecture of Hyperledger Fabric. The endorsing peers will execute the transactions and send an endorsement back to the client. Then after validating the endorsement policy, client will send the endorsed transaction to an ordering service to achieve the sequential consensus. However after the block is generated by the orderers, the peers including the

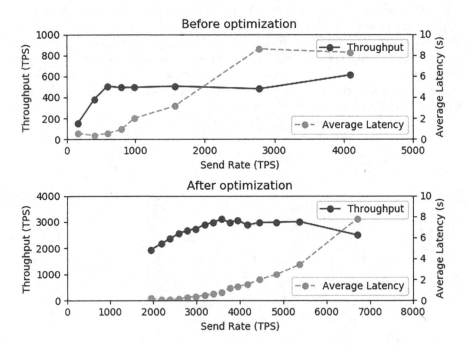

Fig. 5. On the same cloud servers, the available testing throughput for the original framework is only around 500 TPS in the upper plot. After the optimization with the layered consensus mechanism, the throughput is arised to larger than 3000 TPS in the lower plot.

---

[1] https://www.hyperledger.org/projects/fabric.

committing peers must validate the transactions in this block again, since the results of transactions may be changed after ordering service.

This workflow of the consensus mechanism brings two issues. One is that the low performance since a transaction must be validated twice to achieve the consequential consensus. Another is that the misleading response to the client when the client has already received the successful endorsement but the transaction is finally not written into the new block. The new layered consensus mechanism can solve these two problems and provide a better decentralization, scalability and security.

We use the ordering service to reach the sequential consensus at first. Then the nodes are reconstructed and can execute transactions in a pool with a struct of process tree. After broadcasting the hash value of read and write set (RWSet in Fabric), the endorsing nodes can achieve the consequential mechanism. Finally after a random process, the eventual consensus is achieved to generate the new block. The optimization of performance is shown in Fig. 5 where the available throughput in TPS (Transactions Per Second) is increased from 500 to larger than 3000 in the same testing cluster where the red lines show the average latency representing the availability of system.

For the issue of misleading response, the transaction response can be fed back to the clients just after the achievement of consequential consensus instead of the eventual consensus. Without the block informations like block number and block hash value, the transaction can be still responsed as a success or failure since the relevant nodes have achieved the consequential consensus. The block consensus is only a checkpoint in the form of block, and it is hardly failed in the enterprise scenario exactly with the limited business trust and additional artificial supervision. This ealier response will also speed up the blockchain applications in the service layer where the responsed transaction facilitates the process of subsequent business and the applications can then query the block and blockchain information later if needed.

4.2   Some Examples for Enterprise Applications and Services

Modern Enterprise Architecture. The modern enterprise architecture is a best practice to promote the governance of consortium blockchain. A modern enterprise architecture has the board of directors, administrative departments and the board of supervisors. Enterprise architecture applies architecture principles and practices to guide organizations through the business, information, process, and technology changes necessary to execute their strategies. These practices utilize the various aspects of an enterprise to identify, motivate, and achieve these changes. With the layered consensus mechanism, we can govern the consortium blockchain and the enterprise federation in an enterprise-like architecture. If considering the nodes of the consortium blockchain as the shareholders of an enterprise, the nodes involved in the sequential consensus are just like the board of directors where they usually don't care about the details of everyday transactions but determine the directions of the system. The nodes involved in the consequential consensus are just like the administrative departments who are responsible for handling the detail business and make sure the coordination of the organization. Finally the nodes involved in the eventual consensus are just like the board of supervisors where they usually don't involvd in the management of enterprise (the consortium blockchain) but act as the final barrier to protect the interests of shareholders (the blockchain system). The governance of a modern enterprise has been widely and deeply studied, but not the enterprise federation. Through the introduction of a modern enterprise architecture, it can better promote the application and development of the consortium blockchain in the federated commercial field.

Enterprise Service Bus. An important component of SOA is the enterprise services bus (ESB) [20]. P2P communication normally has issues with scalability. These issues are further fused with increased systems. ESB implements a communication system between mutually interacting software applications in SOA. ESB as a middleware technology is a Bus-like architecture used to integrate distributed and heterogeneous systems. ESB promotes agility and flexibility with regard to high-level protocol communication between applications. Using the layered consensus mechanism, a consortium blockchain can actually establish an cross-enterprise service bus. Compared to the original centralized governance, the cross-enterprise service bus provides a method to construct the connectivity and sharing of data and resources in multiple enterprises which will greatly facilitate the service integration and collaboration across the different enterprises. For an example, the relevant enterprises in a supply chain can integrate and connect their production resources, inventory resources and sales resources though the cross-enterprise service bus. Crucially, the unique features of the blockchain like the access control and irreversible can protect the reality and security of high-value enterprise data. So such an efficient model of enterprise federation would be an important technology to integrate the business ecosystem to discover and create much more business value. This new technology and architecture can be called *Blockchain Service Bus* (BSB) to construct a cross-enterprise resource planning for the newly-developing economy of enterprises federation which is just like ERP (Enterprise Resource Planning) applied to the management of modern enterprise.

5   Summary

In this paper, we briefly summarized the development of the blockchain consensus mechanism and inspired the service-oriented consensus mechanism in consortium blockchain especially for the enterprise scenarios. In the architecture of SOA, we introduced the layered architecture of consensus mechanism which includes sequential consensus, consequential consensus and eventual consensus respectively. Benefit from the new consensus algorithm, the transaction and consensus process in Hyperledger Fabric has been optimized which validates that the performance and scalability have been greatly improved.

As discussed above, the service-oriented and layered consensus mechanism can promote the consortium blockchain to a better balance of decentralization, scalability and security for the enterprise services. These service-oriented technologies should be more practical which can be applied to enterprise services and also the cross-enterprise services with decentralization and extensibility in the principle of enterprise-level security.

Acknowledgement. This work was partially supported by the technical projects No. S-2018-164-503559, No. 2017YFB0802703, and No. JSGG20160331101809920. This work was also supported by NSFC(91646202), the 1000-Talent program.

References

1. Nakamoto, S.: Bitcoin: A peer-to-peer electronic cash system (2008). https://bitcoin.org/bitcoin.pdf
2. Litecoin. https://litecoin.org/. Accessed 25 Mar 2019
3. He, S., Xing, C., Zhang, L.-J.: A business-oriented schema for blockchain network operation. In: Chen, S., Wang, H., Zhang, L.-J. (eds.) ICBC 2018. LNCS, vol. 10974, pp. 277–284. Springer, Cham (2018). https://doi.org/10.1007/978-3-319-94478-4_21
4. Wood, G.: Ethereum, A secure decentralised generalised transaction ledger. Ethereum Project Yellow Paper, pp. 1–32 (2014). https://gavwood.com/paper.pdf
5. Chen, H., Zhang, L.-J.: FBaaS: functional blockchain as a service. In: Chen, S., Wang, H., Zhang, L.-J. (eds.) ICBC 2018. LNCS, vol. 10974, pp. 243–250. Springer, Cham (2018). https://doi.org/10.1007/978-3-319-94478-4_17
6. Back, A.: Hashcash-a denial of service counter-measure (2002). ftp://sunsite.icm.edu.pl/site/replay.old/programs/hashcash/hashcash.pdf
7. King, S., Nadal, S.: PPCoin, Peer-to-peer crypto-currency with proof-of-stake. Self-published paper, 19 August 2012. https://bitcoin.peryaudo.org/vendor/peercoin-paper.pdf
8. Zhang, L.J., Cai, H., Zhang, J.: Services Computing. Tsinghua University Press, Beijing (2007)
9. Cachin, C., Vukolić, M.: Blockchain consensus protocols in the wild. arXiv preprint arXiv:1707.01873 (2017). https://arxiv.org/abs/1707.01873
10. Lamport, L., Shostak, R., Pease, M.: The Byzantine generals problem. ACM Trans. Program. Lang. Syst. (TOPLAS) 4(3), 382–401 (1982). https://www-inst.eecs.berkeley.edu/~cs162/sp16/static/readings/Original_Byzantine.pdf
11. Saleh, F.: Blockchain without waste, Proof-of-stake (2018). https://www.ivey.uwo.ca/cmsmedia/3783185/11-30-18-saleh.pdf
12. Kiayias, A., Russell, A., David, B., Oliynykov, R.: Ouroboros: a provably secure proof-of-stake blockchain protocol. In: Katz, J., Shacham, H. (eds.) CRYPTO 2017. LNCS, vol. 10401, pp. 357–388. Springer, Cham (2017). https://doi.org/10.1007/978-3-319-63688-7_12
13. Ongaro, D., Ousterhout, J.: In search of an understandable consensus algorithm. In: 2014 USENIX Annual Technical Conference (USENIXATC 2014), pp. 305–319 (2014). https://www.usenix.org/conference/atc14/technical-sessions/presentation/ongaro

14. Castro, M., Liskov, B.: Practical Byzantine fault tolerance. In: OSDI 1999, pp. 173–186 (1999). https://www.usenix.org/legacy/events/osdi99/full_papers/castro/castro_html/castro.html
15. Barborak, M., Dahbura, A., Malek, M.: The consensus problem in fault-tolerant computing. ACM Comput. Surv. (CSur) **25**(2), 171–220 (1993). https://doi.org/10.1145/152610.152612
16. Lamport, L.: The part-time parliament. ACM Trans. Comput. Syst. (TOCS) **16**(2), 133–169 (1998). https://courses.cs.washington.edu/courses/csep590/04wi/papers/lamport-part-time-parliament.pdf
17. Clement, A., Wong, E.L., Alvisi, L., et al.: Making byzantine fault tolerant systems tolerate byzantine faults. In: NSDI 2009, vol. 9, pp. 153–168 (2009). http://static.usenix.org/events/nsdi09/tech/full_papers/clement/clement.pdf
18. Larimer, D.: Delegated proof-of-stake (DPOS). Bitshare whitepaper (2014). https://www.bitshares.foundation/papers/BitSharesBlockchain.pdf
19. Kwon, J.: Tendermint: Consensus without mining. Draft v. 0.6 (2014). https://cdn.relayto.com/media/files/LPgoWO18TCeMIggJVakt_tendermint.pdf
20. Chappell, D.A.: Enterprise Service Bus. O'Reilly Media, Inc., Sebastopol (2004)

Digital-Physical Parity for Food Fraud Detection

Sin Kuang Lo[1,2(✉)], Xiwei Xu[1,2], Chen Wang[1], Ingo Weber[1,2], Paul Rimba[1], Qinghua Lu[1,2], and Mark Staples[1,2]

[1] Data61, CSIRO, Sydney, Australia
{sinkuang.lo,xiwei.xu,chen.wang,ingo.weber,paul.rimba,
qinghua.lu,mark.staples}@data61.csiro.au
[2] School of Computer Science and Engineering, UNSW, Sydney, Australia

Abstract. Food fraud has an adverse impact on all stakeholders in the food production and distribution process. Lack of transparency in food supply chains is a strong factor contributing to food fraud. With limited transparency, the insights on food supply chains are fragmented, and every participant has to rely on trusted third parties to assess food quality. Blockchain has been introduced to the food industry to enable transparency and visibility, but it can only protect the integrity of a *digital representation* of physical food, not the physical food directly. Tagging techniques, like barcodes and QR codes that are used to connect the physical food to its digital representation, are vulnerable to attacks. In this paper, we propose a blockchain-based solution to link physical items, like food, to their digital representations using physical attributes of the item. This solution is generic in its support for different methods to perform the physical checks; as a concrete example, we use machine learning models on visual features of food products, through regular and thermal photos. Furthermore, we use blockchain to introduce a reward system for supply chain participants, which incentivizes honesty and supplying data. We evaluate the technical feasibility of components of this architecture for food fraud detection using a real-world scenario, including machine-learning models for distinguishing between grain-fed and grass-fed beef.

Keywords: Blockchain · Machine learning · Food fraud

1 Introduction

Food fraud is a US$40 billion per year industry, which has a significant negative impact on all stakeholders in the food production and distribution process. Food fraudsters leverage consumers' perceived safety, trust, and value associated with prominent brands and certifications to charge premium prices for inferior, or even dangerous, food products. However, it is difficult, if not impossible, to eliminate the fraud industry considering the big profit it generates for beneficiaries.

© Springer Nature Switzerland AG 2019
J. Joshi et al. (Eds.): ICBC 2019, LNCS 11521, pp. 65–79, 2019.
https://doi.org/10.1007/978-3-030-23404-1_5

Lack of transparency and visibility of the food supply chain is a strong factor contributing to food fraud. Food supply chains are complex multi-party systems that involve different participants, such as farmers, food production processors, and retailers. However, regulations in major markets, such as the US, the EU, and China generally only require one-up and one-down traceability regarding supply chain participants [1]. In a food supply chain with limited transparency, insights are fragmented and thus each consumer or producer has to rely on trusted third party agencies to monitor food quality across the whole food supply chain.

Blockchain technology has been applied to food supply chains [3,5] to enable transparency and visibility because every participant within the blockchain network has access to all the records and historical movements of information in the entire system. For instance, a blockchain-based traceability system has been proposed for tracking food products along international supply chains [8]. However, blockchain only guarantees the integrity of the digital representation of food but not the integrity of the physical attributes of a food product.

Commonly used tagging technologies, like barcodes, serial numbers, and QR codes can connect physical food to its digital representation. Such techniques are vulnerable to attacks, e.g., a counterfeit product with authentic packaging and tag[1]. To counter fraud, it is necessary to enable supply chain participants to verify the connection between the food itself and the digital information.

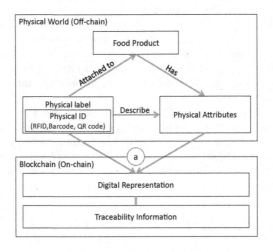

Fig. 1. Conceptual overview of food fraud detection

A conceptual overview of the relation between a food product, its physical label, ID, attributes and a digital representation is shown in Fig. 1. The integrity we seek to establish is between the physical food product and its digital representation. We approach this goal by connecting the physical item via its label and

---

[1] https://www.news.com.au/finance/business/retail/empty-tin-sales-a-new-low-in-baby-formula-saga/news-story/b269717700fa9128470803cb34363705.

physical attributes to the digital system (links marked (a) in Fig. 1). Conceptually, this architecture takes a similar approach as in multi-factor authentication and biometric cryptosystems where physiological and behavioral features are used for identifying a user [7]. The difference is mainly on that the physical characteristics of a food product is rich and diverse, which is difficult to capture using a closed system.

Stable isotope ratio analysis is one technique in this direction: chemical isotope levels on physical food products, e.g., on muscles of cows [4], can be analyzed to verify claims of origin. However, isotope analysis is not economically feasible at large to tackle food fraud issues. Similarly, a national lab for drug substance testing recently tested honey samples sourced from supermarkets and markets in Australia; adulteration was detected in 18% of the 38 samples [10]. While independent labs may provide test results, the confirmation of their discovery takes time. Test methods need to be fast and cheap enough to enable widespread use.

We propose using machine learning techniques to assess food products through exploiting distinct visual features to verify their physical attributes. Machine learning models provide an effective way to encapsulate knowledge of differentiating objects based on features. Data can be collected from cameras, smartphones, X-ray, and ultrasound scanners. By training models and performing feature extraction across training data, we can verify the physical attributes of a food product against its digital information. Recipients in the supply chain can check food authenticity based on features they collect.

In this paper, we make the following contributions:

- We propose a blockchain-based architecture that enables checking the parity of physical items and their digital representation. The proposal is generic in its support for methods to check physical attributes against the digital claims about these attributes.
- As one concrete method, we propose machine learning on distinct visual features of food. In this method, we provide the exposure and knowledge about food fraud to the consumers by machine learning models.
- We devise incentive mechanisms that distribute coins to food supply chain participants to reward honest behavior and supplying data. These rewards can further be shared with machine learning developers, who contribute models that allow fraud detection.

We evaluate the technical feasibility of components of this architecture for food fraud detection using a real-world scenario, including machine-learning models for distinguishing between grain-fed and grass-fed beef. To the best of our knowledge, there is no related work that use machine learning and blockchain to link between the physical attributes of physical food products and their digital representations.

The remainder of the paper is organized as follows. The overview of the generic architecture is listed in Sect. 2, followed by the resulting system design in Sect. 3. Section 4 provides technical details of the system. The evaluation with a beef case study is described in Sect. 5. Finally, Sect. 6 concludes the paper and outlines the future work.

2   A Generic Architecture for Food Digtal-Physical Parity

2.1   Overview

The generic architecture for food digital-physical parity is shown in Fig. 2. The architecture aims to connect the physical items in a supply chain with their digital representation. The attributes of a physical items (e.g., visual features, geographical location and chemical composition) can be assessed via various techniques. There is no perfect solution that fits all different kinds of food products: for some, it might be more suitable to check their visual attributes but for others it might only be possible to check via their chemical composition. Hence, our generic architecture allows the use of different types of assessment methods to verify the claimed attributes on physical products. For the digital representation of the physical items, blockchain is chosen due to its immutable and transparent nature and ability to span across dynamic networks of parties. Functionally, blockchain can be used as a data storage and a computational infrastructure in a software system [9]. As a data storage, blockchain stores all transactions that have ever occurred in the network, which cannot be deleted or modified. As a computational infrastructure, blockchain can run programs called *smart contracts*, the result of which is stored in the distributed trusted data storage.

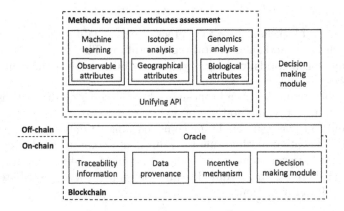

Fig. 2. A generic architecture for food digital-physical parity

The claimed attribute assessment methods requires computational resources that can currently not be fulfilled by blockchain. Therefore, the computation of the assessment is done off-chain. Data required for the execution of assessment are also stored off-chain.

Information related to the food supply chain, such as the claimed attributes of food products, the details about stakeholders on the supply chain are being recorded on blockchain. The transactions on blockchain enables the recipients to trace the originality and the processing activities on the food product in the corresponding supply chain. Incentive mechanism would be deployed as a smart contract on the blockchain to motivate active participants to contribute to the supply chain. The results from the assessment of the claimed attributes will be used as the input for the incentive mechanism to determine the reward to the contributors.

As blockchain is unable to communicate with the external world, an *oracle* is required to enable the interaction between blockchain and the off-chain components. The oracle is connected to a unifying API, which can interact with the different attributes assessment methods.

There is a decision making module in our generic architecture that decides whether an item is considered authentic or not: it takes the different assessments for the available methods and decides whether the claimed physical attributes match the observed ones well enough. The decision making module can be either deployed on-chain or off-chain, depending on the specific situation. In the context where decision is done in a proprietary, confidential way by a single authority, the decision making module would be kept off-chain. If the decision making has been established by consensus from a set of authorities, and its workings need not be kept confidential, the decision making module can be kept on blockchain to ensure the transparency of its rules and implementation.

2.2 Food Fraud Detection

Food fraud encompasses the deliberate and intentional substitution, addition, or misrepresentation of food, food ingredients or food packaging for economic gain. Introducing blockchain into supply chain with Internet of Things (IoT) [6] enable real-time monitoring of physical movement via tags on products and immutable food provenance recorded on blockchain. In additional, the smart contract on blockchain can be used to enable compliance checking. The provenance information or the authenticate food can be used to detect *simulation*, where the illegitimate product is designed to look like the legitimate product with the same label, or *overrun*, where the legitimate product is made in excess of production agreements. In these two types of food fraud, there are duplicated labels. Although it is difficult to determine which one is authentic, and which one is simulation or overrun based on the digital representation only. *Diversion* means the sale or distribution of legitimate products outside of intended markets. If the condition of sale and distribution associated with the products is recorded in blockchain, smart contract can help to do automatic compliance checking against legislation. However, other types of food fraud, like *adulteration*, where a component of the finished products is fraudulent, can not be detected by using provenance information because the coupling between the physical food and its digital representation is loose when only basic tagging techniques are used. Adulteration becomes automatically detectable when the binding between the physical food and its digital representation is tighten by any of the attributes assessment techniques.

3   Food Fraud Detection System Design

We instantiate a food fraud detection system design based on the proposed generic architecture. The system helps to manage the knowledge of differentiating fraud from non-fraud. The knowledge about food fraud is accumulated through analysis of multimodal data (regular camera, thermal camera, and specially designed sensors) as well as the interaction between food producers, independent food experts, and recipients in a food supply chain. A more detailed machine learning assessment module of the system is shown in Fig. 3. Although we demonstrate the system design using an image processing technique, the architecture can use other machine learning techniques.

As discussed above, the existing methods of assessing the integrity of the physical attributes of food products are either expensive (some require complicated lab procedures) or vulnerable to attack (an adversary can easily swap the RFID tag for the physical food products). This food fraud detection system focuses on visible, distinguishable features of food product that can be captured by a regular camera, thermal camera, or other specially designed sensors. Take wild salmon as an example. Wild salmon get their characteristic colour from what they eat. The unique colour reflects the diet of shrimp and krill. Salmon from different geo-location consumes a different proportion of carotenoid-rich creatures, which affects how pink or red salmon becomes.

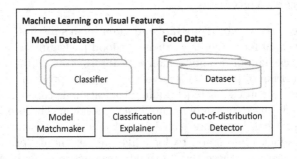

Fig. 3. Machine learning assessment of our food fraud detection system

The main components of this system is a data repository, a knowledge base that captures the differences between fraud and non-fraud food products and a blockchain-based trust management module. The knowledge is represented as machine learning models that make use of food product data collectible by food suppliers and recipients to classify frauds. The data and models are often provided by food suppliers or independent parties. A consumer can make use of these models to classify whether the food product she purchases is fraud.

There are incentives for a high quality food product supplier to provide data containing identifiable features to differentiate their high quality products. Similarly, food fraudsters also have the motivation to control and manipulate the data/model in the system to confuse the consumers to gain benefit.

3.1 Users

The users in the system are:

1. Food product suppliers and experts who are knowledgeable about the difference between fraudulent and authentic food products.
2. Recipients in a food supply chain who can collect data of a particular food product.
3. Machine learning developers that provide services for recipients to check food fraud based on the data provided by recipients.

3.2 Data Provenance

For food products with potential digital features, aggregating various test methods for transparency and reproducibility is essential. As mentioned in Sect. 2, we apply the blockchain technique to enable tracking data and model provenance and linking them to the party for accountability.

All the datasets within the food database and the classifiers within the model database are registered on the blockchain, thus, publicly available to all the users of the system. Other than registration, all the activities conducted on the datasets and the models have separate records on the blockchain. The tamper-proof log of events on blockchain provides the connection between the data (as the digital representation of the food product) and the historical activities executed on the data. Machine learning models are viewed as a type of data.

A simplified data analytics life cycle is depicted in Fig. 4a. Food suppliers and recipients contribute to this process by uploading batch data or new data item of a food product. Machine learning developers contribute to this process by cleaning the raw data and training/re-training models that capture the knowledge from the food experts. The data analysts register all the analytic activities, for example, who does cleaning on which dataset at what time. Every activity record on blockchain is signed by the person who conducts the activity using their digital signature. Such information allows tracing back to data analysis activities that have been conducted on a particular data. It allows the system users to track the changes of food fraud detection knowledge represented by the data and the models and the system to quantify the contribution activities towards the final model.

The incentive mechanisms discussed in Sect. 3.3 uses the data provenance and food traceability information recorded on blockchain to distribute reward to the contributors and honest participants in the supply chain.

3.3 Trust Management Through Incentive

We use blockchain to provide an incentive infrastructure for the food fraud detection system. With cryptocurrency, blockchain can also provide a trading infrastructure that enables contingent payment implemented as a smart contract for trading items registered on the blockchain. In the context of incentive, honesty and trust is the "tradable" item. We introduce two coins as the incentive mechanisms. *Contribution-coin* is the incentive for ML scientists and experts to use the system and share their knowledge and data. *Honesty-coin* is used as the reward to the honest recipients in the supply chain.

Reward to Contribution. There are two mechanisms to reward contribution. One is a rule-based automated mechanism that rewards the users of the platform based on their contribution. The contribution to the platform can be roughly quantified based on metrics proposed by machine learning experts. The value of data is determined by its size and diversity. A data has more value if it is different from any of the data in the system, for example, data from a new food product, or data from a new feature of a food product. Model with higher accuracy has more value to the system. How to calculate the contribution based on these or more metrics is our future work. Point-to-point reward model as shown in Fig. 4a will be implemented. The reward to a certain model is split between the developer who cleans the data and the developer who trains the model if more than one developers are involved in this data analytics process. How to split the reward is decided by machine learning developers.

The second is a human-driven point-to-point reward mechanism, like the digital reward system on social media where rewards can be sent between users arbitrarily. There will be constraints for the reward, as the monetary limit. Since all the reward transactions are recorded on the blockchain, they are transparent for public auditing. For example, ML scientist A is rewarded x Contribution-coins from supplier B, a *link* is established between A and B with weight x. If the supplier is fraudster or colluding with ML scientist, it is supposed to have unusual patterns [2].

Reward to Honesty. The food fraud detection is primarily to check compliance between the authenticity information on blockchain and the food product data uploaded by recipients. As shown in Fig. 4b, any participants in supply chain can report a potential fraud case via our system. In the case that the food product complies with the authenticity information provided by the farm, some *honesty-coins* are rewarded equally to all the participants in the supply chain according to the food traceability information on the blockchain, With this incentive reporting mechanism, it motivates every participant in the same line of supply chain to cross check the product that arrived at their position.

However, in the case of negative result, the result of fraud detection does not indicate which participant in the food supply chain is the fraudster. In the case that the food product does not comply with the authenticity information, a food expert is selected and requested to validate the result. If the result is invalid, a machine learning developer is alerted and requested to re-train the model. If the food expert confirms the validity of the result, the honesty-coin own by all the previous participants in the supply chain will be minused off to pay the reporter. This mechanism punishes all the participants in the supply chain as an

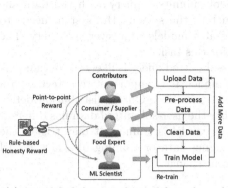
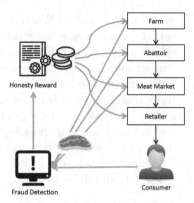

(a) Simplified data analytics life cycle and contribution coin distribution

(b) Simplified beef supply chain and honesty-coin distribution

Fig. 4. Coins distribution

incentive for honest participants to find out the food fraudster or partner with other participants with a higher balance of honesty coin.

3.4 Off-Chain Components

As the blockchain does not have the scalability to execute computation heavy process on-chain nor it could store big size of raw data on-chain, we have chosen to execute our machine learning model and store all the dataset for the model off-chain. The inherent disadvantage of using off-chain is that there are no native way for blockchain to fetch data from off-chain. Hence, the interoperability between the off-chain components and blockchain can be achieved with the use of an oracle. Oracle is needed to inject data from off-chain into blockchain. Details are discussed in Sect. 4. The training dataset and the model are all stored off chain. Off-chain databases and modules are being described below:

- *Food database*—A collection of datasets that show the difference between fraudulent and non-fraudulent of various food products. Food fraud is a huge market, and a continuous data collection mechanism is vital to help detection techniques keeping up with fraud techniques with new data collection devices and knowledge built on top of new datasets;
- *Model database*—Storing various classifiers and their associated metadata. We assume that the classifiers are learned of the system, based on the datasets within the food database. Every classifier is aimed to distinguish fraudulent food from non-fraudulent food under certain circumstances. The definition of fraud is context specific. One example is to distinguish grain-fed beef from grass-fed beef, as discussed in Sect. 5. All the newly uploaded product data and the corresponding detection results are stored, and a machine learning developer is selected regularly to double check and confirm the result. Such dataset with a label will be used to improve the performance of the models.

– *Model matchmaker*—When a recipient submits a query with the data she collects about a specific food product to the system, the system needs to search for its model database for suitable models to answer the query. The "model matchmaker" is responsible for this task.
– *Out-of-distribution detector*—A user-submitted query is likely to contain patterns that has never been seen by a model. It is important to detect such a mismatch to avoid arbitrary classifications. The "Out-of-distribution detector" is responsible for checking whether the user-submitted data has different distribution with the data on which a model is trained. It may trigger the re-training of a model based on changing data or training of a new model when data distribution has a significant change.

4   Implementation

An overall deployment architecture of the food fraud detection system is shown in Fig. 5. It has four main components: (1) a blockchain with registries and incentives implemented in smart contracts; (2) classifiers and an out-of-distribution detector which are hosted on AWS; (3) an Amazon S3 bucket for storing images uploaded from the users and other datasets; and (4) an Oraclize-based oracle as the main connector between the blockchain and AWS.

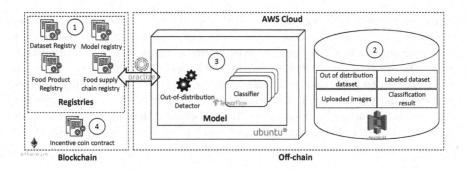

Fig. 5. Overall deployment diagram

4.1   Registries as Smart Contracts

We implemented the food fraud detection system with Ethereum Rinkeby Testnet. All the datasets within the food database and the classifiers within the model database are registered to smart contracts called *dataset registry* and *model registry*. The registries store the metadata of the datasets (description, ownership, the location of the data) and the classifiers (description, ownership, purpose, accuracy). The raw data (the machine learning models and photos of food products) are stored off-chain in the Amazon S3 bucket. A registry, *food supply chain registry*, is used to establish the relationship of all the participants in the supply chain for a food product. The stakeholders of a supply chain play an essential role in ensuring a customer gets a genuine product as described on the its label by the food supplier. Hence, all the details of related participants for food products will be recorded on the blockchain. Another registry, *food product registry*, is used to register the metadata of the food product image submitted by the recipient. Metadata includes the checksum of the image and a pointer that links to the raw image. Once a food product image is labeled and used to train a model, it is removed from the food product registry and is registered in the dataset registry as part of a dataset.

4.2 Incentive Mechanisms as Smart Contracts

We introduced *contribution-coin* and *honesty-coin* to incentivize the honesty of food supplier and contribution of participants towards the system. Both coins are implemented in smart contracts that are compliant to the ERC20 token standard[2]. All the balance of token owners will be recorded by the token contract.

We have a *ratioConfig(address tokenOwner, uint ratio)* function to allow authorized admins (e.g., verified ML scientists) to adjust the ratio pertaining to the distribution of the tokens. For contribution-coin, the experts that verify the accuracy of the newer model will be permitted to set the coin distribution ratio according to the task description entered by the ML scientist. Some of the tasks related to retraining a model include preprocessing and cleaning dataset.

Contribution-coin is rewarded to the ML scientists for their contributions to improve and maintain the machine learning model. Experts are also rewarded for checking the result of the classifier and label given on the training datasets periodically. The initial distribution ratio of coin is set to 6:4 between the ML scientist and experts that verify the classifier and label. Honesty-coin is given to participants of the supply chain for their honesty in supplying genuine food products to the public. If the classifier determined that a food product is genuine as stated on its food label, every participant in the supply chain for that food product will be rewarded Honesty-coin based on the weight predefined in the food supply chain registry

4.3 Off-Chain Storage and Model Execution

The images of food products uploaded by recipients are stored in off-chain storage. In our prototype, we have opted for AWS S3 due to its availability and resilience of the stored data. A pointer that links to the image stored in AWS S3 and checksum of the image will be recorded on the blockchain. Storing only the metadata of images on the blockchain eliminates the high cost of storing images on and the storage limitation of blockchain while allowing detection of any tampering of the images. The pointer and the checksum of the images will be stored on-chain via a transaction.

---

[2] https://theethereum.wiki/w/index.php/ERC20_Token_Standard.

The trained models and the training datasets are also stored off-chain. The execution environment of the ML model is running on an Ubuntu 16.04 LTS AWS EC2 instance. The machine learning model is written in the Python language with TensorFlow. This module provides two main operations: (1) image data upload; and (2) image data classification. The latter returns classification results together with saliency maps of the result as well as the confidence that the input image is within the knowledge scope of this model used.

4.4   Oracle for On-Chain and Off-Chain Interoperation

An oracle is a mechanism that fetches data from the external world to the isolated execution environment of a blockchain. We have selected Oraclize[3] for our oracle implementation. It provides various proof mechanisms to ensure the validity of the information acquired from the data source. In our prototype, Oraclize is used to obtain the result of the ML classifier for food fraud detection and distribution of the reward coins to the participants. It is triggered once the result is generated from the model classifier. The oracle will inject the result of the classification into the blockchain and use it as an input for the incentive coin distribution.

5   Example Case Study

We use a simple case study of a beef supply chain to demonstrate the feasibility of our food fraud detection system, which is used to distinguish grain-fed beef (lower quality and price) from grass-fed beef (higher quality and price).

Using the food fraud detection system, a beef recipient can verify the claimed attributes of the beef product (written on the label of in the digital representation). To use the system, the recipient needs to take photo of a full top view of the beef product under good lighting, currently without plastic packaging or other covers, and upload the image to our system. Once the image has been uploaded successfully, the checksum of the image will be calculated, and a script will invoke the Food Product Registry smart contract to add a data item. The pointer to the image and the checksum of the image will be entered as input data on the smart contract to record them on the blockchain. The off-chain ML system is triggered once the data has been recorded on the blockchain. It will retrieve the input data from the blockchain (pointer and checksum) to download the picture, verify the checksum and run the image through the classifier to check whether it is a grain-fed beef or grass-fed beef. The result is checked against the claim, and a threshold-based decision is made and recorded in the result database, triggering the incentive mechanisms.

5.1   Machine Learning for Classifying Beef Types

Grain-fed beef and grass-fed beef are visually different as grain-fed beef has more fat. However, the difference can be subtle and overwhelm consumers. Examples

---

[3] http://www.oraclize.it/.

of the two types of beef are shown in Fig. 6. We trained a classifier based on a small set of grass-fed and grain-fed beef images to help detect the fraud.

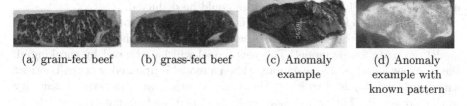

(a) grain-fed beef   (b) grass-fed beef   (c) Anomaly
                                                example   (d) Anomaly
                                                            example with
                                                            known pattern

Fig. 6. Beef images

We built a neural network-based classifier to distinguish grain-fed beef and grass-fed beef based on the meat texture in input images. The binary classifier contains two convolutional layers with 24 and 32 filters at the first and the second layer respectively, and with a kernel size of dimension (5,5), two *max pooling* layers, one drop-out layer and two fully connected layers with 64 units and 2 unites respectively. The texture difference can be learned using a small amount of training data obtained from supplier and supermarket websites. The model accuracy is 92.5% on a dataset randomly picked from the Web. The amount of training data grows as recipients or producers keep collecting and contributing data to the platform, which enables the classifier to be tuned to distinguish a greater variety of beef of the two types. The data diversity enhances the capability of the classifier, thereby enriching the knowledge about food product differences accumulated in the platform.

The learned "knowledge" of a model is useful when a recipient-collected image preserves the pattern known by the classifier even though the machine learning model may not be directly trained from the same type of images. When a beef steak is cooked, the features differentiating grass-fed from grain-fed are not visible, as shown in Fig. 6c. However, when a recipient uses a thermal camera to take a picture of the beef and submits the image, as shown in Fig. 6d to the system to check, the pattern of grain-fed beef becomes highly distinguishable as the fat part has a higher temperature, and thus, a specific model can classify it correctly. This demonstrates the knowledge capturing capability of machine learning models in food fraud detection scenario.

5.2   Incentive Mechanism

In the proposed incentive mechanism, the two types of coins are the Honesty-coin and Contribution-coin, which are distributed as follows. Honesty-coin will be distributed to all the participants recorded on the supplier registry via their accounts if the product bought by the final recipient is verified to be genuine. Once the result from the classifying process is available, the system triggers the incentive coin smart contract. If the result shows "genuine", the smart contract will distribute Honesty-coin to participants according to a predefined split. In the implementation and the case study, we have set equal split for every participant. If the result indicates fraud, the involved participants could be penalized; however, in a decentralized system, that would require the participants to put up a stake upfront from which penalties could be deducted.

The system tracks out-of-distribution cases. Once the occurrence reaches a certain threshold, the ML scientists will be notified to check and tune their model or create a new model. The new model will be adjusted by checking all the recipient-submitted image input. When a model is updated, a smart contract with oracle will be used to inject the model's performance in term of accuracy to the blockchain. The actual model will be stored in cloud data registry. If the updated model achieves higher accuracy than the previous one, contribution-coin will be distributed to the scientist, data contributors and experts who help to verify the performance of the updated model. Currently, the coins are split among all parties in a pre-defined fix ratio.

5.3   Discussion

Our system provides a transparent platform for recipients to verify claims about a food product against its physical attributes. It ensures the originality and integrity of uploaded data and allows tracing back to all participants in case of food fraud. By using incentives, the system encourages participants continuous engagement.

Our design takes future needs into consideration. The classifiers are loosely coupled with other components within the system, thus allowing for ML models to be swapped and modified according to the needs and data. Furthermore, the architecture supports other methods for assessing physical attributes of a product, like isotopic or genomic analysis.

There are limitations arise from using blockchain and machine learning for food parity. There are chances where the beef classifier itself might be rigged for maximum economy benefit for all the participants in the supply chain except the buyer. Although we added the *expert* role as a trusted intermediary to verify and ensure the trustworthiness of the dataset and classifier, but influential supply chain market player might still be able to find way to manipulate the result or machine learning model outside of blockchain and supply chain. As partipants on blockchain are transparent, supply chain participants might be able to communicate wth each other outside of the supply chain to gain mutual consensus to work together to commit fraud. Another problem would be malicious recipients submitting fake beef product. For example, they could have gotten good quality product, but ended up substituting beef from others as input to the system for personal gain or to purposely jeopardize the partipants in the supply chain.

6   Conclusion and Future Work

We proposed a generic architecture that connects physical food products in a supply chain with their digital representation. The architecture uses blockchain for immutability and an incentive system. We instantiate this architecture with a concrete system using machine learning on visual features of beef, to check if the digital claims on the beef product match the physical attributes. By evaluating our system with a real-world scenario on distinguishing the types of beef, we determine that it is feasible to implement the components in our proposed generic architecture to achieve parity between a physical food product and its digital representation. To the best of our knowledge, this is the first research work that combines physical attribute of food products with their digital representation via blockchain and machine learning. Our future work will focus on rewarding participants relative to their contribution, and on introducing a reputation coin that can be used to assess the trustworthiness of participants.

Acknowledgements. This research is supported by the Science and Industry Endowment Fund of Australia.

References

1. Food fraud vulnerability assessment and mitigation-are you doing enough to prevent food fraud? Technical report, PWC (2016)
2. Fleder, M., Kester, M.S., Pillai, S.: Bitcoin transaction graph analysis. arXiv preprint arXiv:1502.01657 (2015)
3. Lo, S.K., Xu, X., Chiam, Y.K., Lu, Q.: Evaluating suitability of applying blockchain. In: The 22nd ICECCS, November 2017
4. Osorio, M.T., Moloney, A.P., Schmidt, O., Monahan, F.J.: Beef authentication and retrospective dietary verification using stable isotope ratio analysis of bovine muscle and tail hair. J. Agric. Food Chem. **59**(7), 3295–3305 (2011)
5. Staples, M.: Risks and opportunities for systems using blockchain and smart contracts. Technical report, Data61 (CSIRO), Sydney (2017)
6. Tian, F.: A supply chain traceability system for food safety based on HACCP, blockchain & internet of things. In: The 14th International Conference on Service Systems and Service Management, June 2017
7. Uludag, U., Pankanti, S., Prabhakar, S., Jain, A.K.: Biometric cryptosystems: issues and challenges. Proc. IEEE **92**(6), 948–960 (2004)
8. Xu, X., Lu, Q., Liu, Y., Yao, H., Zhu, L., Vasilakos, T.: Designing blockchain-based applications: a case study for imported product traceability. Futur. Gener. Comput. Syst. **92**, 399–406 (2019)
9. Xu, X., et al.: The blockchain as a software connector. In: The 13th Working IEEE/IFIP Conference on Software Architecture, April 2016
10. Zhou, X., Taylor, M.P., Davies, P.J., Prasad, S.: Identifying sources of environmental contamination in european honey bees (Apis mellifera) using trace elements and lead isotopic compositions. Environ. Sci. Technol. **52**(3), 991–1001 (2018)

Blockchain Interoperable Digital Objects

Babu Pillai[1(✉)], Kamanashis Biswas[1,2(✉)],
and Vallipuram Muthukkumarasamy[1(✉)]

[1] Griffith University, Gold Coast, Australia
babu.pillai@griffithuni.edu.au,
kamanashis.biswas@acu.edu.au, v.muthu@griffith.edu.au
[2] Australian Catholic University, Sydney, Australia

Abstract. The future of distributed ledger technology such as blockchain is dependent on its ability to interact and integrate with other systems. Therefore, interoperability has become a fundamental issue that needs to be addressed. The emerging category of crypto-assets are managed and understood using different frameworks. There is, therefore, a need for a unified classification of crypto-assets. This work aims to bring some clarity to and understanding on interoperable crypto-assets and their characteristics. This paper categorizes digital crypto-assets for the purpose of implementing interoperability. The categorization of crypto-assets is based on their functionalities and their purpose. An interoperability scenario has been given for the defined crypto-asset classes.

Keywords: Blockchain · Distributed ledger technology · Interoperability · Digital assets · Crypto-assets · Crypto-coins · Crypto-tokens

1 Introduction

The blockchain technology has emerged as a disruptive technology, that enable trust among untrusted network nodes in the digital world. Blockchain the underlying technology behind bitcoin has enormous potential for enhancing the trustworthiness of data in a distributed environment, [1] and is foreseen as a possible solution to a number of challenging problems across many domains [2]. The technology adds trustable value to digital entities in the Internet domain and makes it possible to transfer value, rather than information over the network [3, 4]. These unique characteristics open a new form of cryptographic assets, which have generated significant interest in another type of digital assets. With the promise of trustability, transparency, and traceability of digital objects registered in the system, the blockchain technology has attracted significant research studies and industrial attention [5].

A diverse ecosystem of blockchain projects with different protocols and cryptographic structures offering a variety of solutions has emerged to serve the needs of the digital world. However, these blockchains remain isolated, operating in their own respective silos, each one with its own ecosystem, consensus model, and network. Many of these projects offer a solution to a specific problem [6] such as the decentralized marketplace[1], and open-bazaar[2]. Thus, it has become clear that there will exist many more independent networks of blockchains designed for specific problems. The applications developed on these networks need to cross communicate with each other to provide real services in a broad range of situations. This emerges as a new paradigm of "establishing connections between isolated blockchain networks" creating the concept of interoperability [4].

Interoperability is generally referred to as the ability of different systems to communicate with each other in a distributed environment to exchange or retrieve information/data. The application that operates on each system must interpret the data and understand the meaning of the exchanged information. In the case of blockchain based system, the most significant obstacle to be overcome in the creation of this interoperable network of blockchains would be the preservation of what makes each chain unique when the value moves from one chain to the other. A recent study conducted by Hileman and Rauchs [7] suggests that "Interoperability will be essential for the massive adoption of blockchain and distributed ledgers." Therefore, whether a public or private type of blockchain, interoperability across blockchain systems will become a core requirement [8].

The concept of interoperability among blockchain based systems is not fully understood and it is vital for the future growth of the blockchain industry. It has been seen that interoperability solutions are viewed from the perspective of a generalized information system [9, 10]. However, this perspective of interoperability has been failed to achieve true and adequate levels of interoperability for every situation. Hence, a concept of a systematically categorized perspective is needed. Therefore, we need to look at the design philosophy of this technology and categorize the type of digital crypto-assets the system is holding that require interoperability. Thus, there is a clear requirement for a unified classification of interoperable asset classes. The purpose of this classification is to provide an independent type of crypto-assets in order to guide the design and implementation of interoperability. In this paper, we propose a classification of crypto-assets, based on the purpose and the type of value the asset carries, which helps to understand the crypto-asset landscape.

The rest of the paper is structured as follows. Section 2 introduces interoperability, its challenges, goals, approaches and mechanisms. Section 3 discusses blockchain and digital objects classifications. Section 4 describes a crypto-asset classification for blockchain based systems. In Sect. 5, we formalize the classification and map the crypto-asset class with an interoperability scenario, and finally, Sect. 6 concludes the paper.

---

[1] https://coincentral.com/decentralized-marketplace-blockchain/.
[2] https://openbazaar.org/.

2 Interoperability

Interoperability refers to the ability of two or more systems to provide service or accept service from the other system and to utilize the service of a common exchange effectively together [11]. The linkage should allow these connected systems to exchange data accurately, effectively, and consistently [12]. That means the application that operates on each system must understand the functionality, which is available for the other system. Software level interoperability is essential since it allows information to be shared without an intermediary. Furthermore, a common standard will enhance the possibility of in-built interoperability [4, 13].

For a blockchain technology-based system, interoperability refers to cross-communication between different blockchains that enables to exchange or retrieve information or values. This deals with information obtained from another system and makes a change to the state of that system based on the received information. However, inherently the blockchain is an 'append only' model, and the state can only be appended through transactions, by nodes within its own network using their consensus mechanism [1, 13–16]. Therefore, here the underlying assumption is that "cross-communication is not intended to make direct state changes to another blockchain system. Instead, a cross-communication should trigger some set of functionalities on the other system that expected to perform an operation within its own network", as an example, verifying the authenticity of information requested within its own network. However, for the process of interoperability cross-communication remains a challenge - because interoperability requires the integration of different interlinked information sources [17].

2.1 Challenges

Considering the Internet or intranet as an overall network and blockchain as platforms with sub-networks within it holds a variety of digital assets. The current state-of-the-art blockchain technology is architectured in such a way that it operates as a standalone system. It is designed so that a network of node participants, who are the stakeholders, decide on the current state of the system based on an agreed protocol [15]. This protocol dictates the value and the consensus model. Most importantly the value has been created by and exists only within the system and its nodes [13]. This means, enabling interoperability is a way to exchange value from one blockchain system to another system. However, validating data from another system is challenging because each systems' value is unique and no cross-chain standard classifying crypto-assets' value exists. Therefore, each blockchain system has its own idiosyncratic interoperability issues that cannot be addressed using a general information systems perspective. This is the main challenge we address so that data and digital assets can be exchanged between sub-networks.

2.2 Goals of Interoperability

Generally, interoperability is developed through functional design principles and standards thus it forms a base for different applications to communicate and helps to automate the process. Many approaches have been proposed to achieve interoperability such as: Integrated approach – where a commonly agreed format of data structure exists; the Unified approach – where a common format with semantic understanding exists; and the Federated approach – where connections established accordingly [18]. A common goal of the interoperability approach is to enable cross-communication using different types of technologies.

Interoperability seems to be a strategical concept, where different systems cross-communicate to achieve a common goal. Here the desired goal is to connect separate networks of ledger systems and facilitate cross-chain communication in order to interact and transfer data. To understand the interoperability goal, it is first necessary to identify the scenarios for interoperability: an active mode – where systems must be able to engage in the interaction to send and receive data; and a passive mode where systems able to receive data [4]. Therefore, the desired interoperability generally falls into two categories, identified as:

- Cross-chain 'transfer\exchange' - a cross-chain transfer process aims to transfer various types of assets or value from one blockchain system to another. That means the systems must be in active mode and have a common understanding of the semantics so that the transfer occurs meaningfully.
- Cross-chain 'validation\verification' – a cross-communication process aims to provide the ability to verify assets, value or information between the blockchain systems.

In order to facilitate cross-communication, many techniques such as sidechain, relay, notary schemes and hash-locking are under development [19]. A variety of approaches have been proposed to achieve interoperability [4, 8], but nearly all of them lead to the violation of the principles of decentralization. The core benefit of a blockchain technology-based system is to overcome the risk of centralization.

2.3   Approaches for Interoperability

Interoperability approaches aim to address interoperability barriers however, we must consider how these barriers are removed [18] because some approaches may lead the system to change its security model. Considering the decentralized nature of the architecture, where multiple nodes participate in the process to reach finality, nodes must retain the same result. For that, nodes must have or be given the information in order to process the transaction. If the nodes are set to fetch data from other blockchain systems, the dynamic nature of values would interfere with the consensus. Therefore, the exchange process must be carefully designed in accordance with the system goal. This leads to the interoperability focuses on two types of approaches: centralized and decentralized.

- In a centralized approach, the cross-communication operation is triggered by a single entity and operates directly between the sender and the receiver blockchain. This results in the cross-communication process in a closed environment. The inner communication is facilitated through some trusted/credible nodes acting as notaries to verify whether a specific event has happened on one chain and taken agreed action on another chain [4, 19–21].

- A decentralized approach assumes that the cross-communication occurs automatically at a protocol level through smart contracts in a distributed environment. For example, when Bob invokes a transfer transaction on his chain, it will automatically be credited in Alice's chain.

Current research is experimenting several mechanisms with the aim of achieving interoperability among networks of blockchains.

2.4   Interoperability Mechanisms

Many research groups and industries are actively investigating multiple blockchain architectures and protocols that allow blockchains to cross-communicate between different networks and thus facilitate the exchange of transactions. Many FinTech start-up companies are also working on various blockchain architectures and protocols to address interoperability.

Pegged side-chain is an addition to the bitcoin protocol and enables assets to be transferred back and forth between multiple blockchains [22]. Generally, this can be implemented in any blockchain system that holds an asset, token or cryptocurrency. The 'parent' chain, known as the main blockchain is connected by a new blockchain called a side-chain. There is little interaction between the two. The side-chain as the custodian of assets from the parent chain, and this same asset is locked in the main chain to prevent double spending. However, the advantage of this side-chain is that it can perform instant transactions at a higher speed and volume. Micropayments are the most common use case for side-chains. In this system, it is not necessary to record every transaction between two parties on the main blockchain. If only a handful of parties are concerned about a recurring transaction, it is not necessary for all the other nodes to be aware of those transactions. Instead, a direct connection should be created between the two pairs which perform transactions on a recurring basis for a certain period of time and only the final balance is recorded on the blockchain [23].

Relay is a mechanism where a 'Chain A' actively listens to and keeps a record of part of the information such as block header from another 'Chain B'. This will be useful for a light client to verify block headers belonging to 'Chain B' by using a standard verification process [19].

Hash-locking is another technique for the exchange of digital assets without a trusted third party. The mechanism utilizes a hash time [24] locked system which puts a time lock on the transaction so that both the obligations are fully met, otherwise the transaction cannot occur – atomic transaction [19].

Bridges or gateways are the intermediate mechanism aim to provide interoperability between systems. The objective here is to bridge the differences between various data standards, and middleware. To perform a conversion between the protocol of the sending system and the protocol of the receiving system, the gateway can be expanded with the use of plug-ins.

3 Blockchain and Digital Objects

At their core, blockchains are decentralized databases maintained by a network of computers. Blockchain technology enables the digital representation of assets and their secure transfer of value [25]. By design, the security of the value transfer is guaranteed by the interaction protocol itself and obviates the need for trusted transaction intermediaries [13]. Bitcoin has emerged as the first blockchain application of a decentralized crypto-currency system [25]. Even though Bitcoin blockchain was implemented as a decentralized currency system, the application is, in fact, a software system that executes a scripting language in a distributed environment. To think beyond the payment system required new developments in the technology itself which lead to the development of the Ethereum project [26]. Ethereum was developed as a platform that could run programmed applications on blockchain through smart contracts [27]. Thus, it created a wide variety of decentralized applications which opened the technology to the possibility of digital assets and tokens [28–30]. With the ability to tokenize and decentralize not only cryptocurrency but also other scarce assets the blockchain technology significantly expanded its disruptive potential [29].

Blockchain technology offers a verifiable way to track digital transactions. This makes this technology useful for digital asset management systems. Such functionality offers the storage and transacting of crypto-assets [25]. This is a use case where a system holds a crypto-asset and the user will be able to transfer the asset between systems. Blockchain also allows crypto-assets to be distributed while protecting them from being copied. Thus, the technology is useful to track assets as they move through the systems in a distributed environment [31]. The advantage of a low transaction fee and not having to rely on a single entity are the main benefits of this technology [13].

3.1 Digital Object Classification

Digital objects [32] are an essential part of a modern information system that strives towards technology-independent and future-proof automated operations between software and computer systems. Digital objects exist solely in the digital space and carry a state of information [32]. Further, they can be classified into different digital asset classes to fully bridge the gap between physical and digital mixed world.

Primarily, there are two ways of representing digital objects, tangible and intangible objects. Tangible items are classified as objects with physical existence, such as car, house, and they are unique. In the context of the blockchain, a tangible object represents an asset which has a physical existence as well represented in a digital form. The classification of asset objects is based on the tangibility of the assets. Intangible items are those items that do not have a physical nature such as service and are represented as abstract objects within the system. Further, as referred in Table 1, within the type of the tangible and intangible objects, there are 'fungible' and 'non-fungible' objects [33].

Fungible objects belong to a digital object class which are exchangeable and are built using a common standard, value and characteristics, such as currency and ERC[3]-

---

[3] Ethereum Request for Comments.

20^4 tokens. Cryptocurrencies are perfect examples of fungible tokens, in fact, fungibility is the essential feature of any currency. However, if we take the fungibility out of it, then it becomes a non-fungible token, which is a unique, non-interchangeable special type of objects, such as a birth certificate, passport and ERC-21[5] tokens.

Table 1. Characteristics of assets

Characteristics	Definition	Examples
Tangible	Has a physical existence	Land, property
Intangible	Items are concepts that represent things	Services, ID
Fungible	Built using a common standard	ERC-20 tokens, Currency
Non-fungible	Type of objects that are unique	Birth certificate, passport

4 Crypto-Assets

The generic definition of an asset is a resource which an individual or organization owns or controls and which is expected to produce future economic value. Assets used to be classified as tangible objects, such as buildings, and intangible objects such as intellectual property [34]. The proliferation of digital technology has created a new class of assets known as Data Assets or Digital Assets which exist in binary format, examples of which are digital pictures and Facebook accounts. In the context of this paper, we refer asset as a digital representation of an item that is being created and exists in a blockchain.

Blockchain technology and its services have given birth to a new cryptographic form of assets termed as crypto-assets [29, 35]. Crypto-assets are a type of digital assets, recorded on a blockchain ledger, which utilize techniques such as cryptography, distributed consensus, peer-to-peer network, and smart contract [36] in order to create, transact and verify in a decentralized manner [30, 37], such as BTC and ETH [17]. They derive their names from the cryptographic security mechanisms used within the distributed systems.

The concept of crypto-asset [14] in blockchain systems is essentially a technology that produces virtual tokens that represent value in a closed network. The primary weakness of such crypto-asset token-based systems is its inability to operate outside of its network. Currently, it is being facilitated through third-party intermediaries. Crypto-assets are also referred to as crypto-tokens or crypto-coins, which are primarily based on the asset's functionality. In the context of this paper, 'coin' refers to a cryptographic asset used as a medium of value exchange, whereas the term 'token' refers to an abstract category of digital assets, that acquires specific features depending on the context.

The primary purpose of these crypto-assets is to be used as a medium of exchange independent of any central bank, and with a specific value [37, 38], such as currency, a

---

[4] https://theethereum.wiki/w/index.php/ERC20_Token_Standard.

[5] https://medium.com/crypto-currently/the-anatomy-of-erc721-e9db77abfc24.

place holder for digital representation of objects and services. There are different classifications of these assets based on their functionalities and purposes [30, 39]. There are frequent discussions on whether the crypto-assets can be classified as money or assets [37, 40]. However, this paper does not cover the legal or accounting sides of crypto-assets.

Crypto-assets and their taxonomy are arguably the most important component for enabling interoperability in the blockchain space. Many forms of crypto-assets exist however when you separate them based on the type and functionality most crypto-assets fall into one of the following categories as shown in Table 2.

Table 2. Classification of crypto-assets

Asset class	Definition
Crypto-coin	Representation of digital objects that express the purpose of acting as a medium of exchange or unit of account and implemented at a protocol level, for example, BTC, ETH
Asset-token	Representation of an object that has some characteristics, for example, a car, property
Utility-token	Representation of digital objects that provide the right to access or utilize the value derived from it, for example, a service or subscription

The Fig. 1 represents the relationship between the existing category of assets and the classification of blockchain crypto-assets. For example, an asset-token can represent a tangible or intangible item, however, a crypto-coin represents an intangible object. Each of these crypto-assets can be considered 'digital objects' with their own individual properties.

In the blockchain space, crypto-asset is a new concept. To the best of our knowledge, there is no generally accepted standard for asset classification in the crypto space. Therefore, apart from these three basic categories shown in Table 2, there is much potential for the creation of new asset classes because crypto-assets are digital representation of objects. These objects achieve shape and inherit characteristics when they are mapped to an appropriate digital object. A brief description of the given asset class and their properties are described in the following subsection.

4.1   Crypto-Coins

Crypto-coins are also referred as crypto-currencies, a new form of money, implemented on the blockchain for the purpose of a medium of exchange independent of any central control such as a bank. Crypto-currencies such as BTC or ETH are called native currencies. Because they are developed for and exist within the system and are used to pay for the computational service offered by the system. These are also used as payment-currency where payments can be made for goods or services [41]. Crypto-coins such as BTC and ETH are built into the system as part of the protocol. Therefore, they are not directly exchangeable between other systems, instead they can only be traded.

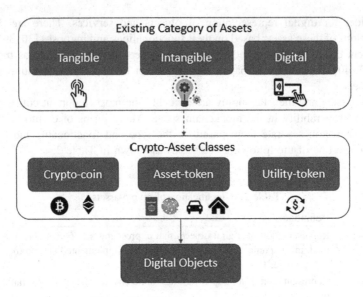

Fig. 1. Blockchain crypto-asset classes

4.2 Asset-Tokens

Unlike crypto-coin, asset-tokens are not native to a blockchain they are created on top of a blockchain and can be used to represent a wide range of assets beyond currencies. Asset tokens are commonly implemented in the smart contracts that may have physical existence such as car, property or may be without a physical existence such as company shares. The domain of digital technology including supply chain is increasingly dependent on the effective management of digital assets which have been managed by central entities [42]. However, these entities have used proprietary techniques which are usually slow, costly, insecure and vulnerable to abuse. Blockchain would be an effective solution to manage digital assets more effectively. CryptoKitties[6] are a classical example of non-fungible tokens that are digital collectables and unique to each other. Some other use cases are Know Your Customer ID[7] for digital academic certificates and copyright [43], supply chain tracking, software licenses, and more.

4.3 Utility-Tokens

Utility tokens are a type of system or network, distinct digital token that represents a unit of product or service. They are also presented as tokens that enable future access to a product or service [44]. Utility tokens are not designed for investment [45]; rather they are designed to be used as a service which can be purchased. In the blockchain

---

[6] https://www.cryptokitties.co/.

[7] https://home.kpmg/ie/en/home/insights/2018/02/blockchain-kyc-utility-fs.html.

space, ERC20 compatible tokens on the Ethereum platform are considered utility tokens. Other utility-tokens such as TRC10 and TRC20[8] also exist.

5 Mapping of Crypto-Assets

Irrelevant of varies category of assets, digital objects are represented in the same form. However, when we map with a particular type of asset class (crypto-coin, asset-token or utility-token), the digital object gets its form and inherits the characteristics of the assets. Therefore, it is essential to determine and understand the appropriate asset class to represent objects in an interoperable environment. Based on the characteristics (tangible, intangible, fungible and non-fungible) and classification (crypto-coin, asset-token and utility-token) of crypto-assets, we propose a crypto-asset classification framework as shown in Fig. 2.

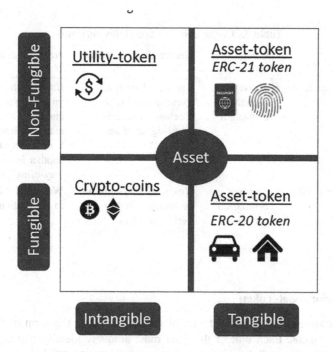

Fig. 2. Crypto-asset characteristics framework

5.1 Scenario: Crypto-Coin

Generally, crypto-coins are divisible and intangible in nature, unless they have been assigned to different purposes or combinations for a specific purpose. Crypto-coins are

---

[8] https://tron.network/.

formed and exist in a ledger of a distributed system in the form of transaction. Each distributed system runs its own independent ledger and has coin native to it. Therefore, validating one coin from another system is challenging. Currently third-party exchanges facilitating the exchange who has access/share on both the network and act as a liquidity provider facilitating the swapping [40]. There two types of exchanges exist: centralized and decentralized. A centralized exchange dependent on a third-party or intermediary to hold the coin and process the exchange. They offer to swap of a variety of crypto-coins mainly through exchange them against fiat currency. Therefore, the centralized exchange is often expensive, inefficient and vulnerable to attack whereas decentralized exchanges do not rely on a third-party service to facilitate the swap. Instead, it occurs directly between users (peer-to-peer) through an automated process. Such a system can be established through a decentralized network using multi-signature, hatch-lock and other solutions. A mapping of crypto-coin with the inter-operability approach of centralized and decentralized scenario has been given in Table 3.

Table 3. Crypto-coin interoperability scenario

Crypto-coins	Centralized approach	Decentralized approach	Proposed direction
Cross-chain transfer of crypto-coins	Through centralized exchanges	Through decentralized exchanges using a mechanism such as multi-signature and hash-lock	If two systems operate on one crypto-currency, then it is a matter of transferring from one system to another in an agreed way using gateways
Validation/verifiability	Through centralized services such as a notary	Yes, a relay system can be implemented to verify the block	Web3 and API access to verification

5.2 Scenario: Asset-Token

Asset-tokens are a digital representation of tangible items in the form of fungible or non-fungible tokens. Each unit of the asset must uniquely identify and hold characteristics based on its asset class, such as, for a car, registration number, model, year of manufacture; and for a property, its ID, land area, land location. Additionally, if the assets are of fungible nature, each unit of the asset must uniquely identify and hold the same characteristics within both systems. An example such as Colored Coin [46] describes a class of methods for representing and managing real-world assets on top of the Bitcoin network. A mapping of Asset-token with the interoperability approach of centralized and decentralized scenario has been given in Table 4.

Table 4. Asset-token interoperability scenario

Asset-token	Centralized approach	Decentralized approach	Proposed direction
Cross-chain transfer	Yes, but centralized, using an intermediary to process the transfer	Yes, but the token that representing the asset must have the same semantics	Common data standard and protocol such as ERC 20 and ERC 21 tokens
Validation/verifiability	Centralized validation through notary	Yes, a relay system to verify the block data	Web3 and API access to verification

5.3 Scenario: Utility-Token

Utility-tokens are not generally made for exchange purposes; however, there might be a use case where the same product or service may have to exchange information with each other. There is more chance that the exchange may happen between users within the network. Because the token holds the service value, but the network is the one that provides the service. The tokens are designed for spending within a specific blockchain ecosystem. A mapping of Utility-token with the interoperability approach of centralized and decentralized scenario has been given in Table 5.

Table 5. Utility-token interoperability scenario

Utility-token	Centralized approach	Decentralized approach	Proposed direction
Cross-chain transfer	The value has to be recreated in the other system	Not directly transferable, it has to be recreated in the other system	Cross-chain bridge or gateways for burning the value in one chain and recreate the value in another chain
Validation/verifiability	Centralized validation through notary	Can use cross-chain bridge and relay	Web3 and API access to verification

Moving forward, it will be vital to distinguish between different cryptographic digital objects that function as crypto-coins, asset-tokens or utility-tokens. A digital crypto-asset can fall into three or more of these categories based on its actual characteristics– and additional categories may not have been invented yet. Therefore, it is difficult to create a lasting category of crypto-assets. However, we assume our classification of crypto-assets will serve as a base for ongoing discussion of current and emerging digital crypto-asset classes.

6 Conclusion

In this paper, we identified the basic category of interoperable crypto-asset classes for blockchain based systems. Further, we provided some clarity on their characteristics and analyzed the current state of interoperability and its proposed directions. Crypto-graphic assets management is a promising use case for blockchain technology. Adding the concept of interoperability through cross-chain communication enables the transfer of digital assets from one blockchain to another. Assets may be of tangible or intangible in nature, may be implemented at protocol-level or in a smart contract, may be in the form of fungible or non-fungible tokens. Irrespective of the various categories or types, digital objects are represented in the same form as series of binary 1 s and 0 s. However, when we map with a particular type of asset class, the digital object gets its shape and inherit the characteristics and attributes of the assets. Therefore, it is important to determine and understand the appropriate digital asset class to represent objects. With a clear view of different types of crypto-assets and underlying values, an appropriate interoperability approach can be determined for an expected outcome.

References

1. Xu, X., et al.: A taxonomy of blockchain-based systems for architecture design. In: 2017 IEEE International Conference on Software Architecture (ICSA), pp. 243–252. IEEE (2017)
2. Peterson, K., Deeduvanu, R., Kanjamala, P., Boles, K.: A blockchain-based approach to health information exchange networks. In: Proceedings of NIST Workshop Blockchain Healthcare, vol. 1, pp. 1–10 (2016)
3. Chen, C.P., Zhang, C.-Y.: Data-intensive applications, challenges, techniques and technologies: a survey on big data. Inf. Sci. **275**, 314–347 (2014)
4. Jin, H., Dai, X., Xiao, J.: Towards a novel architecture for enabling interoperability amongst multiple blockchains. In: 2018 IEEE 38th International Conference on Distributed Computing Systems (ICDCS), pp. 1203–1211. IEEE (2018)
5. Hwang, G.-H., Chen, P.-H., Lu, C.-H., Chiu, C., Lin, H.-C., Jheng, A.-J.: InfiniteChain: a multi-chain architecture with distributed auditing of sidechains for public blockchains. In: Chen, S., Wang, H., Zhang, L.-J. (eds.) ICBC 2018. LNCS, vol. 10974, pp. 47–60. Springer, Cham (2018). https://doi.org/10.1007/978-3-319-94478-4_4
6. Anceaume, E., Del Pozzo, A., Ludinard, R., Potop-Butucaru, M., Tucci-Piergiovanni, S.: Blockchain abstract data type. arXiv preprint arXiv:1802.09877 (2018)
7. Hileman, G., Rauchs, M.: 2017 Global Blockchain Benchmarking Study (2017)
8. Hardjono, T., Lipton, A., Pentland, A.: Towards a Design Philosophy for Interoperable Blockchain Systems (2018)
9. Gordon, W.J., Catalini, C.: Blockchain technology for healthcare: facilitating the transition to patient-driven interoperability. Comput. Struct. Biotechnol. J. **16**, 224–230 (2018)
10. Zhang, P., White, J., Schmidt, D.C., Lenz, G.: Applying software patterns to address interoperability in blockchain-based healthcare apps. arXiv preprint arXiv:1706.03700 (2017)
11. Vernadat, F.: Interoperable enterprise systems: architectures and methods. IFAC Proc. Vol. **39**(3), 13–20 (2006)
12. Geraci, A., et al.: IEEE Standard Computer Dictionary: Compilation of IEEE Standard Computer Glossaries. IEEE Press, Piscataway (1991)

13. Tasca, P., Tessone, C.J.: Taxonomy of blockchain technologies. Principles of identification and classification. arXiv preprint arXiv:1708.04872 (2017)
14. Alqassem, I., Svetinovic, D.: Towards reference architecture for cryptocurrencies: bitcoin architectural analysis. In: 2014 IEEE International Conference on, and Green Computing and Communications (GreenCom), IEEE and Cyber, Physical and Social Computing (CPSCom) Internet of Things (iThings), pp. 436–443. IEEE (2014)
15. Zheng, Z., Xie, S., Dai, H., Chen, X., Wang, H.: An overview of blockchain technology: architecture, consensus, and future trends. In: 2017 IEEE International Congress on Big Data (BigData Congress), pp. 557–564. IEEE (2017)
16. de Kruijff, J., Weigand, H.: Understanding the blockchain using enterprise ontology. In: Dubois, E., Pohl, K. (eds.) CAiSE 2017. LNCS, vol. 10253, pp. 29–43. Springer, Cham (2017). https://doi.org/10.1007/978-3-319-59536-8_3
17. Staples, M., et al.: Risks and opportunities for systems using blockchain and smart contracts. Data61. CSIRO, Sydney (2017)
18. Chen, D.: Enterprise Interoperability Framework. In: EMOI-INTEROP (2006)
19. Buterin, V.: Chain interoperability. R3 Research Paper (2016)
20. Alipour-Hafezi, M., Horri, A., Shiri, A., Ghaebi, A.: Interoperability models in digital libraries: an overview. Electron. Libr. **28**(3), 438–452 (2010)
21. Chen, D., Doumeingts, G., Vernadat, F.: Architectures for enterprise integration and interoperability: past, present and future. Comput. Ind. **59**(7), 647–659 (2008)
22. Back, A., et al.: Enabling blockchain innovations with pegged sidechains (2014). http://www.opensciencereview.com/papers/123/enablingblockchain-innovations-with-pegged-sidechains
23. Poon, J., Dryja, T.: The Bitcoin lightning network: scalable off-chain instant payments. Technical report (draft) (2015)
24. Herlihy, M.: Atomic cross-chain swaps. arXiv preprint arXiv:1801.09515 (2018)
25. Rohr, J., Wright, A.: Blockchain-based token sales, initial coin offerings, and the democratization of public capital markets. Hast. LJ **70**, 463 (2018)
26. Wood, G.: Ethereum: a secure decentralised generalised transaction ledger. Ethereum Proj. Yellow Pap. **151**, 1–32 (2014)
27. Szabo, N.: The idea of smart contracts. Nick Szabo's Papers and Concise Tutorials, vol. 6 (1997)
28. Knirsch, F., Unterweger, A., Engel, D.: Implementing a blockchain from scratch: why, how, and what we learned. EURASIP J. Inf. Secur. **2019**(1), 2 (2019)
29. Chen, Y.: Blockchain tokens and the potential democratization of entrepreneurship and innovation. Bus. Horiz. **61**(4), 567–575 (2018)
30. Masnavi, S.: CryptoCompare Publishes 'Cryptoasset Taxonomy Report 2018' (2018). https://www.cryptocompare.com/media/34478555/cryptocompare-cryptoasset-taxonomy-report-2018.pdf
31. ElMessiry, M., ElMessiry, A.: Blockchain framework for textile supply chain management. In: Chen, S., Wang, H., Zhang, L.-J. (eds.) ICBC 2018. LNCS, vol. 10974, pp. 213–227. Springer, Cham (2018). https://doi.org/10.1007/978-3-319-94478-4_15
32. Hui, Y.: What is a digital object? Metaphilosophy **43**(4), 380–395 (2012)
33. Faget, A.: Fungible vs Non-fungible Tokens: What's the Difference? (2018)
34. Public Sector Accounting Standards Board: Definition and recognition of the elements of financial statements. Australian Accounting Research Foundation (1992)
35. Maas, W.: Classification and valuation issues for crypto-assets (2018)
36. Dinh, T.T.A., Wang, J., Chen, G., Liu, R., Ooi, B.C., Tan, K.-L.: Blockbench: a framework for analyzing private blockchains. In: Proceedings of the 2017 ACM International Conference on Management of Data, pp. 1085–1100. ACM (2017)

37. Söderberg, G.: Are Bitcoin and other crypto-assets money? Econ. Comment. **5**, 14 (2018)
38. Deikun, L.: Explain me like I'm five: what is cryptocurrency (2018)
39. mybitcoin. Blockchain Digital Asset Classification: Types Of Cryptocurrencies? (2018)
40. Demertzis, M., Wolff, G.B.: The economic potential and risks of crypto assets: is a regulatory framework needed? Bruegel Policy Contribution, no. 14 (2018)
41. Huckle, S., Bhattacharya, R., White, M., Beloff, N.: Internet of things, blockchain and shared economy applications. Procedia Comput. Sci. **98**, 461–466 (2016)
42. Hui, K.L., Vance, A., Zhdanov, D.: Securing digital assets (2016). https://www.misqre searchcurations.org/. Accessed 02 Mar 2019
43. Savelyev, A.: Copyright in the blockchain era: Promises and challenges. Comput. Law Secur. Rev. **34**(3), 550–561 (2018)
44. Katalyse.io.: Security Tokens vs. Utility Tokens—How different are they? (2018). https://hackernoon.com/security-tokens-vs-utility-tokens-how-different-are-they-22d6be8901c2
45. Middelman, M. (ed.): Why utility tokens will not make you rich (2018)
46. Rosenfeld, M.: Overview of colored coins. White paper, bitcoil. co. il, vol. 41 (2012)

Patient Privacy and Ownership of Electronic Health Records on a Blockchain

Debasish Ray Chawdhuri(✉) (iD)

Talentica Software (India) Pvt. Ltd., Pune, India
debasish.chawdhuri@talentica.com
http://www.talentica.com/

Abstract. Blockchain technology has found application outside of cryptocurrency in recent times. The development of patient-centric storage of medical records on a blockchain has recently gained momentum. However, there have been few developments in providing a solution towards giving up full control to the public so that the concentration of power by only a small group of validators can be avoided. In this paper, we discuss a solution that enables patient-driven interoperability of medical records on a public blockchain while maintaining privacy using new cryptographic constructs and truly giving up control to the general public.

Keywords: Electronic Health Record · Blockchain · Privacy

1 Introduction

In recent times, medical information has been predictably moved to standardized formats in the form of EHR or Electronic Health Records [1]. EHR systems should enable easier and faster sharing of medical information among different health care providers serving the same patients. EHR also should eliminate duplicate medical tests, like different blood tests, ECG, or tomography, that are often repeated by different health-care providers. However, the existing EHR systems are fragmented and are incompatible with one another. The EHR systems typically are provided as service to certain health care providers. Collaboration among different health care providers becomes a challenge if the same patient seeks care from different providers.

Privacy is another significant concern when different providers share health information of any patient. The patient must own the data, and she must be ensured that she consents before her data are shared. The patient may only choose to share information with the provider of her choice, and this needs to be guaranteed. In the current systems, the health care providers are responsible for storing and managing the data and need to be trusted to first share the information with the patient and then not to share the information with anyone else without the consent of the patient.

J. Joshi et al. (Eds.): ICBC 2019, LNCS 11521, pp. 95–111, 2019.
https://doi.org/10.1007/978-3-030-23404-1_7

Since the start of Bitcoin [2], the crypto-currency has been very popular. Bitcoin works by using a distributed ledger in which every validating node must store a copy of all the transactions. Such a system distributes the trust requirement over a large number of validators so that a small group of them cannot conspire to modify or manipulate the data in a way that is not appropriate (for example pay the same money to two different parties or create money from thin air). In recent years, different uses of blockchain technology have been proposed other than the cryptocurrency application.

Blockchain has been considered by a number of studies as a mechanism for sharing medical records in electronic form because of the distribution of trust and immutability so that as long as a certain percentage of independent parties maintaining the records are trustworthy, the integrity of the data and modifications is maintained even when the other parties are malicious. The blockchain is the best-known way to give control back to the general public.

This paper considers a modification of the CryptoNote [3] protocol to store medical records of individuals in a way so that a link between consecutive records cannot be established. However, unlike currency, it is required that the individual may want to disclose part of her medical records (or all of it entirely). She should be able to prove that those medical records indeed belong to her interactively in such a way that the proof is not transferable. This proof should work across different situations, for example, when she wants to buy medicine using her prescription, prove her records to an insurance provider, or before a judge in case of a dispute. When she is sharing the entire chain, she should be able to prove that the chain contains her entire record.

The following are the advantages of the framework presented.

- Since the records live on a public blockchain, a patient does not have to depend on any private organization to gain access to her data. She will always be able to prove her records even if the provider later goes out of business, moves to a different jurisdiction that does not mandate disclosure or refuses to provide the data.
- The data being on the public network ensures that a group of large private organizations cannot tinker the data, especially in case of a law-suit.
- A verifiable encryption provided in this paper ensure that they are not visible to unintended parties, while still being provable to the intended parties.
- A stealth address and a mixing provided in this paper ensure that it cannot be tracked how many times a patient visits a particular health-care provider or if how many times she visits a doctor in general.

2   Our Contribution

We make the following contribution over the existing literature we could find.

- In our opinion, storing the content of the medical records in any system that is privately controlled defeats the cause of the public control of the data. Therefore, we move away from storage of a simple hash of the data to storing the medical record on the chain to enable complete public control.

- We create a minor variation of the CryptoNote signature, which is a variation of the Traceable Ring Signature [4], to enable masking the links while
enforcing the fact that there is no branching or merging in a patient's records.
- We propose a new IND-CCA2 secure (a.k.a. non-malleable) verifiable encryption that allows one to prove the correctness of decryption through an interactive zero-knowledge protocol so that the transcript of the proof would not
convince a third party. This is a property which is essential to restrict the
unauthorized sharing of private data as much as possible. We use this technique to encrypt the medical records of a patient. Albeit being a relatively
simple construction, to the best of our knowledge, there is no encryption
available in the literature with these specific properties.
- We propose a simple protocol to attach a masked ownership marker which
allows the patient to provide a zero-knowledge interactive proof of ownership.
- Together with the above, we propose a blockchain system for storing EHR
records on the blockchain that truly gives control to the public.

3   Electronic Health Records or EHR

Before electronic systems were invented, health care providers would maintain
patient records in handwritten charts and keep them in files. Every department in
a hospital or every clinic would have their own files. This would, of course, mean
that a patient must be re-diagnosed in every clinic or every health care provider,
and the same tests would be conducted by each organization redundantly. The
patient would then have to make sure to maintain the reports and take it to
any other provider, from which she would seek health care service. Sometimes
certain health care providers would not share full information with the patient,
and hence the data would be unavailable to other organizations.

As a solution to these problems, electronic medical records or EMR systems
[5] evolved to enable electronic recording of medical data of a patient per department or organization. A step further was the electronic health care records or
EHR system [1] which would be able to consolidate a patient's information as
a whole that can be used across different departments in the same organization and sometimes even across different organizations, from which the patient
is seeking health care. In the past decade, in the United States, there has been
significant adoption of EHR systems. Some other countries are also following the
same path. However, these systems generally do not interoperate making it difficult to share information between different organizations. Another problem with
these systems is that the health care providers often do not share all information
with the patients, or transfer patient data to different departments without the
consent of the patient.

The US government is currently tackling these privacy and ownership issues
in the form of HIPAA rules [6,7]. HIPAA requires a health care provider only to
strive to protect the privacy and ownership rights of the patients. The fact that
HIPAA rules do not guarantee the protection of privacy and ownership rights
illustrates the complexity of the issue at hand. We can summarize the primary
objectives of the HIPAA rules as follows -

- The patient has ownership of all her health-related personally identifiable records. She can choose to disclose it to any party of her choice for availing medical care, for claiming insurance cover, for subscribing to an insurance provider to prove her existing conditions or for any other purpose.
- No health care provider or party may disclose the patient's personal health information without her consent. It is notable that HIPAA requires only an informal consent which leaves a grey area in this regard.

We consider that the patient sometimes needs to make some disclosures that must come with the proof of correctness. For example when providing information to an insurance provider to claim benefits. So such requirements must be automatically imposed when designing such a system. In the case of EHR systems controlled by the health care providers, the provider directly provides this information to the insurance provider, thus putting a virtual stamp of validity along with it. When it is in control of the patient in any system, such information must be proved to be correct to the party with whom it is being shared.

4   Blockchain Technology

The blockchain idea came to light after the publication of a whitepaper on Bitcoin [2] under the pseudonym Satoshi Nakamoto. Since then, there has been a plethora of work on variations of blockchain systems. There has been some recent work on storing and managing of EHR records on blockchains.

A blockchain is an evolution of traditional database applications. The purpose of a blockchain is to eliminate a centralized system that validates transactions and to replace it with several independent validators that do not trust one another. For example, in a traditional banking system, we can transfer funds between two parties. However, both parties involved in the transaction have to trust the bank completely. In a blockchain system like Bitcoin, the bank is replaced by a large number of independent validators that do not trust one another. The only thing that it needs is that a certain percentage of those independent validators have to be honest and rational (working in their own best interest). The transacting parties also do not have to trust any particular validator; they only have to trust that some specified percentage of the validators are honest and rational.

A blockchain can be of the following types based on who can read or write to the blockchain.

- **Permissionless:** Any party can join, read and write in a permissionless blockchain and the blockchain protocol itself can verify the required condition for joining the system. In such a blockchain, anyone is allowed to validate whether all transactions are as per the protocol. In other words, public verifiability is available.
- **Permissioned:** In this case the participants are chosen externally to the blockchain, and not anyone can be a part of it to read or write. In this kind of a blockchain, the access to validation is restricted. Hence public verifiability is not available in such a blockchain system.

A permissioned system exposes us to the risk of the validators conspiring to edit the records if a single entity controls them. We must ensure that the validation is at the hands of the public and the right to validate must not be at the hands of a few privileged users. We identify the writers with the protocol we design and an external authority providing only an identity service, whereas the protocol itself manages all authorization. This is why we use a public blockchain for this purpose. However, it requires cryptographic security to protect the privacy of the data, which we also describe in this paper.

5   Current Blockchain Solutions for EHR Records

Although there has been some discussion on the use of blockchain for managing medical records, only a few solutions are provided for the same. One class of implementation concentrates on managing access permissions on the blockchain while keeping the data elsewhere [8–10]. MedRec [8] only stores permissions and access logs on the blockchain while keeping the data in private systems. In the paper [9], the content of the medical data is stored in a cloud service and the database of the health care provider. The data stored in the database is encrypted using the patient's key. In the case of [10], a set of trusted third parties called healthcare data gateways or HDGs regulate access to the data. In all three of those cases, there must be some trusted third parties that follow the access rules and allow access to the data accordingly. This, in our opinion, takes away the control from the patient as she is no longer in a position to ensure that her permissions are always appropriately obtained before giving access to some specific data.

On the other hand, some systems like [11] agree with us in this regard. They ensure public verifiability of the data by storing a hash of the actual data on the blockchain. However, due to privacy concerns, they store the health care data in cloud storage and only the hash of the data in the blockchain. So, even though the cloud data cannot be modified by the trusted third party managing the cloud-based storage without invalidating the particular transaction, it can be removed. This may be a problem for a patient who is, for example, trying to claim insurance protection. It can be particularly inconvenient for the patient if the insurance provider can see that there exists a record in her chain, but she is not disclosing it (or cannot disclose it). To resolve this issue, the paper asks the patient to maintain a copy of all of the data herself as well which makes the patient responsible for the safe storage of the data.

Another problem is that even if the medical records cannot be snooped on by an attacker, the number of times a patient goes to a health care provider, in and of itself, is sensitive information. For example, if a health care provider specializes in cancer treatment and a given patient visits there regularly, it is not hard to conclude that the patient has cancer. To the best of our knowledge, no existing proposal safeguards the patient from this kind of a data leak. This problem cannot even be countered by merely masking the particular institution the patient is going to. For example, if the patient gets too many health records in a short time, either she is very sick, or she is paranoid. It is thus essential to be able to mask the very fact that the patient received some healthcare service.

6 Design Requirements

In this section we outline the design requirements of our solution. A blockchain is essentially a verification system, that does a public verification of a fixed and previously agreed upon computation. In the following, we list the facts that we verify about the medical records in our blockchain system and the privacy properties that we ensure.

- **Prohibition of merging or branching of record chains (continuity):** Our system enforces that a single patient has one continuous chain of records. It prohibits branching of this chain or coalescing two different chains by enabling the patient to prove the continuity of records to any agency, for example, an insurance provider as the proof of existing medical history.
- **Ownership of records:** Every record in our system has cryptographically masked reference to the patient to whom it belongs.
- **Privacy of content:** The records are encrypted and cannot be seen by any third party without the cooperation of the patient.
- **Privacy of linkage:** As discussed earlier, the privacy of the content is not enough privacy. Even the ownership of the records and the linkages must not be known to a third party without the cooperation of the patient in our system.
- **Zero-knowledge interactive provability:** When required, the patient can prove the content of a part or the whole of her record chain to any desired party using zero-knowledge proof. Both the content of the records and the continuity of the linkages, along with the ownership of the records can be proved interactively.

7 Implementation Overview

We depend on some cryptographic constructs that we describe in this section. We have three cryptographic constructs, namely zero-knowledge verifiable encryption, zero-knowledge provable mixing, and zero-knowledge provable ownership.

- **Zero-knowledge verifiable encryption:** The encrypted content can only be read by the patient and the party that created the encryption. So, when the patient provides the decrypted plain text, she needs to be able to prove that the encrypted content has been correctly decrypted. We have described such a public key encryption mechanism so that the patient can execute an interactive zero-knowledge verification algorithm with any third party to verify the correctness of the decryption process. The transcript of such an interactive protocol will not convince any third party of the correctness of the decryption. This property makes the proofs non-transferable and hence immune to being shared without the patient's consent.

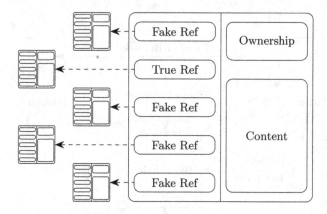

Fig. 1. A record in the blockchain

- **Zero-knowledge provable mixing:** We use a mixing similar to what is used in CryptoNote [3] protocol to fudge the chain linkages. The idea is to hide the actual chain linkage within fake linkages. The records are stored in the form of a chain of UTXOs. However, the link between a record and its previous record is fudged by cryptographically hiding it in a number of fake previous records which are records in the chain but not belonging to the current patient. This property is achieved using the one-time ring signature with proof of trace described later in this paper.
- **Zero-knowledge provable ownership:** We provide a way to ensure that records are always marked to the owner so that ownership can be proven even without showing the entire chain. This mark is cryptographically hidden, but the patient can provide a zero-knowledge interactive proof to any party to whom the patient wants to prove her ownership.

After we describe the cryptographic constructs, we will detail the actual implementation of the design goals.

In Fig. 1, we can see the structure of a single record in the blockchain. It has three components namely the previous record, an ownership marker, and the content. The previous record is fudged using the zero-knowledge provable mixing technique, the ownership marker is hidden using the zero-knowledge provable ownership technique, and the content is encrypted using the zero-knowledge verifiable encryption technique.

7.1 Typical Interactions for Interoperability

Interoperability is achieved in our system through common storage of medical data on the blockchain and interactive proofs. We will now discuss the typical usecases that enable interoperability. Figure 2 shows some of the basic usecases the system supports. They are described in this section.

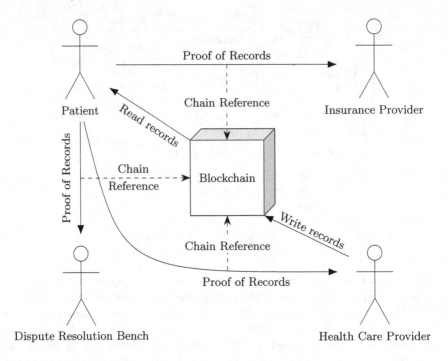

Fig. 2. Chain interactions in the typical usecases - refer to Sect. 7.1 for details.

Registering for the System: There is a need to match the identity of the patients on the chain to actual people, and an ID service provider is necessary for this purpose. This service provider is the only centralized control in the system. The following is the process.

1. The patient approaches the ID service.
2. The ID service verifies documents/takes biometric data.
3. The patient generates a key-pair (sk, pk) and gives pk to the ID service.
4. The ID service provider generates an electronic ID, puts the identification information along with pk in it and signs it.
5. The patient then creates a new record chain in the blockchain using the ID as the starting point. All records for this person must be added to this chain in the future.

Getting Service from a Health Care Provider:

1. First the patient describes her problem to the health care provider.
2. The health care provider asks her to reveal certain health care records possibly involving continuity.
3. The patient provides the records and proves their correctness with zero-knowledge interactive proofs.
4. Now that the provider is confident that information is validated, the provider starts the service.

5. The patient provides a forward space by creating a one-time ring signature with proof of trace and privately communicates the signature to the health care provider.
6. The provider adds the encrypted content, creates a new record and publishes them in the blockchain.

Subscribing to an Insurance Scheme:

1. The patient approaches an insurance provider.
2. The insurance provider asks to reveal all the records since a certain past date.
3. The patient discloses the records and proves the correctness of the content and the continuity (proving those are the only records in that time frame) using zero-knowledge proofs.
4. The insurance provider proposes certain policy price and benefits to the patient which the patient is free to buy or to bargain more.

Claiming Insurance:

1. The patient sends the claim to the provider.
2. The patient proves that her claim qualifies for the policy using zero-knowledge proofs on content, continuity, and ownership.
3. The insurance provider has now proofs required for the claim and hence process the claim.

Dispute Resolution: In case there is a dispute or a case of medical malpractice, a competent bench may want to look at the records provided by multiple providers. The patient can prove these records to the bench using the same three cryptographic constructs.

8 Crytographic Constructs

We first describe an interactive proof technique and then we will use this to develop the three cryptographic constructs that we have used in our system. For brevity, we only describe them in short, and we only provide informal proofs of security. We intend to publish the complete proofs as a technical report.

8.1 Notations

We assume that $\mathbb{G}$ is an elliptic curve group with prime order q and with DDH hardness assumption. We assume that $\mathbb{F}_q$ is the field of integers modulo q. All operations on the members of $\mathbb{F}_q$ are assumed to be modulo q. $\mathbb{F}_q^*$ is $(\mathbb{F}_q \setminus \{0\})$. G is a fixed point in the group. H_β, H_g, H_q are hash functions from any bit-string to a β bit string, a member of $\mathbb{G}$ and a member of $\mathbb{F}_q$ respectively modeled as random oracles. $Pr(Z)$ means the probability of the event Z and $Pr(Z|\alpha)$ means the conditional probability of Z given α.

For any probabilistic polynomial time algorithm (PPTA), we use a concise notation to describe it. $x \leftarrow Y$ means x is chosen randomly from the set Y with a uniform probability distribution. If Y is a PPTA, then x is the result of a single execution of Y. A PPTA is defined as $\{\mathbf{S}_1; \mathbf{S}_2; ...; \mathbf{S}_n; \mathbf{R}\}$ which means $\mathbf{S}_1, \mathbf{S}_2, ..., \mathbf{S}_n$ are statements to be executed in order and $\mathbf{R}$ is the return value. The expression $if(C)\{\mathbf{P}_1\}else\{\mathbf{P}_2\}$ where $\mathbf{P}_1, \mathbf{P}_2$ are sequence of statements followed by a return value and C is a boolean expression, represents a conditional expression that evaluates to $\mathbf{P}_1$ if C is *true*, else it evaluates to $\mathbf{P}_2$. The construct $loop\_n\_times\{\mathbf{P}_1\}$ represents a loop that iterates n times executing $\mathbf{P}_1$ unless a return value is encountered. The sign = reprensents assignment, $\overset{?}{=}$ reprensents an equality check, the symbol $\oplus$ represents a bitwise OR operation, and the symbol $\perp$ represents an error.

8.2   Generalized Zero-Knowledge Proof of Linear Dependence

Here we describe a variation and generalization of Chaum's undeniable signature protocols [12] adapted to an elliptic curve group and simplified into a random oracle model. We define the linear dependence between n-tuples of curve points $(M_1, M_2, M_3, ..., M_n)$ and $(N_1, N_2, N_3, ..., N_n)$ to mean there exists $r \in \mathbb{F}_q^*$ such that $N_i = rM_i$ for all $i \in \{1..n\}$. We define $ZkPLD_r(M_1, M_2, M_3, ..., M_n | N_1, N_2, N_3, ..., N_n)$ to be an interactive protocol for zero knowledge proof of the fact that $M_i = rN_i$ for some fixed r for all $i \in \{1..n\}$. In some cases, we omit the subscript r when the private key is not known or not important for the discussion. The prover must know the value of r, but would not have to disclose this value.

$ZkPLD_r(M_1, M_2, M_3, ..., M_n | N_1, N_2, N_3, ..., N_n)$ This is a 4 message communication protocol. The following describes how it works.

1. The verifier chooses n random values $c_1, c_2, c_3, ..., c_n \leftarrow \mathbb{F}_q^*$ and sends $Y = \sum_{i=1}^{n} c_i M_i$ to the prover.
2. The prover computes $Z = rY$ and sends $h = H_q(Z)$ to the verifier.
3. The verifier sends $(c_1, c_2, ..., c_n)$ to the prover.
4. The prover checks $Y \overset{?}{=} \sum_{i=1}^{n} c_i M_i$. If the check succeeds, the prover sends Z to the verifier.
5. The verifier verifies $Z \overset{?}{=} \sum_{i=1}^{n} c_i N_i$ and $h \overset{?}{=} H_q(Z)$. If the equalities hold, the verifier accepts the verification, rejects otherwise.

The transcript of the protocol is $(Y, h, c_1, c_2, ..., c_n, Z)$. It is also known as the view of the protocol.

Proof of Security: The definition of completeness, soundness and zero-knowledge are defined in [13]. We present the theorems as below.

Theorem 1. *Proof of completeness: If it is true that there exists an r such that $N_i = rM_i$ for all $i \in \{1...n\}$, and the prover knows of the witness r, the prover will be able to generate a valid proof that would be accepted by an honest verifier with a probability 1.*

Proof. Since $Y = \sum_{i=1}^{n} c_i M_i$ and $Z = rY$, if $N_i = rM_i$ for all i, then $Z = rY = r\sum_{i=1}^{n} c_i M_i = \sum_{i=1}^{n} c_i r M_i = \sum_{i=1}^{n} c_i N_i$ and $h = H_q(Z)$. Hence the verifier checks succeed.

Theorem 2. *Proof of Soundness: Under the random oracle model, in* $ZkPLD_r(M_1, M_2, M_3, ..., M_n | N_1, N_2, N_3, ..., N_n)$, *if there is no r such that $N_i = rM_i$ for all $i \in \{1...n\}$, the prover can produce the valid proof with a maximum probability of $1/q + 1/q(1 - 1/q) < 2/q$.*

Proof. Suppose, the prover can produce the correct proof, it must either have computed $Z = rY$ in step 2 correctly, or H_q produced the same output for two different values. Without loss of generality, let us assume that (M_1, N_1) and (M_2, N_2) are not linearly dependent. Suppose $M_2 = kM_1$. Since our group is of prime order, such a k always exists. Now, it could happen that the verifier had sent the value $Y' = \sum_{i=1}^{n} c'_i M_i$ where $c'_1 = c_1 - kt$, $c'_2 = c_2 + t$ for some t and $c'_i = c_i$ for all i other than 1 and 2. This means $Y' = (c_1 - kt)M_1 + (c_2 + t)M_2 + \sum_{i=3}^{n} c_i M_i = c_1 M_1 + c_2 M_2 + \sum_{i=3}^{n} c_i M_i = Y$.

However, given $Y = c_1 M_1 + c_2 M_2 + \sum_{i=3}^{n} c_i M_i$ and $Z = c_1 N_1 + c_2 N_2 + \sum_{i=3}^{n} c_i N_i$ as the verifier checked, there is only one value of c_1 that would satisfy the verifier checks unless (M_1, N_1) and (M_2, N_2) are linearly dependent (otherwise one can solve for c_1 and c_2 given the other values with infinite computational power). Since the prover could only see Y, it cannot distinguish between c_1 and c'_1; so probability of it computing Z correctly is at most $1/q$. The probability of a different Z having the same hash is $1/q$. Hence, the probability of a successful verification for a non-linear set of pairs of points is at most $1/q + 1/q(1 - 1/q)$. $\square$

Theorem 3. *Proof of zero-knowledge:* $ZkPLD_r(M_1, M_2, M_3, ..., M_n | N_1, N_2, N_3, ..., N_n)$ *is a black box computational zero knowledge protocol in the sense defined in [13].*

Proof. To prove it, we must construct a deterministic algorithm **M** such that given a black box access to any arbitrary program acting as a verifier **V***(possibly malicious), **M** is able to generate transcript that is computationally indistinguishable from an actual transcript of the interaction, i.e. $(Y, h, c_1, c_2, ...c_n, Z)$, by any arbitrarily powerful **A**.

Our simulator **M** works as follows with black-box access to **V***.

1. **M** receives Y from **V***.
2. **M** generates $h' \leftarrow \mathbb{F}_q^*$ and sends to **V***.
3. **M** receives $(c_1, c_2, ..., c_n)$ from **V***.
4. **M** checks $Y \overset{?}{=} \sum_{i=1}^{n} c_i M_i$, and computes $Z = \sum_{i=1}^{n} c_i N_i, h = H_q(Z)$ and outputs the transcript $(Y, h, c_1, c_2, ...c_n, Z)$.

Since $Y = \sum_{i=1}^{n} c_i M_i, Z = \sum_{i=1}^{n} c_i N_i, h = H_q(Z)$, if it is true that $N_i = rM_i$ for all i for some fixed r, we have $Z = \sum_{i=1}^{n} c_i N_i = \sum_{i=1}^{n} c_i r M_i = r\sum_{i=1}^{n} c_i M_i = rY$. Hence, the generated transcript is indeed indistinguishable from an actual transcript by any PPTA. If there is no such r, the generated transcript cannot be computationally distinguished from an actual interaction due to DDH assumption. If the protocol should have been aborted as disclosed by $(c_1, c_2, ..., c_n)$, a corresponding transcript is generated by $\mathbf{M}$.   □

8.3 Zero-Knowledge Verifiable Encryption

Our encryption enables an interactive proof of decryption such that the transcript of the proof cannot be used to convince a third party of the correctness of decryption. We use the notion of plaintext-awareness as defined in [14] for IND-CCA2 security with a variation of ElGamal encryption to construct our Zero-knowledge verifiable encryption. Our encryption system requires two EC key-pairs. Following are the procedures of the encryption system.

- **Key generation:** This step involves generation of two EC key-pairs $(p_1, P_1), (p_2, P_2)$ in the following way.
  $\{p_1, p_2 \leftarrow \mathbb{F}_q^*; P_1 = p_1 G; P_2 = p_2 G\}$.
- **Encryption:** The encryption of a β bit message m is generated by the program $Enc_{P_1,P_2}(m) = \{r, w \leftarrow \mathbb{F}_q^*; R = rG; M_1 = rP_1; M_2 = rP_2; c = m \oplus H_\beta(M_1) \oplus f(M_2); A = wG; b = H_q(R, A); a = w - rb; V = (a, b); (R, V, c)\}$, where f is the β bit representation of the curve-point passed to it.
- **Check validity:** The validity is checked by the program $ChkVld(R, V, c) = \{(a, b) = V; A = aG + bR; b \stackrel{?}{=} H_q(R, A)\}$.
- **Decryption:** Decryption is done by the program $Dec_{p_1,p_2}(R, V, c) = \{if(ChkVld(R, V, c))\{M_1 = p_1 R; M_2 = p_2 R; m = c \oplus H_\beta(M_1) \oplus f(M_2); m\}else\{\bot\}\}$.
- **Verification:** The verification of decryption of (R, V, c) to m is done in the following steps.
  1. The verifier runs $ChkVld(R, V, c)$. If it returns $false$, the verifier rejects the proof, else continues.
  2. The prover shares the values M_1, M_2.
  3. The prover and the verifier execute $ZkPLD_{p_1}(G, R|P_1, M_1)$ and $ZkPLD_{p_2}(G, R|P_2, M_2)$. If any of them fails, the verifier rejects the proof, else continues. Notice that since the prover knows p_1, p_2, the prover can provide these proofs.
  4. The verifier computes $c' = m \oplus H_\beta(M_1) \oplus f(M_2)$ and checks if $c' \stackrel{?}{=} c$.
  5. If all the conditions are satisfied, the verifier accepts the proof, otherwise the verifier rejects it.

The view of the verification protocol consists of the views of $ZkPLD_{p_1}(G, R|P_1, M_1)$ and $ZkPLD_{p_2}(G, R|P_2, M_2)$ combined with the values M_1 and M_2.

Proof of Security: Given an optional oracle $\mathcal{O}$ and an adversary PPTA $\mathcal{A} = (\mathcal{A}_1, \mathcal{A}_2)$, the general security definition for IND-XXX is as follows.

$$Adv^{IND-XXX}(\mathcal{A}) = \{p_1, p_2 \leftarrow \mathbb{F}_q^*; e \leftarrow \{0,1\}; P_1 = p_1 G; P_2 = p_2 G;$$
$$(m_0, m_1, s) \leftarrow \mathcal{A}_1^{\mathcal{O}}(P_1, P_2); (R, V, c) = Enc_{P_1, P_2}(m_e);$$
$$e' \leftarrow \mathcal{A}_2^{\mathcal{O}}(m_0, m_1, s, R, V, c);$$
$$|Pr(e' = 0|e = 0) - Pr(e' = 0|e = 1)|\} \quad (1)$$

In case of IND-CPA security, $\mathcal{O}$ is a do-nothing program and in case of IND-CCA2, $\mathcal{O}$ is a decryption oracle that decrypts any valid encryption unless that encryption is (R, V, c).

Theorem 4. *The advantage $Adv^{IND-CPA}(\mathcal{A})$ of the adversary is negligible.*

Proof. Suppose the adversary $\mathcal{A}$ does have a non-negligible advantage predicting e. Since H_q is a random oracle, if the input is not known, the output of H_q is indistinguishable from random. So, unless the adversary is able to compute M_1, the values $c = m_e \oplus H_\beta(M_1) \oplus f(M_2)$ and $V = (a, b), A = aG + bR, b = H_q(R, A)$ are indistinguishable from random. Also, since the random oracle could return any other value, c cannot possibly contribute anything to the computation of M_1 as all values of c should produce the same result. Since V is simply a CrytoNote signature with a single public key, V does not contain any computable information about r, so V also cannot help compute M_1. Hence the adversary must have a sub-algorithm $\mathcal{A}'$ that computes M_1, given G, R, m_e, M_2, P_1, P_2 with some non-negligible advantage ϵ. We represent the computation by $\mathcal{A}'(G, R, m_e, M_2, P_1, P_2)$. We will use this to construct an algorithm $\mathcal{A}''(G, S, T)$ that finds $U = sT$ given $G, S = sG, T$ where $s \leftarrow \mathbb{F}_q^*$. This is the Computational Diffie-Hellman problem that is assumed to be hard.

$\mathcal{A}''(G, S, T)$ is defined as $\{P_1 = S; R = T; p_2 \leftarrow \mathbb{F}_q^*; m_e \leftarrow \{0,1\}^\beta; P_2 = p_2 G; M_2 = p_2 R; M_1 = \mathcal{A}'(G, R, m_e, M_2, P_1, P_2); M_1\}$.

The above algorithm will return the value of U with the same advantage ϵ.

Theorem 5. *In the encryption protocol, $Adv^{IND-CCA2}$ is negligible.*

Proof. Since the oracle H_q could either provide b or b' as the result of the query after the input (R, A) is passed to it (i.e. R and A are fixed), if the adversary would produce valid a and a' respectively in each case, then we must have $aG + bR = a'G + b'R$, i.e $a + rb = a' + b'r$ or $r = \frac{a - a'}{b' - b}$. Once, r is known, the plain text can be computed $m = c \oplus H_q(rP_1) \oplus f(rP_2)$. This means, the probability of creating a valid encryption without being able to compute the plaintext is negligible, and hence decryption oracles do not help in breaking the security. Hence IND-CCA2 game is reduced to the IND-CPA game.   □

Theorem 6. *The verification protocol is black box computational zero-knowledge in the sense defined in [13].*

Proof. We have to produce a PPTA $\mathcal{M}$ such that, given the encryption (R, V, c), plain text m, it will produce a transcript that is computationally indistinguishable from the view of the verification protocol. We construct the following PPTA that generates the placeholder for the values M_1, M_2 named M_1', M_2' respectively.

$\{loop\_N\_times\{$
$r' \leftarrow \mathbb{F}_q^*; M_1' = r'P_1; F = m \oplus c \oplus H_\beta(M_1'); if(\exists f^{-1}(F))\{$
$M_2' = (f^{-1}(F)); return(M_1', M_2')\}\}\bot\}$

We then use the M_1', M_2' values to generate the pseudo-transcripts of $ZkPLD(G, R|P_1, M_1')$ and $ZkPLD(G, R|P_2, M_2')$ the same way as in Theorem 3.

If the probability of f^{-1} being non-invertible is ϵ, the probability of the PPTA failing is ϵ^N which is negligible on the parameter N. To see that the pseudo-transcript generated by the PPTA is computationally indistinguishable from a real transcript, we observe that the pseudo-transcript for the $ZkPLD$ protocol already have a black box computational zero-knowledge property, and the values of M_1', M_2' cannot be distinguished from M_1, M_2 (given R, P_1, P_2) due to DDH assumption. $\qquad\square$

Encryption of Multiple Blocks of Text: We have until now only used a β bit block of message. For a longer message, a standard padding can be first used to obtain a message in multiple of β bits. Say $m = m_1 m_2 ... m_n$. To save space on the randomness marker $R = rG$ and the validation V, we use the same randomness r, but use different public keys. Instead of only two private keys p_1, p_2, every patient chooses $2u$ public keys $p_1, p_2, ..., p_{2u}$ and declares the corresponding public keys $P_1 = p_1 G, P_2 = p_2 G, ..., P_{2u} = p_{2u} G$. For a plaintext with less than u blocks, we can encrypt as $c_i = m_i \oplus H_\beta(rP_{2i-1}) \oplus f(rP_{2i})$ for $i \in \{1..u\}$. For messages with more than u blocks, we start over with a new randomness after every u blocks.

8.4   One-Time Ring Signature with Proof of Trace

We use a slight variation of the one-time ring signature as described in the CryptoNote protocol [3] to sign a message m. The CryptoNote protocol has four operations **GEN, SIG, VER** and **LNK**. Our variation makes sure that the record chain belongs to a single owner, we also modify the signature a bit so that the block verifier can verify this while still not being able to know the real signer.

- **GEN:** $\{x \leftarrow \mathbb{F}_q^*; B \leftarrow (\mathbb{G} \setminus \{0\}); P = xB; (x, (B, P))\}$. x is the private key and (B, P) is a public key. For any $r \in \mathbb{F}_q^*$, (rB, rP) is also a public key for the same private key.
- **SIG:** The signer selects a random set of other public keys (B_i, P_i), her own signing keys $(x, (B, P))$. She computes $I = xH_g(B, P); r \leftarrow \mathbb{F}_q^*; B' = rG; P' = rxG$. Let s be her own secret index such that $P_s = P, B_s = B$.

She picks random $q_i, w_i \leftarrow \mathbb{F}_q^*$ for all $i \in \{1...n\}$. She then computes the following.

$$L_i = \begin{cases} q_i B_i & \text{if } i = s \\ q_i B_i + w_i P_i & \text{if } i \neq s \end{cases} \qquad M_i = \begin{cases} q_i B' & \text{if } i = s \\ q_i B' + w_i P' & \text{if } i \neq s \end{cases}$$

$$R_i = \begin{cases} q_i (H_g(B_i, P_i)) & \text{if } i = s \\ q_i (H_g(B_i, P_i)) + w_i I & \text{if } i \neq s \end{cases}$$

She then computes the non-interactive challenge
$\mathfrak{c} = H_q(m, I, B_1, B_2, ..., B_n, P_1, P_2, ..., P_n, L_1, L_2, ..., L_n, M_1, M_2, ..., M_n, R_1, R_2, ..., R_n)$
She finally computes c_i, d_i for all i as follows;

$$d_i = \begin{cases} w_i & \text{if } i \neq s \\ \mathfrak{c} - \sum_{i \in \{1..n\} \setminus \{s\}} w_i & \text{if } i = s \end{cases} \qquad c_i = \begin{cases} q_i & \text{if } i \neq s \\ q_s - d_s x & \text{if } i = s \end{cases}$$

The signature is $\sigma = (I, c_1, c_2, ..., c_n, d_1, d_2, ..., d_n)$. I is called the key-image.
- **VER:** The verifier computes $L_i' = c_i B_i + d_i P_i$, $M_i' = c_i B' + d_i P'$, $R_i' = c_i H_g (B_i, P_i) + d_i I$. After that, the verifier checks whether $\sum_{i=1}^{n} d_i \overset{?}{=} H_q(m, I, B_1, B_2, ..., B_n, P_1, P_2, ..., P_n, L_1', L_2', ..., L_n', M_1', M_2', ..., M_n', R_1', R_2', ..., R_n')$.
- **LNK:** The verifier checks that the same key-image I has not been used before for any signature.

Proof of Security: The linkability, exculpability and unforgeability properties remain the same as proved in CryptoNote [3] and the proofs remain identical in our protocol. The proof of the anonymity property is also very similar to the one provided in the CrytoNote paper. We prove a new property that we call chain-continuity that restricts anyone from merging or branching patient record chains.

Theorem 7. *Chain continuity: Given a set of public keys S and a valid signature $\sigma = (I, c_1, c_2, ..., c_n, d_1, d_2, ..., d_n)$, it is impossible to have the next public (B', P') and the current signing public key (B, P) correspond to different private keys under the random oracle model.*

Proof. Suppose they belong to different private keys x and y respectively. So, $(P = xB)$ and $(P' = yB')$. If the secret index of the public key is j, we have $L_j = c_j B + d_j P \Rightarrow L_j = c_j B + d_j x B$ and $M_j = c_j B' + d_j P' \Rightarrow M_j = c_j B' + d_j y B'$. Let $L_j = sB, M_j = tB'$. Since $\mathbb{G}$ is of prime order, such s, t always exist. So, we have $s = c_j + d_j x$ and $t = c_j + d_j y$. Unless $y = x$, this fixes c_j, d_j just like c_i, d_i for all other i. So, the sum $\sum_{i=1}^{n} d_i$ is also fixed and cannot match the output of the random oracle. So, it must be that $x = y$. $\qquad\square$

9 Implementation of the Design Objectives

We now describe the implementation of the three design goals as follows.

- **Prohibition of merging or branching of record chains (continuity):**
  When signing (with the unlinkable one-time ring signature) for the public
  keys (B, P),the patient generates (B', P') and creates a signature and shares
  that to the provider. The provider then adds the encrypted content and adds
  the record to the chain with a blockchain transaction. (B', P') then becomes
  the next UTXO. Theorem 7 makes sure that (B, P) and (B', P') correspond
  to the same private key which prohibits merging of a different patient's record
  in the chain. We also have the same check as CryptoNote that the validators
  check that the same key-image I has not been used before for any signature,
  which prohibits branching of the chain.
- **Ownership of records:** The patient initially creates the primary key-pair
  $(x, P_0 = xG)$ for a fixed base G and gets it certified from the identity provider.
  Now we can use the next public key (B', P') as the ownership marker.
  Privacy of content: The privacy of content is achieved using the zero-
  knowledge verifiable encryption. Notice that in Theorem 6, we can simulate a
  verifier to create a pseudo-transcript, which means that any party can claim
  any text of the same length as being the plaintext of the encrypted message
  and provide a pseudo-transcript for it (unless of course an actual interactive
  proof is demanded). This means the proof transcript is not transferable, i.e.,
  the transcript will not convince a third party that the decryption is correct.
  Privacy of linkage: This is achieved using the one-time ring signature with
  proof of trace.
  Zero-knowledge interactive provability: The patient can prove the linkages for **n** consecutive transactions, for which the true signing public keys
  are $(B_1, P_1), (B_2, P_2), ..., (B_\mathbf{n}, P_\mathbf{n})$ (among the fakes) and the key images are
  $I_1, I_2, ..., I_\mathbf{n}$. The patient does this by first sharing the true signing pub-
  lic keys and then using $ZkPLD_x(H_g(B_1, P_1), H_g(B_2, P_2), ..., H_g(B_\mathbf{n}, P_\mathbf{n})|I_1,$
  $I_2, ..., I_\mathbf{n})$ where x is the private key. The ownership of the record can be
  proved using $ZkPLD_x(G, P_0|B', P')$ for any ownership marker (B', P') where
  P_0 is the primary public key of the patient. The content can be proved using
  the verification protocol of the encryption.

10 Conclusion and Future Work

This paper provides a solution to store EHR records on a blockchain. To truly
give control to the patients, we think it is necessary to put the records on a
publicly maintained blockchain, which requires the use of strong cryptography
to provide the patient with true privacy. We provide cryptographic constructs to
achieve full privacy for the patient including the information about how many
times a patient visits a health care provider along with the actual medical records
of the patient.

However, since we store all records on the blockchain, it would be infeasible to store large diagnostic raw data, like a tomograph, in our proposed system. This requires another publicly maintained datastore that the current system may refer to where we can use the same encryption algorithm for storage of the data. While there are some related works, we intend to explore and design such systems in the future to enhance the capability of the proposed system.

References

1. Health it and health information exchange basics. https://www.healthit.gov/topic/health-it-and-health-information-exchange-basics/health-it-and-health-information-exchange
2. Nakamoto, S.: Bitcoin: a peer-to-peer electronic cash system. http://bitcoin.org/bitcoin.pdf
3. van Saberhagen, N.: Cryptonote v 2.0. https://cryptonote.org/whitepaper.pdf
4. Fujisaki, E., Suzuki, K.: Traceable ring signature. In: Okamoto, T., Wang, X. (eds.) PKC 2007. LNCS, vol. 4450, pp. 181–200. Springer, Heidelberg (2007). https://doi.org/10.1007/978-3-540-71677-8_13
5. Electronic medical record systems. https://healthit.ahrq.gov/key-topics/electronic-medical-record-systems
6. HIPAA administrative simplification. https://www.hhs.gov/sites/default/files/hipaa-simplification-201303.pdf
7. Summary of the HIPAA privacy rule. https://www.hhs.gov/hipaa/for-professionals/privacy/laws-regulations/index.html
8. Azaria, A., Ekblaw, A., Vieira, T., Lippman, A.: MedRec: Using blockchain for medical data access and permission management. In: 2016 2nd International Conference on Open and Big Data (OBD), pp. 25–30, August 2016. https://doi.org/10.1109/OBD.2016.11
9. Dubovitskaya, A., Xu, Z., Ryu, S., Schumacher, M., Wang, F.: Secure and trustable electronic medical records sharing using blockchain. In: AMIA Annual Symposium Proceedings. AMIA, August 2017
10. Yue, X., Wang, H., Jin, D., Li, M., Jiang, W.: Healthcare data gateways: found healthcare intelligence on blockchain with novel privacy risk control. J. Med. Syst. **40**, 1–8 (2016)
11. Jiang, S., Cao, J., Wu, H., Yang, Y., Ma, M., He, J.: BlocHIE: A BLOCkchain-based platform for healthcare information exchange. In: 2018 IEEE International Conference on Smart Computing (SMARTCOMP), pp. 49–56 (2018)
12. Chaum, D.: Zero-knowledge undeniable signatures (extended abstract). In: Damgård, I.B. (ed.) EUROCRYPT 1990. LNCS, vol. 473, pp. 458–464. Springer, Heidelberg (1991). https://doi.org/10.1007/3-540-46877-3_41
13. Goldreich, O., Oren, Y.: Definitions and properties of zero-knowledge proof systems. J. Cryptol. **7**(1), 1–32 (1994). https://doi.org/10.1007/BF00195207
14. Bellare, M., Rogaway, P.: Optimal asymmetric encryption. In: De Santis, A. (ed.) EUROCRYPT 1994. LNCS, vol. 950, pp. 92–111. Springer, Heidelberg (1995). https://doi.org/10.1007/BFb0053428

Blockchain Federation for Complex Distributed Applications

Zhitao Wan$^{(\boxtimes)}$, Minqiang Cai, Xianghua Lin, and Jinqing Yang

Institute of Advanced Technology Research, Ge Lian Corporation, Hangzhou, China
wan@pku.edu.cn

Abstract. Blockchains are immutable distributed ledger systems usually without a central authority. Blockchains enables people to establish trusted application among untrusted parties. But, the performance of blockchain is a challenge for massive applications. There are many researches to improve the performance of blockchain including side blockchain, interconnection of blockchains. In fact, a distributed application usually needs resource of computing, storage and transportation, even with possible permissioned access. It means that any current blockchain cannot satisfy all the demands simultaneously. This paper proposes a new Blockchain Federation that consolidates several blockchains to support complex distributed applications. Two typical application scenarios are implemented following the proposed concept of Blockchain Federation. The new emerging blockchain technology are combined together to meet the demands of complex peer-to-peer applications. And, the conclusions are drawn and future direction of Blockchain Federation evolution, Federation Blockchain, is discussed as well.

1 Introduction

1.1 The Evolution of Blockchain

When a signed chain was used as an electronic ledger for digitally signing documents in 1991 the core idea of blockchain emerged. The idea is in a way that could easily show none of the signed documents had been changed [1]. It was first applied to digital cash in 2008 in the initial paper describing the Bitcoin electronic cash solution, which was published pseudonymously by Satoshi Nakamoto. Bitcoin is the first milestone of blockchain implementation and application. Blockchain enabled Bitcoin to be implemented in a distributed way and there is no single user or organization controlled the blockchain system. There is no single failure point existed in the blockchain system as well. The distributed miners joined freely maintained the Bitcoin blockchain system. Bitcoin blockchain created a complete transparency system, which promoted trust and credit in its wide adoption. All transactions are transparent within the Bitcoin blockchain system. Each transaction must be censored by massive miners and consensus reached before it was recorded in blockchain permanently, which avoided double spend of digital assets. Blockchain enabled business to be conducted with

© Springer Nature Switzerland AG 2019
J. Joshi et al. (Eds.): ICBC 2019, LNCS 11521, pp. 112–125, 2019.
https://doi.org/10.1007/978-3-030-23404-1_8

untrusted and unknown parties. With the more and more blockchains emerging, projects aim to connect the separated blockchains were founded. They intend to reduce fees and try to provide inter-blockchain transaction with high usability, scalability, and reliability.

There is a common three-stage taxonomy of blockchain 1.0, 2.0 and 3.0, which is typically represented by the Bitcoin[1] as e-cash, Ethereum[2] with smart contract, and blockchains[3] stand on more solid application ground respectively.

Blockchains are applied in AI, audit, big data, cloud computing, finance, governance, health care, intellectual property, IoT, security, smart cities, transportation, 5G and mobility, and more fields.

1.2 The Diversity of Blockchain

Generally, blockchains can be classified into three major categories.

Private Blockchain is basically closed and exclusive that serves organizations or simple businesses. It is usually implemented in a small range and the topology is relatively simple.

Consortium Blockchain serves related parties have a common goal, and related organizations can join the consortium blockchain on common agreements.

Public Blockchain has no restrictions on join/leave blockchain.

Apart from the main stream classical blockchains, there are many other blockchain variants which cooperate with other blockchain, usually called as main chain, as work around to improve the performance or reduce transaction fee.

Side Chain is a protocol that enables developers to connect side chains to the main chain. The side chain enables transactions between the main chain and side chain. These side chains can have different properties from main chain [2].

Off Chain works with off main chain transactions. Off chain transactions are recorded locally that will be synchronized to the main chain later on to avoid the transition jam on main chain [3].

Alternative Chain implements separate blockchain to achieve distributed consensus and may use a different token as intermedia of transactions. Alternative chains to scaling other than sharding include state channels, side chains, multi-chains and off-chain computation[4]. Some implementations share miners with the main blockchain.

---

[1] https://www.bitcoin.org/.

[2] https://www.ethereum.org/.

[3] https://www.stateofthedapps.com/.

[4] https://github.com/ethereum/wiki/wiki/Scaling-projects-and-proposals-and-other-crypto-infrastructure-projects.

The calssical blockchains such as Bitcoin adopts single chain structure that avoid any fork which offers a double spending free guarantee from data structure angle. DAG(Directed Acyclic Graph) aims to make blockchains more scalable for higher transaction rate in a sense of parallelization or permissioned fork. There are two typical implementations.

Block DAG includes blocks referencing multiple predecessors, thus, blocks with long propagation time are also acceptable in the network. It increases the transaction volumes and throughput [4]. A key facet of this inclusive protocol is the rewarding of the blocks creator with transaction fees, although the block is not from the main chain.

Transaction DAG[5] is formed with each transaction containing a list of previous transactions hashes[6]. A single chain transaction blockchain would not scale with high transaction rate, orphan chains or blocks that will be obsoleted and lower priority transactions will probably not fit in the blockchain. Transaction DAG alleviates this problem.

Different consensus algorithms or models are adopted by different blockchains to meet the design principles or targets.

PoW(Proof of Work) usually let a mining node gets the right to publish the next block when it solved a computationally intensive puzzle. The solution to this puzzle is the proof of it has performed work. The puzzle is designed such that solving the puzzle is difficult, but easy to check that a solution is valid or not. This enables all other mining nodes to validate any proposed next blocks easily, and any proposed block that does not satisfy the puzzle will be rejected.

PoS(Proof of Stake) is based on the idea that the more stake a node has in the system, the more likely it will want the system to succeed. Stake is the relative value held by the node. PoS blockchain systems use the amount of stake a node has as a determining factor for new block creation [5].

Round Robin relies on the existence of some level of trust between mining nodes. There is no need for a complicated consensus mechanism to determine which node to publish the next block to the chain. This consensus model is often used for private blockchains where nodes take turns in creating blocks. To handle situations that a mining node is not available when it is its turn to publish block, usually an element of randomness is given to enable available nodes to publish block. An unavailable node will not obstruct blockchain operation.

Voter is a probabilistic model describing opinion dynamics on a graph. Each node in the blockchain system has an opinion, which changes from time to time by adopting the opinion of a random neighbor. Different selection models for the opinion updates result in different behavior of the population's opinions over time [6].

---

[5] https://bitcointalk.org/index.php?topic=1504649.0.

[6] https://dagcoin.org/whitepaper.pdf.

There are many new or improved consensus algorithms emerged fitting for different application scenarios with more blockchain variants.

UTXO(Unspent Transaction Outputs) model used in Bitcoin and account based model used in Ethereum are the two major transaction models.

UTXO allows the transfer of assets between mutually trustless counterparties. In this model, every transaction consumes outputs created from earlier transactions and generates new outputs for later consumption by subsequent transactions [7].

Account Based permits interactive processes between mutually trustless counter parties. A smart contract is a non-tokenized script kept on the blockchain with a unique address [8].

Different blockchains provide different mechanisms or supports for distributed applications. Some blockchains provide their own distributed applications with themselves due to their very limited functionality (e.g., Bitcoin). Many other blockchains provide interfaces for distributed application development and running. e.g., Hyperledger[7] Composer REST Server is used to support higher level business abstractions and Hyperledger Fabric SDK REST Server to support lower level fine control. It is convenience to be integrated with current Web services to construct permission applications.

There are many researches intend to find out which attributes, such as immutable, trustless and anonymous, of blockchains are important for a given application, and how to determine which elements of an architecture should employ blockchain technologies. But for a standalone distributed application, the absence of researches on blockchain based functionalities integration obstructs the adoption of blockchain. Methodologies and best practices are absent. There are still many open issues in how to develop distributed applications that supported by blockchains or blockchain functionalities.

1.3 The Diversity of Distributed Application

A distributed application is software that is executed or run on multiple computers within a network. These applications interact in order to achieve a specific goal or task. It does not rely on a single system or server(s). There is no center(s) needed to support a distributed application any more. But, the resource needs for any distributed application still exist and should be allocated locally or from peer(s). If a node that is running a particular application copy goes down it will not impact the whole distributed application system.

Adopting blockchain technologies is a way to develop distributed applications. But, most of current blockchains can only provide very limit resources for distributed applications. Consequently, the blockchain enabled distributed application scenarios are relative simple and very limit. e.g., only token based value exchange, gambling, ledger based data sharing, notarization and so on are

---

[7] https://www.hyperledger.org.

applicable. The network connection and data storage capacity cannot support distributed applications with relative higher resource consuming. New emerging blockchains try to solve the problem but they are usually limited to a specific direction. Coordinating different blockchains is a way to solve the problem. A complex distributed application usually consumes variant resources intensively which typically include:

Computing resources in this context means CPU, GPU, FPGA, ASIC or any other computational resource accessible to distributed applications rather than broad-sense computing including the following items.

Network resources refer to the protocols and connections that can be accessed by a group of nodes with computing resources and related software stacks and hardware devices.

Storage resources provide the process of storing information in a computer memory or on a magnetic tape or disk.

Other applications/services resources provide accessible functionalities via interfaces to distributed applications.

A complex distributed application in this paper usually consumes the mentioned resources one or several orders of magnitude higher than Ethereum can offer.

Most of current blockchains only provide very limit single type resource for distributed applications. e.g., Bitcoin provides transaction with short memo which is practice impossible for active distributed application to store application data. To meet the gaps between traditional blockchains and distributed applications there are many dedicated blockchains emerged. IPFS(Inter-Planetary File System)[8] based blockchains declared to use Proof of Replication and Proof of Space. NKN[9] is a kind of P2P network connectivity protocol powered by a public blockchain. It uses incentives to motivate Internet users to share their spare network connection and bandwidth. But, there does not exist one fit all total solution blockchain can meet complex distributed application demands. In this paper, we propose an innovative Blockchain Federation to integrate current blockchains for complex distributed applications. Blockchain Federation provides not only a realistic way for distributed application development but also a way of blockchain evolution. The rest of this paper consists of the following sections: Section 2 raises the problems of current blockchain. Section 3 proposes the concept of Blockchain Federation to solve the problems by meeting the gap of functionality, performance, security and acceptability. Section 4 uses two examples to demonstrate how the Blockchain Federation works and Sect. 5 draw the conclusions and indicate the future works.

2   Problems

Blockchains are distributed digital ledgers fit for basic distributed application. Transactions are cryptographically signed and grouped into blocks to be stored

---

[8] https://ipfs.io/.

[9] https://www.nkn.org/.

that provides little flexibility for external data storage. Each block in a blockchain is cryptographically linked to the previous block with validation which is undergoing a consensus decision by given consensus algorithm or mechanism. And, any possible conflict is resolved automatically using predefined rules. Every new block is replicated across all copies of the ledger in the nodes within the blockchain network. Compare with other standalone digital ledger system, it is obvious that a blockchain needs more copies of ledger, extra consensus and conflict resolving. The direct consequences are the higher storage cost, higher latency of replication across the network and, more uncertainty of data storage process. All blockchain data and source code are usually public accessible and the security risk is relative higher.

2.1 The Performance Limitations of Blockchain

Block propagation in network is necessary for blockchains. For a blockchain system, propagation delay implies a longer time until consistency on the block is reached. Furthermore, the efficiency of PoW depends on fast information propagation [9]. Consequently, the delay significantly impacts the performance of distributed applications based on blockchain. The major performance measures of blockchain are following.

Transaction Rate measures how many transactions per second are added to the memory pool of transactions awaiting confirmation. In fact, it may drastically increase or decreases from the declared rate, this can be caused by network congestion, or a major nodes experiencing downtime.

Storage Capacity is obvious much higher in blockchains comparing with applications only keep local copy of data. Each block will be duplicated as many times as blockchain active node number even though there are lot of nodes in blockchain network will not keep full data copy.

Consistency Delay of blockchain includes the propagation delay in the network, consensus process delay and conflict resolving delay.

The distributed consensus, data storage of blockchain skyrockets the cost and delay of blockchain. The blockchain based applications should be elaborately designed especially in how to utilize blockchain(s).

2.2 The Function Limitations of Blockchain

The blockchain nodes are interconnected by P2P to form a network. Taking Bitcoin as an example, each node can transmit and verify data and has a routing function to ensure information interaction and block spread throughout the network. Blockchain nodes can join or leave the blockchain network without impact on the blockchain operation. Blockchain nodes are equal to communicate without intermediate entities. But, a newbie has to download all related data before it can perform as a normal node of blockchain and it usually will cost a couple of days. And, blockchains only support given transaction and possible smart contract. The major function limitations of blockchain are following.

Identity in server centric system allow users to access a given online service or different services by adopting federated identity management, which also known as SSO(Single Sign On). Permissionless blockchains provide anonymity that is not sufficient for some distributed application scenarios. And, the distributed application may erode the anonymity of permissionless blockchains.

Join/Leave Blockchain for permissionless blockchains usually cannot be interfered by the blockchain itself or any other node if any node is joining in proper manner. But, the implied requirements of blockchain such as computing, storage and networking hedge the new node join and may interrupt the distributed application connection and access.

Transaction Type of current blockchains are usually focus on value transfer.

Ledger Data Structure of a blockchain is usually strictly predefined.

Smart Contract is computer code intends to facilitate, verify, or enforce a digital contract. A smart contract allows the performance of transactions without third parties involved in trackable and irreversible manner. These transactions are partially or fully self-executing and/or self-enforcing. But, to connect with real world an Oracle is usually needed.

The function limitations hedge the wide application of blockchain. The consequence is that most current distributed applications are very simple or rely on other centric service(s).

2.3   The Security Issues of Blockchain

A permissionless blockchain maintains a global state and allow modification of that state by users of the blockchain system. Users formulate changes to the state as transactions, which are published, distributed, verified and stored on the distributed network. A permissioned blockchain can only be used by authenticated users. The major security issues of blockchain are following.

Identification is used to establish permits to exchange sensitive data with an authentication mechanism, which is usually basing on password, trusted hardware, trusted third party or user characteristic and so on. Blockchain authentication can use smart contract which is code deployed to blockchain. The need for a third party to authenticate transactions is eliminated. Costs can be reduced while security and privacy are greatly enhanced. Effort of hijacking the authentication process would be much greater in the distributed environment.

Encryption and Hash Algorithm play key roles in maintaining blockchain. Bitcoin used the SHA-256 algorithm for hash. Due to the advent of mining of graphics cards, FPGA and then ASIC. The mining pools make the problem of centralization worse. The SCRYPT algorithm uses CPU idle time for calculations [10]. Heavycoin[10] attempts parallel algorithms for games on

---

[10] https://heavycoin.github.io/.

the blockchain. Ethereum uses the transition algorithm Ethash[11]. The algorithms are mainly used to resist the computing hegemony. Primecoin[12] seeks large prime numbers. If it passes the Fermat and EulerCLagrangeCLifchitz test it will be considered a prime number. This approach does not guarantee every number that passes the tests is a real prime number. The system will operate normally even with a wrong result[13].

Network of blockchains should prevent disclosure of application layer information by IP address for anonymity and prevent DoS(Deny of Service) attack caused interruption of connection and information propagation. All the traditional network attacks somehow impact blockchains but the robust of blockchains are relatively higher than centric servers.

Data Exposition is a common issue to permissionless blockchains. Asymmetric encryption and hash algorithms are the foundation of blockchains to build trust on untrusted network. Asymmetric encryption algorithms are used for encryption, signature, and authentication. The hash algorithms are used to construct the blockchain data structures and sometimes for PoW. Due to all the data of blockchains are exposed to all permission parties. The cracking and tampering are inevitable.

Smart Contract is the basis for forming the logical chain of information, and also the bridge between the lower logical chain and the upper services. A smart contract is a self-assurance mutual distributing agreement between parties to the transaction. Smart contracts come in many forms, such as token systems [11], wallets, multi-signature smart contracts, etc. A study of the security of smart contract points out that 8833 of the existing 19,366 contracts in Ethereum were vulnerable [12]. A set of Oyente[14] for identifying potential security vulnerabilities was proposed as well. As short piece of code deployed in blockchain each smart contract should be checked carefully.

The one-time pad is the optimum encryption system with theoretically perfect secrecy. Due to the data exposition of blockchain and public system, any sensitive data should not be submitted to a blockchain.

2.4   The Developer and End-User Acceptability of Blockchain

The developer and end-user are two important factors that impact the adoption of blockchain. From the developers angle, besides the fundamental functions, incentive mechanism, development language, API, ecosystem, community and others are taken into consideration.

Incentive Mechanism is used to ensure the continuity and attractiveness of the blockchain. Public blockchains usually have proposed incentives. Establishing a token issuing and value equilibrium mechanism to attract and

---

[11] https://github.com/ethereum/ethash.
[12] http://primecoin.io/.
[13] http://primecoin.io/bin/primecoin-paper.pdf.
[14] https://oyente.tech.

keep enough active participants. Reward for miners, currency exchange and token appreciation reinforce the blockchains and provides solid ground for distributed applications.

Development Language of the mainstream blockchains are vary. Most main stream blockchains usually provide more than one different development language implementations such as C/C++, Python, JavaScript, Go and so on.

API of blockchains is a key factor for developers. Main stream blockchains provide SDKs for different development languages.

Ecosystem of blockchain is important because no single party can take over the all opportunities of blockchain. Users, organisations, miners, developers and investors are actors of blockchain ecosystem.

Community is an interesting group of users and developers, epically advocators, of blockchain. A member can complete challenges to grow skill set and reputation and get access to resources, guides, and best practices, discuss content and code with other like-minded developers. be rewarded for contributions and guided through technical journey. Community is very important for blockchain.

The impact of this issue depends on many factors such as actors and other non-technical factors. Generally, for a team with different backgrounds, more choices mean more flexibilities.

3 Blockchain Federation

As discussed in previous section, a current blockchain cannot satisfy all the demands of a complex distributed application. And, the performance, function, security and development issues of current blockchains should be solved to support complex distributed applications. We propose a new Blockchain Federation to fix the gap between current blockchains and the targets of complex distributed applications. Blockchain Federation integrated two or more blockchains and necessary improvements to solve the related problems of blockchains to meet the requirements of complex distributed applications. The Blockchain Federation is a model for integrating multi-blockchain functionalities with possible performance, security, acceptability and other improvement. It enables the support of complex distributed applications basing on current blockchains. The Blockchain Federation has three characteristics, three development models and three deployment models.

3.1 Targets

The core target of Blockchain Federation is to provide a methodology to support distributed applications that cannot be done by a single blockchain. The targets of Blockchain Federation can be generally classified into four groups according to the discussion in previous section.

Function Integration enriches the supporting to distributed applications. e.g., NKN provides a fast blockchain for network connection; IPFS based blockchains provide more flexible data storage. Blockchain Federation enables the cooperation of independent blockchains to maximize the automation and robust of distributed applications. Solving cross blockchain transactions, scalability and atomic validity are the research hotspots. Interledger[15] uses connector to find the recipient's remittance path and transfer funds.

Performance Improvement includes throughput promotion and latency. For a given blockchain it is applicable to duplicate blockchain for parallel processing. The latency of a blockchain can be improved by adopting low latency network connections and more powerful computers. The side blockchain and off blockchain can improve the performance of main blockchain significantly.

Security Improvement of blockchain depends on the integration model. Generally, each blockchain keeps its own security behavior and potentially risks are localized. The inter-blockchain anchor provides extra proof for abnormal detection to keep consistency and correctness.

Acceptability Increase is relative complex because of the human resource related issue is hard to measure. The capacity, preference and experience of developers in a team may vary. The integration of more blockchains provides more room for developers to choose proper blockchains.

In fact, not all the targets can be achieved simultaneously but at least one target should be reached when a Blockchain Federation is designed.

3.2 Characteristics

The Blockchain Federation has three characteristics. The multi-blockchain connection enables the information exchanging. The inter-blockchain anchor enables the mutual proof. And, the Elasticity enables the fast Blockchain Federation deployment and resource allocation and release.

Multi-Blockchain Connection enables information exchange across blockchains.

Inter-Blockchain Anchor is to use other blockchain(s) for existence proof. It provides a way for higher level of tamper resistant. The anchor is a hash value of a blockchain block data is written in another blockchain's block. The later blockchain proofs the existence of block data in the former one.

Elasticity means all blockchains involved in the Blockchain Federation are pluggable, i.e., Blockchain Federation can choose alternative blockchain and will not impact the implementation and operation of current blockchains. Blockchain capabilities can be elastically provisioned and released, i.e., a Blockchain Federation can be applied to a distributed application with minimal configuration effort and can be released instantly.

A Blockchain Federation should keep all above three basic characteristics.

---

[15] https://interledger.org/.

3.3 Deployment Models

The Blockchain Federation includes permissionless, permissioned and hybrid deployment models.

Permissionless Model is provisioned for open access by the general public and all the blockchains involved are permissionless blockchains.

Permissioned Model is provisioned for exclusive use by an organization or interesting group with only permissioned blockchains.

Hybrid Model is a composition of permissionless and permissioned blockchains. Usually full access to any Blockchain Federation's permissioned blockchain is granted.

A permissionless model is used for public used scenarios. A permissioned model is used inside an organization. A hybrid model usually crosses the boarder of an organization.

4 Examples and Evaluations

In this section, we use two on-going projects to demonstrate the application of Blockchain Federation. One is video distribution and copyright protection and, the other is air pollution monitoring and emission quota exchanging.

4.1 Video Distribution and Copyright Protection

Nowadays, Tik Tok[16] and similar short-video sharing platforms make a massive amount of video with copyrights and user-generated pieces. The Fair Use Act[17] gives people the ability to freely use those stuff without compensating the original provider, but the EU voted in a new copyright directive that video-sharing sites need to obtain licenses to show the contents. The video copyright protection rules become stricter. Blockchain can be used to protect Intellectual Property, and it improves efficiency and accuracy with lower costs. We developed distributed applications based video distribution and copyright protection platforms with blockchains.

A video distribution and copyright protection platform consists of three main components including copyright confirmation, content storage and distribution. Figure 1 depicts the implementation of the video distribution and copyright protection distributed application and Blockchain Federation.

We adopt open source video platform Kaltura[18] as the base of prototype for video publish and NKN for content distribution. Hyperledger is used for copyright notarization. Ethereum test network is used for incentive record.

---

[16] https://www.tiktok.com.

[17] https://eur-lex.europa.eu/legal-content/EN/TXT/?uri=CELEX:52016PC0593.

[18] http://www.kaltura.org/.

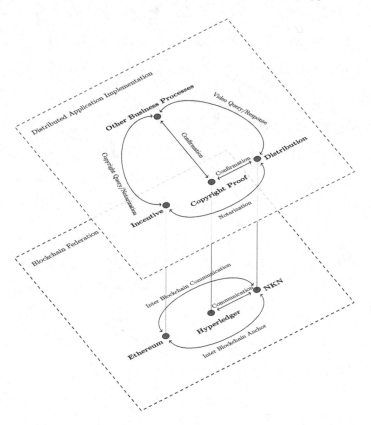

Fig. 1. The video distribution and copyright protection distributed application and blockchain federation

4.2   Air Pollution Monitoring and Emission Quota Exchanging

Current AQM(Air Quality Monitoring) stations take air samples from the emission equipment and a few places throughout a factory. The AQI(Air Quality Index) is created by the pollutants present in the air usually including carbon monoxide, nitrogen dioxide, ozone, sulfur dioxide, lead, PM(Particulate Matter)2.5 and PM10. AQM stations uplink to local control room as well as to local Environmental Protection Agency. Figure 2 depicts the implementation of the air pollution monitoring and emission quota exchanging distributed application and Blockchain Federation.

We use X86 based UP board[19] as the AQM hardware platform and Ubuntu as the software platform to construct low cost AQM station. Hyperledger Fabric is used for data storage and quota exchange. NKN is used for air pollution monitoring and data report. The Hyperledger is used to store AQM data in a factory and all data reported via NKN.

---

[19] https://up-board.org/.

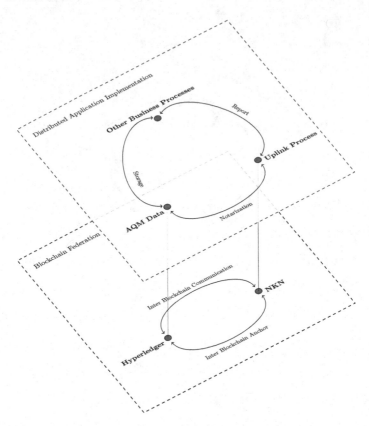

Fig. 2. The air pollution monitoring and emission quota exchanging distributed application and blockchain federation

5   Conclusions and Future Works

Blockchains are immutable distributed ledger systems usually without a central authority. It is intrinsic to support distributed applications. But, the performance of blockchain is a challenge for massive adoption. And, any current blockchain cannot satisfy all the demands of computing, storage and network simultaneously. We propose a new Blockchain Federation that consolidates several blockchains to support complex distributed applications. Two typical application scenarios, one is video distribution and copyright protection and the other is air pollution monitoring and quota exchange, are implemented following the proposed concept of Blockchain Federation. The blockchain technologies are combined together to meet the demands of complex distribution applications. The prototypes demonstrate the Blockchain Federation is realistic for distributed applications.

But, the business logic of Blockchain Federation is managed by glue code rather than native blockchain code. In a permissioned application it is easy to keep the whole distributed application system integrity but for permissionless application it needs extra mechanism to keep the system integrity. It is the possible evolution of the Blockchain Federation. Construct an integrated new single blockchain, Federation Blockchain, to keep the integrity of the current inside blockchain and inter-blockchain transitions is an interesting research direction.

References

1. Narayanan, A., Bonneau, J., Felten, E., Miller, A., Goldfeder, S.: Bitcoin and Cryptocurrency Technologies: A Comprehensive Introduction. Princeton University Press, Princeton (2016)
2. Deng, L., Chen, H., Zeng, J., Zhang, L.-J.: Research on cross-chain technology based on sidechain and hash-locking. In: Liu, S., Tekinerdogan, B., Aoyama, M., Zhang, L.-J. (eds.) EDGE 2018. LNCS, vol. 10973, pp. 144–151. Springer, Cham (2018). https://doi.org/10.1007/978-3-319-94340-4_12
3. Wang, P., Xu, H., Jin, X., Wang, T.: Flash: efficient dynamic routing for offchain networks. CoRR abs/1902.05260 (2019)
4. Danezis, G., Hrycyszyn, D.: Blockmania: from block DAGs to consensus. CoRR abs/1809.01620 (2018)
5. Kang, J., Xiong, Z., Niyato, D., Wang, P., Ye, D., Kim, D.I.: Incentivizing consensus propagation in proof-of-stake based consortium blockchain networks. IEEE Wirel. Commun. Lett. 8(1), 157–160 (2019)
6. Hardwick, F.S., Akram, R.N., Markantonakis, K.: E-Voting with blockchain: an E-Voting protocol with decentralisation and voter privacy. CoRR abs/1805.10258 (2018)
7. Delgado-Segura, S., Pérez-Solà, C., Navarro-Arribas, G., Herrera-Joancomartí, J.: Analysis of the bitcoin UTXO set. In: Zohar, A., et al. (eds.) FC 2018. LNCS, vol. 10958, pp. 78–91. Springer, Heidelberg (2019). https://doi.org/10.1007/978-3-662-58820-8_6
8. Christidis, K., Devetsikiotis, M.: Blockchains and smart contracts for the internet of things. IEEE Access 4, 2292–2303 (2016)
9. Gervais, A., Karame, G.O., Wüst, K., Glykantzis, V., Ritzdorf, H., Capkun, S.: On the security and performance of proof of work blockchains. [13], pp. 3–16
10. Alwen, J., Chen, B., Pietrzak, K., Reyzin, L., Tessaro, S.: Scrypt Is maximally memory-hard. In: Coron, J.-S., Nielsen, J.B. (eds.) EUROCRYPT 2017. LNCS, vol. 10212, pp. 33–62. Springer, Cham (2017). https://doi.org/10.1007/978-3-319-56617-7_2
11. Fröwis, M., Fuchs, A., Böhme, R.: Detecting token systems on ethereum. CoRR abs/1811.11645 (2018)
12. Luu, L., Chu, D., Olickel, H., Saxena, P., Hobor, A.: Making smart contracts smarter. [13], pp. 254–269
13. Weippl, E.R., Katzenbeisser, S., Kruegel, C., Myers, A.C., Halevi, S. (eds.): Proceedings of the 2016 ACM SIGSAC Conference on Computer and Communications Security, Vienna, Austria, 24–28 October 2016. ACM (2016)

Enriching Smart Contracts
with Temporal Aspects

Fabiana Fournier$^{(\boxtimes)}$ ⓘ and Inna Skarbovsky ⓘ

IBM Research - Haifa, University of Haifa, Haifa, Israel
fabiana@il.ibm.com

Abstract. Blockchain technology provides a platform for the decentralized execution of smart contracts. A smart contract is an agreement that is automatically executed when certain conditions are met. Current smart contracts use business rules to express conditions in which transactions occur but lack the capability to reason over time. We present a model-driven approach for creating blockchain applications that can run temporal logic. We present the new concepts required at the model level and explain how these concepts can be translated to a blockchain solution applying Hyperledger Fabric, Hyperledger Composer, and PROTON complex event processing. We illustrate the approach using a pharma cold chain scenario. Cold chain scenarios are typical examples of blockchain cases in which temporal reasoning is required. Here, the blockchain provides transparency, a non-repudiation process, full traceability and trackability of the transactions (provenance), shorter lead times, and authentication and verification of the parties in the supply chain network at each asset transfer. The temporal reasoning is required since decisions about pharmaceutical quality is based on time windows in which the goods have been exposed to certain conditions. Our solution includes the model, the blockchain backend, and a mobile user interface that allows each certified and authorized party in the network to initiate actions, finish their transactions, and track progress. It also includes temperature monitoring to ensure compliance with the proper conditions for transportation and asset transfer.

Keywords: Blockchain · Hyperledger Fabric · Hyperledger Composer · Cold chain · Complex event processing

1 Introduction

Blockchain is a peer-to-peer network and distributed ledger technology that allows any participant in a business network to see THE system of record (ledger). At the heart of any blockchain network is a distributed decentralized ledger, replicated across many network participants, that records all the transactions that take place on the network. A transaction is essentially an asset transfer onto or off the ledger.

In addition to being decentralized and collaborative, the ledger is append-only, using cryptographic techniques that guarantee that once a transaction has been added to the ledger it cannot be modified. This property of "immutability" makes it simple to determine the provenance of information, allowing network participants to be sure

© Springer Nature Switzerland AG 2019
J. Joshi et al. (Eds.): ICBC 2019, LNCS 11521, pp. 126–141, 2019.
https://doi.org/10.1007/978-3-030-23404-1_9

information has not been changed after the fact. Each peer on the network (a network participant) keeps a copy of the transaction ledger and world state database, which reflects the current state of all the assets in the network. The process of keeping the ledger transactions synchronized across the network is called consensus.

A blockchain network uses smart contracts to support the consistent update and controlled access of information, and to enable ledger functions such as transacting and querying. The smart contract concept was proposed by Szabo in 1997 [1]. The main goal of smart contracts is to automatically execute the terms of an agreement once certain conditions are met. For each transaction, the flow of value and transaction state must be defined. Simply stated, a smart contract is code that is stored, verified, and executed on a blockchain [2].

Today's smart contracts express conditions for transactions to occur, such as *if delivery arrives at port, then ownership passes from carrier to port authorities*; or *if temperature in container is above specified threshold, then send alert*. These conditions are expressed in the form of business rules (*IF* <condition(s)> *THEN* <action(s)>). However, many asset transfers in blockchain are related to business events that are also temporally constrained. For example: *if delivery arrives at port with a delay of more than an hour, then ownership doesn't pass from carrier to port authorities*, or *if temperature in container is above threshold for more than an hour, then send alert*.

Our objective is to propose building blocks for defining smart contracts so that temporal reasoning can be done without the use of custom code. To this end, we propose a model-driven approach based on Hyperledger Fabric [3] and Hyperledger Composer [4], which can derive both the business rules and event-driven logic parts of an application. This paper presents our approach and demonstrates it using a supply chain use case.

Supply chain is one of the most suitable use cases for permissioned blockchain technology (see Sect. 4). Blockchain provides transparency, a non-repudiation process, full traceability and trackability of the transactions (provenance), shorter lead times, and authentication and verification of the parties in the supply chain network at each asset transfer. Many supply chain contractual clauses include temporal constraints, such as penalties and escalation policies if delays occur. Furthermore, many scenarios include IoT sensors that monitor and report real-time environmental conditions of the shipment, such as temperature and location. These scenarios are typical examples of cases in which temporal reasoning is required as decisions about product quality in these situations are based on time windows in which the goods have been exposed to certain conditions. For example, exposure for more than a certain amount of time to humidity or temperature, might jeopardize the overall quality of the shipment.

This paper is organized as follows: Sect. 1 introduces the main idea and motivation of our proposed approach. Section 2 briefly describes event processing and blockchain terms used throughout this paper. Section 3 introduces our approach. Section 4 presents our illustrative example while Sect. 5 describes its implementation. We discuss related work in Sect. 6. Section 7 concludes the paper and identifies future plans.

2 Preliminaries

2.1 Hyperledger Fabric and Hyperledger Composer

Hyperledger Fabric [13] and [5] is a blockchain framework implementation and one of the Hyperledger projects hosted by the Linux Foundation. Hyperledger is a collaborative effort created to advance cross-industry blockchain technologies for business. It provides an open source, industrial-grade implementation of a private or permissioned blockchain under the Linux Foundation umbrella. (For a comparison of permissioned and permissionless/public models, see Swanson [6].)

According to a recent HVS report [7], Hyperledger Fabric is the number one open-source production-ready permissioned blockchain designed for enterprises.

Hyperledger Fabric (or simply Fabric) provides a modular architecture with a delineation of roles between the nodes in the blockchain network, execution of smart contracts, and configurable consensus and membership services. At the heart of the framework is a distributed ledger for the immutable recording of transactions occurring in the network. The Fabric infrastructure is designed to deliver high degrees of confidentiality, resiliency, flexibility, and scalability. For a thorough description of Fabric, see Gaur et al. [9].

Hyperledger Composer (or simply Composer) is another open source Hyperledger project hosted by the Linux Foundation (contributed by IBM andOxchains). It is composed of a suite of tools that make it easy to develop blockchain applications. Composer supports Fabric blockchain infrastructure and run-time. Each Hyperledger Composer application in the business network is represented by a chaincode process. The chaincode has a JavaScript interpreter that executes the logic for processing the transaction. Chaincodes are the mechanisms through which smart contracts are defined in the Fabric blockchain implementation.

Hyperledger Composer has several concepts for representing data and defining the transaction processing logic:

- *Participants* represent actors that interact with the blockchain application through transactions.
- *Assets* model the items to be stored in the blockchain. They often represent something of value manipulated by the transactions.
- *Transactions* represent the actual transaction registered on the blockchain ledger, initiated by a participant and related to one or more assets.
- *Transaction processors* are used when a transaction is initiated on the blockchain and it is validated by all nodes of the blockchain. In Hyperledger Composer, transaction processor callbacks are called in all nodes of the blockchain. Consensus algorithms check that all nodes process the transaction the same way, which ensures a consistent update of the ledger and the world state database.
- *Events* are defined in the business network definition in the same way as assets or participants. Once events have been defined, they can be emitted by transaction processor functions to indicate to external systems that something of importance has happened to the ledger.

Participants, assets, events, and transactions are described in Hyperledger Composer by using a dedicated high-level language. The business network definition can be packaged and exported as an archive (*.bna* file) ready to deploy on a Composer blockchain network. Transaction processors are implemented as JavaScript functions that manipulate the resources.

For more information on Hyperledger Composer applications refer to [8].

2.2 Complex Event Processing

Event processing is computing that performs operations on events [10]. An event is an occurrence within a particular system or domain; it is something that has actually happened or considered to have happened in that domain. Examples include the reading of a temperature sensor or the loss of apiece of luggage. The word event is also used to refer to a programming entity that represents such occurrences in a computing system. Common event processing operations include reading, creating, transforming, and deleting events.

Each complex event processing (CEP) engine uses its own terminology and semantics. We follow the semantics presented in Etzion's and Niblet's book [10]. For the sake of clarity, we briefly mention below only the concepts and terms necessary to understand the approach we take.

An Event Processing Network (EPN) is a conceptual model, describing the event processing flow execution. An EPN comprises a collection of event processing agents (EPAs), event producers, events, and event consumers (see Fig. 1). The network describes the flow of events originating at event producers and flowing through various event processing agents to eventually reach event consumers. For example, in Fig. 1, events from Producer 1 are processed by EPA 1. Events derived by EPA 1 are of interest to Consumer 1 but are also processed by EPA, 3 together with events derived from EPA 2.

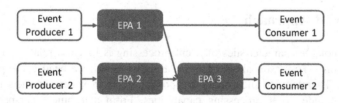

Fig. 1. Illustration of an event processing network

An EPA is a software module that processes input events and looks for matches between these events, using an event processing pattern or some other kind of matching criterion. An *event pattern* is a template specifying one or more combinations of events. Given any collection of events, if it's possible to find one or more subsets of those events that match a particular pattern, it can be said that such a subset satisfies the pattern. Some common examples of patterns include the following:

- *Sequence* - at least one instance of all participating event types must arrive in a specified order for the pattern to be matched.
- *Count* - the number of instances in the participant event set must satisfy the pattern's number assertion.
- *AND* - at least one instance of all participating event types must arrive for the pattern to be matched; the arrival order in this case is immaterial.
- *Trend* - events need to satisfy a specific change (increasing, decreasing, or stable) over time of some observed value; this refers to the value of a specific attribute or attributes.

EPAs process events within predefined contexts. *Context* is a named specification of conditions that groups event instances, so they can be processed in a related way. A *temporal context* consists of one or more, possibly overlapping, time intervals. Each time interval corresponds to a context partition, which contains events that occur during that interval. A *segmentation context* is used to group event instances into context partitions based on the value of an attribute or collection of attributes in the instances themselves.

We denote *event rules* as the natural language representation of an EPA, and (complex) events emitted from the CEP engine as *situations*.

Examples of event rules, include:

- Alert when the temperature has more than three increased readings in the last five minutes (*trend* pattern).
- Alert when the same customer bought and later sold the same stock within 24 h (*sequence* pattern).
- Send a confirmation email if hotel and flights are reserved within 72 h (*AND* pattern).

It's important to note that an EPN is a network of event rules creating a hierarchy of (complex) events at different levels of abstraction; one complex event can serve as input to generate another, more abstract, complex event.

3   Proposed Approach

One of the notable characteristics of event processing is its close relationship to temporal reasoning. To reason about time and time windows, we need event processing capabilities. Therefore, to incorporate temporal aspects in smart contracts means we must also include event processing capabilities. From a technical perspective, this means integrating a CEP engine with Fabric. Our goal is to make this integration as seamless as possible with a unified model. To this end, we propose extending the Composer programming model with EPN building blocks to generate a Composer business network specification and an EPN definition file, along with configuration entries to connect the blockchain network with the CEP engine at run-time.

The idea is to have an external system (CEP engine) process the event-driven temporal logic outside the chaincode. Emitted (complex) events from the CEP engine are encoded and posted as transactions in Composer. Business events resulting from Composer transactions that are required for the event processing logic are posted to the

CEP engine. The next sections describe our approach, and Sect. 4 illustrates it as applied to a pharma cold supply chain scenario in Kenya.

3.1   Build-Time

At the model level, we enrich the Composer programming model as follows. Business events are leveraged to serve as triggers (input events) for the CEP engine, while emitted events from the CEP engine are defined as transactions in the Composer model. We extend Composer with a new concept called *event Rules*; these are part of the model and embody the event-driven logic of the application being built.

The approach at build time is shown in Fig. 2. Emitted events (situations) from the CEP engine are encoded and posted as transactions in Composer, while business events required for the event processing logic are posted to the CEP engine. New objects of type *eventRule* are defined in Composer for the event rules logic (i.e., the EPN). The Composer *bna* file contains all the definitions to run the chaincode in Fabric, except for the *eventRules*, which are translated to a definition file for the CEP engine. The CEP definitions file created at build-time is a JSON file that represents the EPN of the specific event-driven application and contains all required ingredients to run the matching CEP application (the event-driven logic). The transformation from the event rule to EPN and to code follows the model-driven approach described by Etzion et al. [12].

Composer uses *Connection Profiles* to define the system to which it connects. These profiles specify the network participant nodes along with their URLs. Adding the details of a CEP engine as a node in the connection profile allows us to automatically generate URLs within Composer for the emitting events and URLs for consumer definition in the CEP JSON application specification.

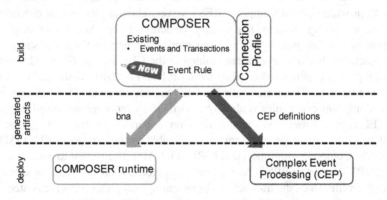

Fig. 2. Overview of the approach at build-time

This approach is general and not tailored to a specific CEP engine. Although we use our open source CEP PROTON[1] as the run-time engine, any other tool that works with

---

[1] https://github.com/ishkin/Proton/.

the EPN programming model can work as well. Furthermore, the generation of code can be carried out for any other specific CEP programming model and engine, following The Event Model (TEM) methodology as described in [12].

3.2 Run-Time

Figure 3 depicts how our approach works at run-time.

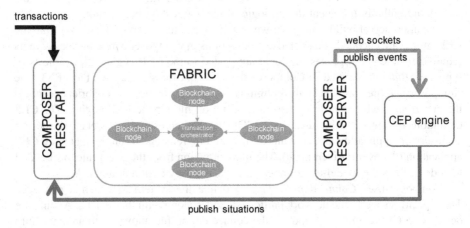

Fig. 3. Overall approach at run-time

At run-time, the transactions are posted to the Composer network through the REST API provided by the Composer REST server. The transactions are processed by transaction processing functions that specify the actions to be taken upon receipt of the transaction in the Composer programming model. As part of these transaction processing functions, business events are emitted to the CEP engine. (The code from the connection profile is generated to place the CEP RESTful URL as the address for the business events sink.) The events enter the CEP engine, where the JSON file generated from the Composer event rules is already loaded. The events are processed and stored in the CEP engine's memory. Once a situation is derived by the CEP engine, it is encoded as a JSON message in a format recognizable by the Composer REST API and posted to the Composer run-time via this RESTful API. The format to encode and the RESTful URL are part of EPN's "consumer" definition and are also generated from the connection profile. Once the transactions representing complex events are posted to the blockchain, they are processed in the same manner as regular transactions, changing the state of the assets on the network according to the business logic specified in the Composer application.

4 Illustrative Example

According to the World Health Organization [11], one in every 10 medical products circulating in low and middle-income countries are either substandard or fake. This means that people are taking medicines that fail to treat or prevent disease. Not only this is a waste of money for individuals and health systems that purchase these products, but substandard or falsified medical products can cause serious illness or even death. The World Health Organization reports show that 700,000 people are killed globally by counterfeit medicines annually. Africa contributes 100,000 of these deaths. One of the causes for substandard medication is problematic transportation or storage conditions. Many pharmaceuticals require the transportation of temperature-sensitive products using thermal and refrigerated packaging methods and the logistical planning to protect the quality of these shipments. A temperature-controlled supply chain for products requiring specific levels of refrigeration is known as a cold chain.

Our scenario illustrated in Fig. 4 is a simplification of a real scenario provided by a pharmaceutical company. In Kenya, pharmaceutical products are delivered from the manufacturers through different distributors to local pharmacies and hospitals. From there, they are distributed to the doctors, located mostly in distant rural areas, who in turn, prescribe the medications and give them to the patients. The distribution of the pharmaceuticals from the local pharmacies to the doctors is usually carried out by individuals using different means of transportation (bicycles, motorbikes, trucks, or on foot) whose trajectory is hard to track. This is the weakest link in the supply chain and most of the counterfeiting and stealing of medication is done at this stage.

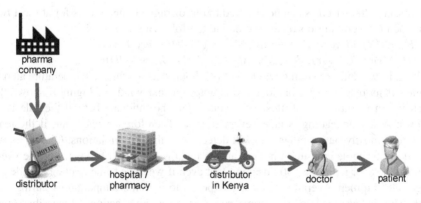

Fig. 4. Pharma supply scenario in Kenya

Our scenario deals with the transportation of Tuberculosis (TB) vaccines in Kenya. TB remains one of the major causes of morbidity and mortality in Kenya. The BCG vaccine is a live bacterial vaccine that protects against TB.BCG vaccine ampoules must be kept refrigerated and transported at temperatures between +2 °C–+8 °C. Our goal is to apply blockchain technology to ensure the trusted delivery of the vaccines and reduce counterfeit. This is done by verifying the provider and receiver of the vaccines at each transfer point, along with a continuous monitoring of the temperature conditions of the product. Application users in Kenya include the pharmacist at the hospital or pharmacy, the distributor or carrier, and the doctor.

4.1   Implementation of a Business Rule for Temperature Control

We assume that the vaccines are transported in a shipment container equipped with a temperature sensor that sends a temperature reading every minute. To detect abnormal sensor readings, we define the following business rule:

IF (temperature_reading < 2) OR (temperature_reading > 8)

THEN update shipment warning array on ledger with TriggerTemperatureWarning

That is, each time a sensor reading is received (every minute), we check whether the temperature in the shipment container (vaccines delivery) is between specified thresholds (+2° to +8° Celsius). In the event of a violation, a warning is written on the blockchain network. Figure 7 shows the definition of this business rule in Composer.

The doctor who receives the shipment checks for violations and rejects/accepts the delivery accordingly. The main problem with this scenario is that individual violations per se don't entirely determine whether the vaccines were compromised. There are other constraints besides a single temperature reading, such as the number of out-of-range temperatures over a given period of time, which are better indications of the quality of the shipment conditions. This challenge is addressed in the next section.

4.2   Extending the Scenario with an Event Rule to Monitor Shipment Conditions

Let's assume the vaccines can be exposed to out-of-range temperatures for at most two hours before becoming obsolete. We define the following event rule:

IF COUNT (TriggerTemperatureWarning) > 50 every 1 h

THEN emit TriggerTemperatureAlert (with the shipmentID)

That is, we define a sliding window of one hour, during which a temperature alert is emitted if more than 50 violations are counted in that window. Figure 8 shows the extension in Composer with this new event rule. The rationale behind the rule is as follows: A sensor reading is taken every minute. Therefore, in one hour, if the temperature is mostly out of range, we will detect more than 50 violations. Of course, we should get 60 violations in an hour if all the readings are out of range. For the event rule, we look for more than 50, meaning that even if we have some readings inside the range, the shipment overall was clearly exposed to extreme temperatures during that hour. This is designed to give some room for corrective actions if possible (e.g., changing the sensor or adjusting the temperature) before the vaccine becomes obsolete. Figure 5 describes the flow of events in the new setting.

Sensor readings enter the system (1) and are checked against a temperature violation in Composer. If a violation occurs (2), then a warning event is written to blockchain and emitted as an input event to the CEP engine. If the event rule is satisfied (more than 50 warnings in one hour), then a temperature alert is emitted from the CEP engine and is processed as a new transaction i.e., the alarm is written on the blockchain for the appropriate delivery (3).

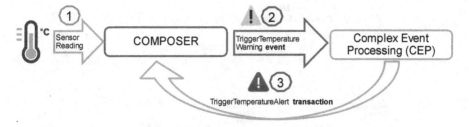

Fig. 5. Event rule end-to-end flow

In this scenario, the doctor receives the alerts in real-time and can reject a delivery accordingly. In our first implementation (business rules only), the doctor sees these warnings only after receiving the shipment and only at that point can the physician accept/reject the delivery accordingly. This is a kind of "post-mortem analysis". We could send warnings in real-time to show the doctor sees these violations as they happen. But, as previously pointed out, a low number of violations doesn't necessarily mean a rejection of the entire delivery. When using more complex rules, we can cover a wider spectrum of situations, such as sending real-time alarms when the shipment might be rejected (as in our second case) or when a rejection is inevitable, allowing the delivery to be aborted (e.g., when the temperature is higher than threshold for more than two hours).

5   Example Implementation

5.1   Blockchain Network

Our implementation includes a network consisting of two peers belonging to two different organizations: carriers and medical facilities (doctors and pharmacies) (Fig. 6) with *certification authority* for each of the organizations and one *orderer*[9]. The end user for the mobile app can be the pharmacist, doctor, or carrier. The mobile app enables the verification of the delivery at each transfer point, the authentication of the user, the rejection or acceptance of the delivery by the user, and the safe transfer of the delivery.

The Composer business network runs on top of Fabric. The mobile application allows the users, such as the carrier or the doctor, to interact with the network (e.g., authenticate, gain access, and post transactions such as acceptance of delivery). The mobile application runs a RESTful backend for posting transactions to the Composer network by using Composer's REST server. We also use a separate RESTful application acting as a simulator to generate temperature sensor readings.

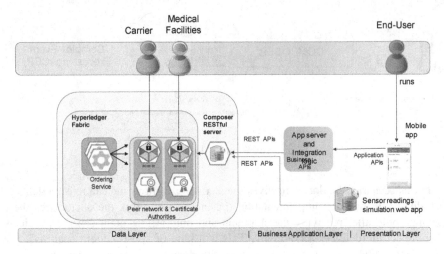

Fig. 6. Solution architecture for the use case

5.2 Model in Composer

As mentioned above, we apply Composer to define business rules and extend it with the definition of the new event rule. Figure **7** shows the screenshot of the business rule definition in Composer along with annotations.

```
 * @param {com.ibm.haifa.pharma.SensorReadingTransaction} tx The sensor reading transaction instance.
 * @transaction
 */
function sensorReadingTransaction(tx) {

    if (tx.temperature < 2 || tx.temperature > 8)          ◄── business rule
    {
      var timestamp = Date.now();
      // Get the asset registry for the delivery
      return getAssetRegistry('com.ibm.haifa.pharma.Delivery')
      .then(function (deliveryRegistry) {
        // Get the factory
        deliveryReg = deliveryRegistry;
        return deliveryRegistry.get(tx.deliveryId);
      })
      .then(function (delivery) {
        var factory = getFactory();
        var warning = factory.newConcept('com.ibm.haifa.pharma', 'TemperatureWarning');
        warning.timestamp = timestamp;
        warning. temperature = tx.temperature;          update of ledger
        delivery.warnings.push(warning);                with warning

        var event = getFactory().newEvent('com.ibm.haifa.pharma', 'TriggerTemperatureWarning');
        event.deliveryId = tx.deliveryId;
        event.temperature = tx.temperature;
        event.timestamp = timestamp;                    TriggerTemperatureWarning
        emit(event);                                    event input for CEP

        deliveryReg.update(delivery);
      })
    .catch(function (error) {
      // Error handling
      throw new Error('Error in adding an warning to delivery'+deliveryId+', reason'+ error);
    });
```

Fig. 7. Composer business rule screenshot

Figure 8 shows the definition of the event rule in Composer. Note, the syntax is still not definitive. More important is the fact that the event rule definition should encompass the three parts required to define an EPA:

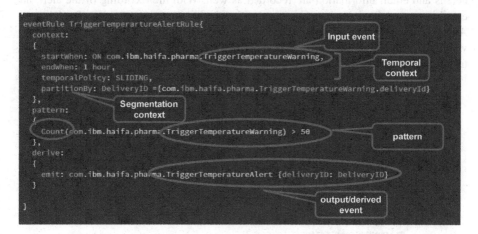

Fig. 8. Composer extension with the new event rule screenshot

- The contexts defined by the time window (temporal context) and the segmentation context (*partitionBy*). The time window is defined by the start and end of the window and the policy. In our case, each new input event (*TriggerTemperatureWarning*) opens a new window (sliding window policy) that ends after one hour.
- The pattern: In our case, COUNT with its assertion (>50).
- The derivation step: once the pattern is satisfied, a situation is emitted (*TriggerTemperatureAlert* with *shipmentID*).

When more than one event rule exists, each event rule is translated to an EPA and the overall event rules to an EPN. The JSON file generated serves as the configuration file for PROTON. At run-time, the engine accesses the file, loads and parses all the definitions, creates a thread per each input and output adapter, and starts listening for input events. At this stage, we manually generate the JSON file from the model. Automatic code generation is possible following The Event Model (TEM) methodology described in Etzion et al. [12] as one event rule definition represents exactly one Event Derivation Table (EDT) in TEM.

5.3   Running of the Network

We ran the implementation applying simulated sensor data fed to Composer at the rate of one temperature event per minute.

Figure 9 presents a screenshot of the Composer RESTful server showing one delivery, including 3 BCG vaccines (serial numbers: b5lwXZgsZ2, 65u3bEo0Uy, and fVepfThIJB), with a temperature alert (*TemperatureAlert*) that was received after 52 warnings (*TemperatureWarning*). The delivery was shipped to Dr. Msia whose address details and email information are recorded as well. With the recording of the alert, an email is sent to the doctor, so she can decide whether to accept or reject the delivery. Additional information to support the doctor's decision-making process is also provided: the number of alarms per delivery, and the maximum and minimum temperatures encountered so far.

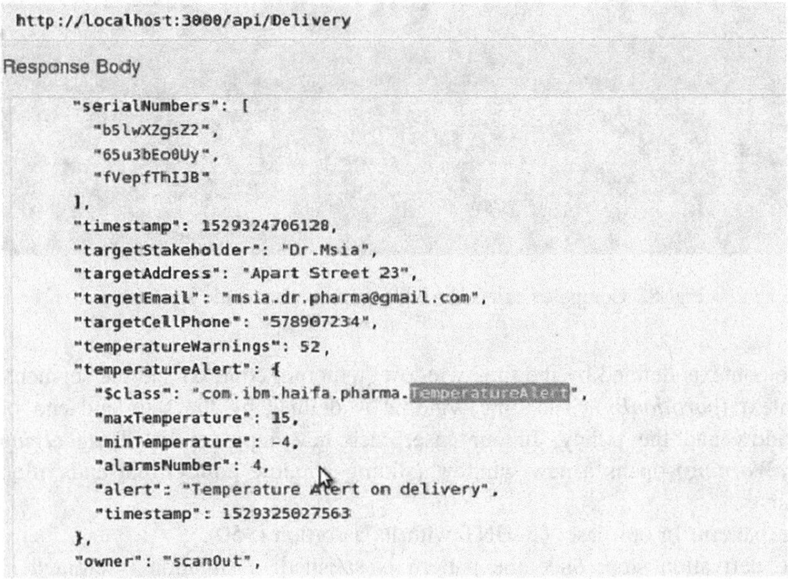

```
http://localhost:3000/api/Delivery

Response Body
        "serialNumbers": [
          "b5lwXZgsZ2",
          "65u3bEo0Uy",
          "fVepfThIJB"
        ],
        "timestamp": 1529324706128,
        "targetStakeholder": "Dr.Msia",
        "targetAddress": "Apart Street 23",
        "targetEmail": "msia.dr.pharma@gmail.com",
        "targetCellPhone": "578907234",
        "temperatureWarnings": 52,
        "temperatureAlert": {
          "$class": "com.ibm.haifa.pharma.TemperatureAlert",
          "maxTemperature": 15,
          "minTemperature": -4,
          "alarmsNumber": 4,
          "alert": "Temperature Alert on delivery",
          "timestamp": 1529325027563
        },
        "owner": "scanOut",
```

Fig. 9. Composer RESTful server screenshot showing the recording of a temperature alert

6 Related Work

Our goal was to follow the Model-Driven Engineering approach [13, 14]. This would allow us to generate executable code out of a computation-independent model that includes temporal aspects for the domain of smart contracts. Consequently, we survey related work in the areas of event processing and smart contract modeling.

In the area of event processing modeling, Cugola and Margara [15] provide a comprehensive survey and comparison of models, including aspects of the functional model, processing model, deployment model, interaction model, data model, time model, and rule model. In general, event processing models contain an event flow model [10], a stream processing model [16], rule-based modeling [17], or visualization (i.e., of the event flows) [18], or are based on logic programming [19]. However, none of these models satisfy the requirement of being computationally independent. The

Event Model (TEM) [12] follows the model-driven approach and can be classified as a computation-independent model in the model-driven architecture. This model can be directly translated into an execution model (platform-specific model) through an intermediate generic representation (platform-independent model), that is, the EPN. To the best of our knowledge, TEM is the only model that satisfies the requirement of being computationally independent in event processing.

Blockchain is a new technology and most of the work in this space has been focusedon the infrastructures themselves, where the business logic of the applications has been tailored or customized to the specific purpose of the application at hand. There are some specific programming models for some of the most popular blockchain platforms, such as Solidity for Ethereum [20] or Composer for Fabric [4], but there is not much research in this area. Boogaard [21] presents a model-driven smart contract development approach in which the requirements of a smart contract are stepwise-developed into a skeleton Solidity smart contract. The platform-independent model is modeled as a finite state machine that is translated into Solidity code. Frantz and Nowostawski [22] present a modeling approach that supports the semi-automated translation of human-readable contract representations into computational equivalents. Their goal is to enable the codification of laws into verifiable and enforceable computational structures that reside within a public blockchain. However, none of these works include temporal reasoning.

7 Summary and Future Work

In this paper, we present a model-driven approach to create blockchain applications that can run temporal logic. The approach uses building blocks to express temporal aspects, without the need to write customized code for each application. We present the new concepts required at the model level and explain how they can be translated into a blockchain solution applying Hyperledger Fabric, Hyperledger Composer, and the PROTON complex event processing programming model and tool. We illustrate the approach using a cold chain scenario of vaccine delivery in Kenya.

Fake or substandard pharmaceuticals can cause death, have unknown side-effects, fail to treat illnesses, and sometimes even add to the spread of disease. Blockchain technology can minimize such counterfeiting by introducing traceability and trackability into the pharma supply chain and ensuring the immutability of information. The proposed solution presented in this paper includes the model, the blockchain backend, and a mobile user interface that enables each certified and authorized party in the network to initiate actions, finish transactions, and track progress. It also includes temperature monitoring to ensure compliance with the proper conditions for transportation and asset transfer.

The approach is exemplified using our CEP engine PROTON, however the approach is general and can support any other CEP tool as long as the event model translation is carried out from the model in Composer to the specific CEP tool programming model. We follow the transformation to an EPN and to JSON format given in [12] so that the code generation is straightforward while applying PROTON.

Our future plans include: the automatic translation of the event-driven generation logic to the JSON file that represents the EPN from the Composer definitions (as explained in [12]), applying the approach in more scenarios, and formalizing the inclusion of the new proposed concepts into Composer.

Acknowledgments. Authors of this paper have received funding from the European Union's Horizon 2020 research and innovation programme under grant agreement No 780732 (BOOST 4.0).

References

1. Szabo, N.: Smart Contracts: Building Blocks for Digital Markets (1997)
2. Stark, J.: Making sense of blockchain smart contracts. In: Coindesk.Com (2016). http://www.coindesk.com/making-sense-smart-contracts/. Accessed 5 Jan 2019
3. Hyperledger Fabric. https://www.hyperledger.org/projects/fabric. Accessed 5 Jan 2019
4. Hyperledger Composer. https://www.hyperledger.org/projects/composer. Accessed 5 Jan 2019
5. Hyperledger: blockchain collaboration changing the business world. https://www.ibm.com/blockchain/hyperledger.html. Accessed 5 Jan 2019
6. Swanson, T.: Consensus-as-a-service: A brief report on the emergence of permissioned, distributed edger systems. http://www.ofnumbers.com/wp-content/uploads/2015/04/Permissioned-distributed-ledgers.pdf. Accessed 5 Jan 2019
7. Gupta, S.: HFS top 10 blockchain platforms, HFS Research report, November 2018
8. Welcome to Hyperledger Composer. https://hyperledger.github.io/composer/latest/introduction/introduction.html. Accessed 5 Jan 2019
9. Gaur, N., Desrosiers, L., Ramakrishna, V., Novotny, P., Baset, S.A., O'Dowd, A.: Hands-On Blockchain with Hyperledger. Packt Publishing Ltd, Birmingham (2018)
10. Etzion, O., Niblett, P.: Event Processing in Action. Manning Publications Company, Shelter Island (2010)
11. WHO: One in 10 medical products in low and middle-income countries are fake. https://www.nation.co.ke/news/Fake-medicine-circulating-in-low-and-middle-income-countries/1056-4207960-14swirrz/index.html. Accessed 3 Jan 2019
12. Etzion, O., Fournier, F., Skarbovsky, I., von Halle, B.A.: model driven approach for event processing applications. In: Proceedings of the 10th ACM International Conference on Distributed and Event-based Systems (DEBS16), pp. 81–92 (2016). https://dl.acm.org/citation.cfm?id=2933268
13. Bodenstein, C., Lohse, F., Zimmermann, A.: Executable specifications for model-based development of automotive software. In: SMC 2010, pp. 727–732 (2010)
14. Brambilla, M., Cabot, J., Wimmer, M.: Model Driven Software Engineering in Practice. Morgan & Claypool, San Rafael (2012)
15. Cugola, G., Margara, A.: Processing flows of information: from data stream to complex event processing. ACM Comput. Surv. (CSUR) **44**(3), 15 (2012)
16. Dindar, N., Tatbul, N., Miller, R.J., Haas, L.M., Botan, I.: Modeling the execution semantics of stream processing engines with SECRET. VLDB J. (VLDB) **22**(4), 421–446 (2013)
17. Bragaglia, S., Chesani, F., Mello, P., Sottara, D.: A rule-based calculus and processing of complex events. In: Bikakis, A., Giurca, A. (eds.) RuleML 2012. LNCS, vol. 7438, pp. 151–166. Springer, Heidelberg (2012). https://doi.org/10.1007/978-3-642-32689-9_12

18. Marquardt, N., Gross, T., Sheelagh, M., Carpendale, T., Greenberg, S.: Revealing the invisible: visualizing the location and event flow of distributed physical devices. In: Tangible and Embedded Interaction, pp. 41–48 (2010)
19. Kowalski, R.A.: Logic programing in artificial intelligence. In: IJCAI, pp. 596–604 (1991)
20. Ethereum. https://www.ethereum.org/. Accessed 5 Jan 2019
21. Boogaard, K.: A model-driven approach to smart contract development, master thesis (2018)
22. Frantz, C.K., Nowostawski, M.: From institutions to code: towards automated generation of smart contracts. In: IEEE 1st International Workshops on Foundations and Applications of Self* Systems, pp. 210–215 (2016)

CloudAgora: Democratizing the Cloud

Katerina Doka[✉], Tasos Bakogiannis, Ioannis Mytilinis, and Georgios Goumas

Computing Systems Laboratory, National Technical University of Athens,
Athens, Greece
{katerina,abk,gmytil,goumas}@cslab.ece.ntua.gr

Abstract. In this paper we present CloudAgora, a platform that enables
the realization of a democratic and fully decentralized cloud computing
market where participating parties enjoy significant advantages: On one
hand, cloud consumers have access to low-cost storage and computation
without having to blindly trust any central authority. On the other hand,
any individual or company, big or small, can potentially serve as cloud
provider. Idle resources, be it CPU or disk space, are monetized and
offered in competitive fees, regulated by the law of supply and demand.
In the heart of the platform lies the blockchain technology, which is
used to record commitment policies, publicly verify off-chain services
and trigger automatic micropayments. Our prototype is built on top of
the Ethereum blockchain and is provided as an open source project.

1 Introduction

The advent of cloud computing has revolutionized the IT sector worldwide, by
allowing organizations and individuals alike to opt for remote resources - be it
storage, computation or applications - instead of costly and hard-to-maintain
local infrastructure. In the last years, cloud computing has indeed prevailed
over traditional on-premise environments as a means of executing applications
and/or offering services for a wealth of reasons, including reduced costs, seemingly infinite resources purchased in a pay-as-you-go manner, scalability, ease
of maintenance, etc., [8]. This fact has highly impacted a multitude of industry
domains in the way they do business and has fundamentally transformed our
everyday lives in the way we work and communicate [5].

Cloud services are mainly based on (a handful of) large providers that act as
trusted entities for the transfer, storage and processing of user or company data.
Thus, despite their reliance on fundamental principles of distributed computing,
they fail to achieve full decentralization. The main disadvantages of this cloud
computing model are summarized in the following:

- It carries the intrinsic weaknesses of any model based on trust: Users take
  for granted that providers act in the interest of their customers rather than
  opportunistically.
- The leading Cloud providers have invested huge amounts of money to build
  massive server farms and consume enormous amounts of energy for running

J. Joshi et al. (Eds.): ICBC 2019, LNCS 11521, pp. 142–156, 2019.
https://doi.org/10.1007/978-3-030-23404-1_10

and cooling them. Although they can provide prices that render infrastructure renting more appealing than on-premise infrastructure operation in the majority of cases, pricing could be even more affordable, had there been a greater competition [21]. Thus, the public cloud market has become a functional monopoly where a few providers define the prices, which are non-negotiable and can be prohibitively high for applications demanding specialized hardware.

– Sovereignty over data and control over computations performed on top of them are surrendered to the big players, who thus accumulate knowledge, gaining significant competitive advantage and strengthening their already privileged position.

The missing traits, i.e., full decentralization, strong guarantees for security and integrity based on proof rather than trust and transparency in any user-provider interaction, are the ones that blockchain technology can provide. Blockchain started off as the driving force behind Bitcoin - a distributed ledger where transactions are ordered, validated and, once recorded, immutable. With the addition of smart contracts - pieces of code which are executed automatically, in a distributed manner - it quickly rose as one of the most groundbreaking modern technologies, offering a new approach to decentralized applications and disrupting a wide range of fields such as finance, IoT, insurance, voting etc., [18].

However, blockchain technology is not a panacea. Especially when it comes to storage and power devouring applications, blockchains fall short of their requirements due to the limited computing and storage capacity they offer. Typically, the most prevalent blockchains, such as Ethereum, support blocks of at most a few Megabytes, achieve a throughput of a few tens of transactions per second and accommodate a limited number of operations per smart contract [9]. As such, blockchains and smart contracts cannot be adopted as storage providers or computing engines per se, but rather as an enabling technology which keeps track of and validates off-chain operations. The challenge in this scenario is to find a secure way to guarantee the correctness of the off-chain service through the use of a publicly verifiable proof [12].

To that end we present CloudAgora, a truly decentralized cloud that allows for on-demand and low-cost access to storage and computing infrastructures. The goal of CloudAgora is to create a blockchain-based platform where participants can act either as providers, offering idle CPU and available storage, or as consumers, renting the offered resources and creating ad-hoc virtual cloud infrastructures. Storage and processing capacities are monetized and their prices are governed by the laws of supply and demand. Thus, CloudAgora democratizes the cloud computing market, allowing potential resource providers - ranging from individuals to well established companies in the field - to compete with each other in a fair manner, maintaining their existing physical infrastructure.

In a nutshell, CloudAgora offers users the ability to express a request for storage or computation and take bids from any potential provider in an auction-style manner. Anyone who can supply storage and/or computing power can become a CloudAgora provider, ranging from individuals or companies offering idle or under-utilized resources to large datacenters, traditionally operating in the Cloud market. Customers are automatically matched to resource providers according to the height of their bid and their reputation. The agreement between providers and consumers is encoded as a smart contract, which allows for traceability of actions and automatic triggering of payments. While storage and processing is performed off-chain, the integrity and availability of stored data as well as the correctness of the outsourced computation are safeguarded through proper verification processes that take place on the chain. Special consideration has been dedicated to offering the necessary incentives for a fair game, both from the provider as well as the customer perspective.

Such a solution offers significant advantages compared to the traditional, datacenter-only based cloud computing model: Providers can exploit existing idle resources for profit while consumers enjoy lower fees due to competition without having to blindly trust any central authority or big company. Through the use of blockchain technology, all services performed in the cloud are recorded and payments are automated accordingly.

Approaches similar to CloudAgora in the competitive landscape either focus exclusively on data hosting [2,20,22] or target specific applications, such as 3D rendering [3]. Other solutions that address secure, off-chain computation have limited applicability due to the restrictions they pose on the type of computation supported [23]. Many of these projects rely on their proper blockchain and native coins, complicating the redemption of rewards. Contrarily, CloudAgora is a fully open-source, based on Ethereum platform, which provisions both storage and computation resources.

In this paper we make the following contributions:

- We propose an open market platform, where users can trade storage and computation resources without relying on any central authority or third party. By enabling any user to become a potential resource provider, our work breaks the monopoly of the few and creates of a truly democratic and self-regulated cloud market.
- We offer a solution that addresses the provision of both storage and compute resources in a unified manner based on smart contracts. The proper publicly verifiable proofs that the off-chain service, either data or computation related, was correctly completed have been identified and incorporated to our platform.
- We implement the proposed platform on top of the most prevalent smart contract blockchain, Ethereum and provide it to the community as an open source project.

2   Architecture Overview

CloudAgora is a system that provides the basic primitives and tools for enabling a truly decentralized cloud infrastructure. Anyone that joins CloudAgora can act either as a cloud user, a cloud provider or both. By taking advantage of blockchain technology, we establish an environment where rational participants do not diverge from their expected behavior, monopoly effects are eliminated and prices dynamically adjust according to market rules. Henceforth, we refer to CloudAgora users that provide resources as *service providers* and to users that consume resources as *clients*.

As we consider that the adoption of a system highly depends on the ease of installation and use, we propose a lightweight design that operates on top of any blockchain technology that supports smart contracts. Although our approach to the design of the system is blockchain-agnostic, we base our prototype implementation on Ethereum, one of the most popular and advanced smart contract platforms, while we keep its internals intact. This way, the whole cloud environment can run as a common application in every public or private Ethereum blockchain.

The system is hierarchically structured in two layers, namely the *market layer*, and the *storage/compute layer*. At the highest level, there is the market layer. This is an abstraction of the way the economy of CloudAgora works. This layer comprises a set of algorithms that define participants' incentives and mechanisms for the regulation of prices. The creation of a new cloud job, the decision on price levels and the assignment to a specific provider all belong to the market layer. The CloudAgora market rules are enforced through a set of smart contracts that work on-chain.

At the bottom layer, actual cloud services are provided: data persistence and computations take place. Furthermore, this layer contains algorithms that can work both on- and off-chain and ensure the provably proper operation of the whole system. The contracts of this layer audit clients and providers and guarantee that none is making profit against the rules of the market. In the following sections, we describe in more detail the two layers of our system. Section 1 presents the market layer, Sect. 4 demonstrates our approach to decentralized storage and Sect. 5 shows how CloudAgora can provide provably correct computations in a decentralized cloud environment.

3   The Market Layer

In a typical cloud scenario nowadays, a user willing to consume resources will have to choose among a few known providers (e.g., Amazon, Google, Microsoft), accept the prices they offer without the right to negotiate it and finally deploy her job. The deficiencies of this approach are twofold: (i) as only a few cloud providers determine price levels, cloud deployments in many cases end up too costly to afford and (ii) large companies accumulate vast amounts of data and get a great head start in races like the ones of machine learning and big data processing.

CloudAgora remedies these drawbacks by enabling a free market where each player can participate on equal terms. Moreover, prices are not fixed but are determined through an auction game. Since potentially anyone can be a service provider, data does not end up in the possession of a few powerful players but are expected to be distributed among all members of the system.

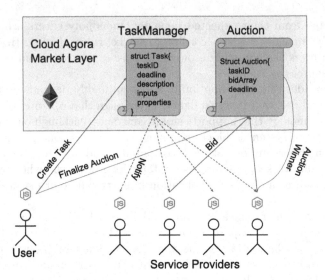

Fig. 1. Market layer

Let us assume a client that needs resources for either storing a dataset D or computing a task T. The client broadcasts a description of D or T and initiates an auction game. Based on this description and the assessed difficulty/cost, anyone interested in providing resources can make an offer. The client finally selects the provider with the most appealing offer (in terms of both price and credibility) and assigns her the job. For guaranteeing integrity and transparency, the market layer is implemented as a set of smart contracts that operate on-chain.

Figure 1 illustrates the workflow followed in a CloudAgora auction. For supporting the required functionality for both clients and service providers, we have implemented the corresponding NodeJS clients. Each CloudAgora client is a Dapp that exposes a specific API and can interact with the blockchain.

Initially, the client interacts with the *TaskManager* contract and creates a new task (storage or computational). Each task comprises a structure that contains a set of mandatory and a set of optional fields. The mandatory fields of a task are: (i) its unique id, (ii) an expiry date, until when the service provider commits to deliver resources and (iii) a description indicative of the tasks's difficulty. For storage tasks, this description can be the size of the dataset the client needs to store and for computational tasks, the amount of required gas if user code is converted to Ethereum Virtual Machine (EVM) assembly. The optional fields may contain task-specific information (e.g., the schema of a dataset, an application parameter, etc.).

As soon as the task is created, the TaskManager contract calls the *Auction* contract and creates a new auction. Every auction carries three pieces of information: (i) the corresponding task id, (ii) bid array: a structure where all bids are maintained and (iii) a deadline. If the deadline expires and a winner has not been found, the Auction contract cancels both the auction and the task.

Auction deadlines are measured in chain blocks. When both the task and the auction are ready, a *taskCreation* event is emitted on the blockchain and all interested parties, i.e., service providers, listen to it. Any service provider that is interested in getting paid for the specific task places her bid at the Auction contract. Upon the receipt of a new bid, the contract checks if the received bid is better than the best it currently maintains in its structure. If not, the bid is discarded. Otherwise, the bid array is updated and a *newBid* event is emitted to both the client and the service providers. The client can inspect the current bid and if it suits her, she can finalize the auction and select provider. A service provider can also inspect the last submitted bid and evaluate if she is willing to make a new offer or not.

We mentioned that only offers better than the current best are inserted into the bid array. A question that naturally arises is what is the criterion for comparing bids. A naive approach would suggest to always choose the provider that offers the lowest price. However, this would encourage malicious players to offer services in extremely low prices. For tackling this problem, in CloudAgora, we employ two distinct mechanisms. When the auction is finalized, the selected provider has to put a collateral until the corresponding task expires. If the provider fails to deliver, the collateral is never returned to her but instead is handed to the client as a refund. The size of the collateral is automatically set to a value greater than the total payoff that the provider will receive if she successfully delivers the task. This way, the provider is incentivized to play by the rules.

Along with the collateral, we also establish a reputation-based system. Providers with a bad reputation should be penalized even when they offer appealing prices and providers that are renowned for their quality of work should have the right to claim higher prices. Thus, for comparing bids we use a function $f(price, reputation) \in \Re$ in order to meet both criteria. The bid that wins the auction is the one with the highest f-value.

However, it is still unclear how reputation scores are computed and assigned. Upon the completion of a task (be it storage or computational) the client calls the *finalize* function of the TaskManager contract. This function takes as input a proof of the task's success and a binary reputation score: 1 denotes success and 0 states that the provider failed to deliver. As the proof of success is sent along with the reputation score, the miners that execute the *finalize* function can verify if reputation is correctly assigned and prevent an *unfair ratings attack* [10]. The aggregate reputation of a provider is calculated by summing up all reputation scores that have ever been assigned to her. It is this aggregate reputation that is used by the f-function in order to compare bids.

4 Storage

In this section we highlight challenges we met and describe our approach to implementing decentralized storage over blockchain in CloudAgora. First, we describe a number of desired properties we consider for a remote data storage system. Then we elaborate on how we provide guarantees for those properties on a trustless environment. Finally, we outline a typical storage workflow in CloudAgora.

4.1 Challenges Specific to Storage

When we consider remote data storage we often come across a wide variety of client requirements. However, all seem to be related to a small number of properties we want a remote data storage system to have. Specifically, in the evaluation of such a system we mostly consider *Data Integrity*, *Data Availability*, *Data Recovery* and *Privacy*. That is the ability to retain our data intact, to access our data at any time, to be able to address data loss and to keep others from accessing our data.

Moving from the more established cloud storage model to a decentralized storage model over blockchain requires us to reconsider our approach regarding the above properties. Existing cloud storage systems are based on trust, reputation and SLAs, however these mechanisms are not directly transferable to a trustless environment such as a blockchain.

At this point we have to note that the blockchain itself can guarantee those properties. However, as we mentioned before, it is not designed to be used as a decentralized storage layer. The cost of storing large data volumes on-chain is prohibitive and its use as a decentralized storage system is impractical since all the data have to be replicated in all the peers. As a result, we have to develop off-chain solutions that can guarantee *data integrity, availability, recovery and privacy* using the blockchain only for bookkeeping, that is only as a distributed ledger that cannot be tampered.

4.2 Our Approach

Given CloudAgora should operate on a trustless environment we have to establish ways to enforce the desired behavior for each one of the participants. Since we base CloudAgora on a open, permission-less blockchain we observe that we cannot enforce any particular behavior. That is because the participants are free to join or leave the process at any time, or even continue with a different identity. As a result we restrict our hypothesis and assume that the participants are rational players that do not exhibit altruistic behaviors. This assumption allows us to use incentives to guide the participants behavior and provide some guarantees related to the desired properties of a remote data storage system. In practice we use a combination of incentives and cryptographic tools to ensure those properties.

In a typical remote data storage scenario we would have a *client* who wants to store data remotely and one or more *providers* who offer data storage. From the *market layer* we have a way to choose one *provider* for a *client*. Therefore, from now on we assume that we have two parties a *client* and a *provider*. They can interact either on- or off-chain, their on-chain interactions are governed by a smart contract. We call this smart contract the *storage contract*, it is a contract between the two parties for storing specific data on the *provider's* side. It has an end date provided by the *client* and the *provider's* payment as it is defined by the *market layer*. The payment amount is transfered from the *client* to the *storage contract* and therefore it is managed by it. Given this configuration, in the following Sections, we describe how we approach and guarantee each one of the properties mentioned.

Data Integrity: To ensure that the data of the *client* will not be tampered while at rest we use two different mechanisms: incentives and Merkle trees.

We first incentivize the *provider* to guarantee the integrity of data by requiring from her to provide collateral in case of data tampering. In order for the *provider* to accept the *storage contract* she has to transfer to the contract a previously agreed upon amount. As a result if the *provider* cannot prove to the *storage contract* that the data have not been tampered, she will lose the collateral.

We further incentivize the *provider* through our reputation system used in the *market layer*. Having in place a reputation system that aids *providers* with good reputation to get better storage deals, we can penalize the reputation of a *provider* that fails to guarantee data integrity. This penalty will influence its future deals and therefore as a rational player she is encouraged to provide good data integrity guarantees.

The mechanism we use to enable the *provider* to prove that she owns the *client's* data is based on Merkle trees [16]. The *client* calculates the Merkle tree of the data to be stored and saves its root hash in the *storage contract*. In the same manner the *provider* verifies the root hash before accepting the contract. As a result, at any point in time the *provider* can send a number of Merkle proofs [16] to the *storage contract*. The contract by verifying that the given proofs match the root hash of the data's Merkle tree, ensures that the *provider* still owns at least part of the original data. Increasing the number of proofs required, increases the probability that the original data remain intact.

Data Availability: To deal with availability we require the *provider* to reply within a certain time frame to random challenges initiated by the *client*. Those challenges involve the *client* asking for a Merkle proof of a specific part of the data. The *client* can perform the challenge either on- or off-chain. In the first case it is the *storage contract* that verifies the proof in the second it is the *client*. If the check is performed on-chain and the *provider* fails to reply within the specified time frame the contract is invalidated and she loses the collateral as well as reputation. That way the *provider* is incentivized to have a certain response time in regard to data availability. Having the response time frame specified as part of the contract gives the *provider* a way to implement hot or cold storage options.

Data Recovery: The incentives provided for *Data Availability and Integrity* could be considered sufficient to cover the case of data loss as well. In such a case the *provider* would not be able to prove that she owned the original data and eventually lose its collateral and reputation. However, given that the

Merkle proofs mechanism can only guarantee the availability of a percentage of the original data, we incorporate erasure codes as a way of lowering even further the possibility of data loss or corruption. In a nutshell, erasure coding expands and encodes a dataset with redundant data pieces and breaks it into n fragments in a way such that the original dataset can be recovered from a subset of the n fragments. There is a large collection of erasure codes available today, we opted for the Reed-Solomon codes [17] because of their popularity and wide use. By erasure encoding the data before sending them to the *provider*, the *client* ensures that retrieving only a part of the stored data is enough to restore all of the original data. This process is transparent to the *provider* and the *storage contract*, that is both the contract and the *provider* treat the *client's* data the same way whether they are erasure encoded or not.

Privacy: The simplest way to handle privacy is at the *client* side by encrypting the data before transmission. As with erasure codes, the *provider* and *storage contract* handle the *client's* data identically whether they are encrypted or not. That gives the *client* the freedom of choosing any encryption algorithm or even not using encryption if not required.

Thus, by assuming rational players and through the use of monetary and reputation based incentives, we are able to guarantee *Data Integrity, Availability and Recovery*. This is enabled by creating Merkle trees on the *client's* data and using erasure codes to lower the probability of data loss.

4.3   Storage Workflow

In this section we describe in detail the remote data storage workflow as well as the life-cycle of a *storage contract* and its state transitions.

Storage Workflow: At this point we assume that the *client* has already interacted with the *market layer* and the corresponding auction is finalized. As a result a *storage contract* is created that binds a *client* with a *provider*. The contract contains the addresses of the *client* and the *provider*, the root hash of the Merkle tree of the *client's* data, the end date of the contract as well as the payment and collateral amounts. Those amounts are transfered to the contract upon its creation and therefore managed by the contract logic. We note that any preprocessing to the data to be stored should be performed by the *client* before the initial auction phase. Typically the data preprocessing includes encryption and erasure encoding as mentioned in the previous section. Given that in the *storage contract* we store the root hash of the Merkle tree of the data we must perform any preprocessing before the Merkle tree calculation.

As a second step, the *client* sets up a server to serve the data. The *provider* downloads the data, computes their Merkle tree and verifies their integrity by matching the root hash of the tree with the one stored in the *storage contract*. If the hashes match, the provider activates the contract. From that point on, the *client* can safely assume that the data are stored remotely.

After the end date of the contract, the *provider* can collect the payment. To do so she has to prove that she still has the data at its possession, he does so by sending a number of Merkle proofs to the *storage contract*, if the proofs are valid the contract releases the funds and transfers them to the *provider's* address. If the *provider* cannot prove that she possesses the *client's* data the contract transfers all the funds to the *client's* address since it assumes that the *provider* lost the data and therefore the *client* should receive the collateral.

At any point in time after the contract activation and before the end date of the contract, the *client* can request its data from the *provider*, this operation is performed off-chain. Although, it is not possible for the *client* to request the data on-chain, she can achieve the same goal by asking a sufficient number of Merkle proofs and restoring its original data from the proofs. This second alternative, however, is not practical but the system's incentives are against it, since providing a Merkle proof to the *storage contract* costs to the *provider* gas.

Additionally, while the contract is active the *client* can challenge the *provider* by requesting a Merkle proof for a specific data block. This process can be performed either on- or off-chain and is used as a safeguard against data tampering.

In the case of an off-chain challenge, we have to note that for the *client* to be able to challenge the *provider* she would have to decide beforehand on a number of challenges and store that number of data blocks locally before serving the data to the *provider*. This is because at the time of the challenge in addition to the Merkle proof the data block that matches that proof is also verified. Thus, when the *client* challenges the *provider* to prove that she owns a specific data block D, the *provider* sends back to the client the given data block D as well as the path of the Merkle tree from D to the root of the tree. At that point, the *client* can verify that the *provider* has D at its possession as well as that D is part of the original data.

In the case of an on-chain challenge, the *client* requires from the *provider* to prove that she owns a number of different data blocks. As a result the *provider* has to send to the *storage contract* a given number of randomly selected data blocks as well as the corresponding Merkle tree proofs. At that point the *storage contract* produces the hash of each data block and combines it with the corresponding proof verifying if the block leads to the Merkle tree root that is stored on the contract. By requesting a given number of Merkle proofs at each challenge the *client* can ensure with good probability that the *provider* has the original data at its possession.

Storage Contract Life-Cycle: The life-cycle of a *storage contract* can be represented by its state transitions as depicted in Fig. 2. The dashed transitions represent actions performed by the *provider* while the solid ones by the *client*.

Transitions t_2, t_4 and t_7 are triggered by the *provider*. In t_2 the *provider* receives the data and proves that she owns it in order to activate the contract. In t_4 the *provider* proves on-chain that she still has possession of the data while in t_7 performs the same proof in order to complete the contract and receive the payment.

Transitions t_0, t_1, t_3, t_5 and t_6 respectively are triggered by a *client* action. In t_0 the *client* through his interaction with the *market layer* creates a new *storage contract* and specifies payment amount, collateral, provider and contract end

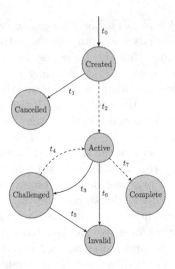

Fig. 2. Storage contract state diagram

date. In t_1 the *client* has the option to cancel the contract before it is accepted by the *provider*. In t_3 the *client* challenges the *provider* by requesting an on-chain proof that she still owns the data. t_5 can be triggered by the *client* in the case the *provider* failed to prove that she owns the data, in that case the contract is invalidated and the collateral is transfered to the *client*. Finally, in t_6 we have the same transition with t_5 only after the contract end date.

5   Compute

Providing secure computations by untrusted parties presents its own challenges. For the following discussion, we make two observations:

(a) In CloudAgora There Exists a Trusted Network (Blockchain) That Correctly Performs Small Computational Tasks. While any algorithm can be developed as a smart contract and executed on the blockchain, we particularly focus on small tasks. Heavy contracts lead miners to the notorious *Verifier's Dilemma*. On-chain verifications that require non-trivial computational efforts will fail to execute correctly in rational miners and the whole chain will be vulnerable to serious attacks [14].

(b) Participants Are Rational in the Sense That They Act To Maximize Individual Profits. A CloudAgora member is eager to solve or verify a task only if she expects to have a monetary profit.

Based on these observations we develop a truebit-like [19] game, where outsourced algorithms are executed off-chain and blockchain is only used for correctness proofs. The outline of such a game consists of the following steps:

– The user announces a task and a task description is placed on-chain.

- Depending on the protocol, a solver is selected for executing the task. In the traditional truebit game, the solver is selected at random. In CloudAgora, a solver/provider is selected based on the auction described in Sect. 3.
- The solver privately performs computations off-chain and only after completion, she reveals the solution on the blockchain.
- While solver is computing the task, any other member of the system can also compute it in private and act as a verifier. If a verifier agrees with the solution provided by the solver, the solver gets paid and the game stops. In case of a disagreement, the verifier can challenge the solver and an interactive proof takes place on-chain. If the solver proves to be malicious, the verifier receives solver's reward and solver looses the deposited collateral we discussed in Sect. 3. If the verifier has triggered a false alarm, she is obliged to pay for the resources wasted due to the interactive game.

5.1   Interactive Proof

In this Section we discuss how disputes are resolved in case of disagreement between a solver and a verifier. First of all, we must be sure that both parties compute exactly the same program and that the architecture of the infrastructure that each party has employed does not affect the result. For this reason, an announced task is first converted to an assembly-like intermediate representation. Then, both parties privately compile a tableau of Turing Machine (TM) configurations, where each time step of the task is mapped to its complete internal representation (tape contents, head position, machine state). The game also determines a parameter c that declares how many configurations the solver broadcasts to the blockchain in each roud and a timeout period within which verifiers and the solver must respond. Failing to do so leads to immediate loss for the non-responding party.

The main loop of the game goes as follows:

- The solver selects c configurations equally spaced in time across the current range of dispute. She then computes c Merkle trees of the Turing tableau where each tree corresponds to the $\frac{1}{c}$ of the current range of dispute. Each leaf of these trees is the complete TM state for a specific time step. The roots of all these Merkle trees are placed on the blockchain.
- The verifier responds on-chain with a number $i \le c$, indicating the first time step in this list that differs from her own.
- The process continues recursively, considering as dispute range the one between the $(i-1)$-st and i-th indexed configurations.

After some rounds, the game converges to the first disputed computational step t. The solver then provides paths from the Merkle tree root to its leaves for the moments $t-1$ and t. The transition of the TM state at time $t-1$ to the one at time t is computed on-chain and the disagreement is resolved by the miners.

6 Prototype Implementation

We implemented a prototype of CloudAgora as a dApp over Ethereum. As a result the contracts that implement the auction and govern the on-chain *client, provider* interactions are in Solidity. All the off-chain logic is implemented in NodeJS using web3.js to interface with the Ethereum blockchain. We used parts of the truebit codebase to implement the compute module of CloudAgora while the Storage is implemented from scratch.

CloudAgora introduces a non-negligible performance overhead to an application execution compared to executing the application over the same hardware without using CloudAgora. This overhead includes the latency of smart contract operations, the latency of committing transactions to the blockchain as well as the overhead attributed to the truebit protocol. Thus, the blockchain of choice heavily determines the performance overhead. Since our prototype relies on Ethereum, CloudAgora inherits its performance characteristics [11].

7 Related Work

CloudAgora is a platform that facilitates the provision of storage and computation resources in a fully distributed and democratic manner, using the Ethereum blockchain to record commitment policies, publicly verify them and automate micropayments. Related work includes blockchain-based projects that offer off-chain computations, data hosting and processing services.

In the domain of data hosting, projects such as Storj, Filecoin and Sia permit users to rent unused storage space, using a blockchain to guarantee the correctness of the service offered. Sia [20] supports smart contracts between storage suppliers and users, which are stored and executed in its proper blockchain. Integrity and existence of a piece of data on a remote host is guaranteed using Merkle proofs and associated final payment is enforced automatically through the contract. Storj [22] is based on Kademlia Distributed Hash Table (DHT) [15] to offer a P2P cloud storage network that builds on top of any smart contract blockchain. Erasure coding is employed as a redundancy mechanism, while audits are based on Merkle proofs. Filecoin [2] relies on zk-SNARK [7], a cryptographic tool for zero-knowledge verifiable computation, to provide what the creators call *Proof-of-SpaceTime*, i.e., evidence that some data has been stored throughout a period of time. This is made possible through iterations of challenges and responses. All the above solutions exclusively address the case of storage provisioning, while CloudAgora provides both storage and computational resources.

Projects such as GridCoin, Enigma, Golem, Dfinity and iExec offer both distributed storage and computation services.

The GridCoin [4] project creates a cryptocurrency as a reward for computations provided to BOINC-based volunteer projects for scientific purposes. It utilizes its own consensus protocol, called Proof-of-Research, which replaces the traditional Proof-of-Work puzzle with useful work. Since it purely concerns volunteer grid computing projects, it is mainly limited to altruistic sharing of resources for scientific research.

Enigma [23] utilizes Multi-Party Computation (MPC) [13] protocols to ensure correct execution while preserving data privacy. Due to the fact that it heavily relies on homomorphic encryption to allow nodes to operate on encrypted shards of data, it poses restrictions regarding the type of computation it can support, thus limiting its applicability and hindering its wide adoption in practice.

Golem [3] is built on top of the Ethereum blockchain. It mainly offers software services and thus focuses on specific computation tasks (e.g., 3D rendering). Proof of correct execution is available through Truebit style challenges, where user reputation is not (yet) taken into account. Contrarily, CloudAgora aims to support any type of task. Moreover, although CloudAgora too employs Truebit as a means of verifying the correctness of the outsourced computation, the reputation mechanism and the auction game it adopts for matching resource requests to providers enhances Truebit's mechanism of allocating tasks to Solvers.

Dfinity [1] is a blockchain aiming to act as a replacement to smart contract platforms like Ethereum by creating a decentralized cloud computer, the "Internet computer", which will host the next generation of Dapps. iExec [6] is a project where computation audits are performed through the so called Proof-of-Contribution. This proof is based on a voting scheme that takes into account user reputation and distributes rewards based on it in a weighted manner. It builds its proper blockchain with trusted nodes using a Proof-of-Stake consensus mechanism. CloudAgora is an open-source platform, based on Ethereum, which is an already popular and widely adopted blockchain.

8   Conclusions

In this paper we presented CloudAgora, a platform that allows for on-demand and low-cost access to storage and computing infrastructures. In CloudAgora participants can act either as providers, offering idle resources, or as consumers, requesting resources. Such requests are expressed as auction smart contracts, where any potential provider can place bids. The height of the offer and the credibility of the provider determines the final choice. The agreement between providers and consumers is encoded as a smart contract, which allows for traceability of actions and automatic triggering of payments. While storage and processing is performed off-chain, the integrity and availability of stored data as well as the correctness of the outsourced computation are safeguarded through proper verification processes that take place on the chain. Our prototype implementation uses Ethereum as the underlying blockchain technology.

Acknowledgments. This research is co-financed by Greece and the European Union (European Social Fund- ESF) through the Operational Programme "Human Resources Development, Education and Lifelong Learning 2014–2020" in the context of the project "Data Sovereignty through the use of Blockchain"(MIS 5004883).

References

1. dfinity: The Internet Computer. https://dfinity.org/

2. Filecoin. https://filecoin.io/
3. Golem. https://golem.network/
4. GridCoin White Paper. https://www.gridcoin.us/assets/img/whitepaper.pdf
5. How cloud computing is changing the world ... without you knowing. https://www.theguardian.com/media-network/media-network-blog/2013/sep/24/cloud-computing-changing-world-healthcare
6. iExec Blockchain-Based Decentralized Cloud Computing. https://iex.ec/
7. Ben-Sasson, E., Chiesa, A., Tromer, E., Virza, M.: Succinct non-interactive zero knowledge for a von neumann architecture. In: 23rd USENIX Security Symposium, USENIX Security 2014, pp. 781–796 (2014)
8. Boss, G., Malladi, P., Quan, D., Legregni, L., Hall, H.: Cloud computing. IBM White Paper **321**, 224–231 (2007)
9. Croman, K., et al.: On scaling decentralized blockchains. In: Clark, J., Meiklejohn, S., Ryan, P.Y.A., Wallach, D., Brenner, M., Rohloff, K. (eds.) FC 2016. LNCS, vol. 9604, pp. 106–125. Springer, Heidelberg (2016). https://doi.org/10.1007/978-3-662-53357-4_8
10. Dennis, R., Owen, G.: Rep on the block: a next generation reputation system based on the blockchain. In: 2015 10th International Conference for Internet Technology and Secured Transactions (ICITST), pp. 131–138. IEEE (2015)
11. Dinh, T.T.A., Wang, J., Chen, G., Liu, R., Ooi, B.C., Tan, K.L.: Blockbench: a framework for analyzing private blockchains. In: Proceedings of the 2017 ACM International Conference on Management of Data, pp. 1085–1100. ACM (2017)
12. Eberhardt, J., Tai, S.: On or off the blockchain? Insights on off-chaining computation and data. In: De Paoli, F., Schulte, S., Broch Johnsen, E. (eds.) ESOCC 2017. LNCS, vol. 10465, pp. 3–15. Springer, Cham (2017). https://doi.org/10.1007/978-3-319-67262-5_1
13. Goldreich, O.: Secure multi-party computation. Manuscript 78 (1998)
14. Luu, L., Teutsch, J., Kulkarni, R., Saxena, P.: Demystifying incentives in the consensus computer. In: Proceedings of the 22nd ACM SIGSAC Conference on Computer and Communications Security, pp. 706–719. ACM (2015)
15. Maymounkov, P., Mazières, D.: Kademlia: a peer-to-peer information system based on the XOR metric. In: Druschel, P., Kaashoek, F., Rowstron, A. (eds.) IPTPS 2002. LNCS, vol. 2429, pp. 53–65. Springer, Heidelberg (2002). https://doi.org/10.1007/3-540-45748-8_5
16. Merkle, R.C.: A digital signature based on a conventional encryption function. In: Pomerance, C. (ed.) CRYPTO 1987. LNCS, vol. 293, pp. 369–378. Springer, Heidelberg (1988). https://doi.org/10.1007/3-540-48184-2_32
17. Reed, I.S., Solomon, G.: Polynomial codes over certain finite fields. J. Soc. Ind. Appl. Math. **8**(2), 300–304 (1960)
18. Swan, M.: Blockchain: Blueprint for a new economy. O'Reilly Media Inc, Sebastopol (2015)
19. Teutsch, J., Reitwießner, C.: A scalable verification solution for blockchains (2017). https://people.cs.uchicago.edu/teutsch/papers/truebit.pdf
20. Vorick, D., Champine, L.: Sia: Simple decentralized storage. White paper (2014). https://sia.tech/sia.pdf
21. Wang, H., Jing, Q., He, B., Qian, Z., Zhou, L.: Distributed systems meet economics: pricing in the cloud (2010)
22. Wilkinson, S., Boshevski, T., Brandoff, J., Buterin, V.: Storj a peer-to-peer cloud storage network (2014)
23. Zyskind, G., Nathan, O., Pentland, A.: Enigma: decentralized computation platform with guaranteed privacy. arXiv preprint arXiv:1506.03471 (2015)

Dual Token Blockchain Economy Framework
The Garment Use Case

Magdi ElMessiry[1] , Adel ElMessiry[2(✉)] , and Malak ElMessiry[3]

[1] Textile Engineering Department, Faculty of Engineering, Alexandria University,
Alexandria, Egypt
mmessiry@yahoo.com
[2] Garment Chain, Nashville, TN, USA
ammessir@ncsu.edu
[3] Vanderbilt, Nashville, TN, USA
malak.a.elmessiry@vanderbilt.edu

Abstract. Over the last few years, the introduction of blockchain technology has brought forth a new set of challenges concerning blockchain token economics and its underlying business needs. Many Initial Coin Offerings (ICOs) have focused on a single token that facilitated the initial project funding but complicated the actual implementation.

Business arrangements can be complex and result in disputes between even the most well-intentioned parties. Supply chain transparency requires careful modeling of a specific implementation of the blockchain technology to correctly capture it.

In this paper, we propose a dual token model that takes into consideration both the financial aspect and the non-fungible nature of complex, real-world industries. Furthermore, we demonstrate the efficacy of our model to accommodate the stages hidden under the umbrella term "supply chain transparency" as it comes to the costing involved in producing the firm's products internal supply chain transparency. We show how this approach increases not only the transparency of the manufacturing process but also the profit and transparency for external stakeholders.

Keywords: Blockchain · Supply chain · Textile · Token economics

1 Introduction

The problem we are addressing in this paper fundamentally pertains to how an economic system can be established and modeled using blockchain technology. In a recent study it was claimed that 80% of all ICOs failed [19]. Another study of the white papers produced by the ICO projects sampled uncovered that [25]:

- 20% failed to convey any information at all about the issuing entity.
- 41% only had the country of origin and a postal address.
- 43% did not provide a valid postal contact.

© Springer Nature Switzerland AG 2019
J. Joshi et al. (Eds.): ICBC 2019, LNCS 11521, pp. 157–170, 2019.
https://doi.org/10.1007/978-3-030-23404-1_11

This is just on the information level of an ICO project and not deeper in the actual process that the blockchain project should model. Naturally, the question is why is there this high level of failure? Why is the process so complicated to model? To have an understanding of the problem we are addressing, we need to first examine the current status of the textile industry and then uncover what blockchain technology is. Finally, we will apply our proposed framework to a real-world problem to solve as a case study.

1.1   Blockchain

A blockchain is a decentralized immutable database that can store references of all types of records [8, 23, 33].

Over fifty percent of participants who run the blockchain network must agree on a transaction before it is added to the network. The data is secured using a hash function, which is any function that can be used to map data of arbitrary size to data of fixed size, more formally defined by Eq. 1, where H is the hash and n is the number of bits returned by the hashing function [27].

$$H : K \times M \rightarrow \{0, 1\}^n \tag{1}$$

A block consists of the following main parts:

Payload, which contains the actual data to be committed to the blockchain.
Previous Block Hash, the digital fingerprint of the previous block.
Current Block Hash, the current digital fingerprint of the current block payload and the previous block hash.

The main concept of the blockchain can be illustrated in Fig. 1.

The transactions can be traced back to the original first block, commonly called the genesis block. The genesis block is the only block that does not reference an actual previous block hash [13].

The most popular blockchain application is Bitcoin, which provides for peer to peer financial transactions. Blockchain removes the need of a middleman as a decentralized system verifies a transaction's authenticity, reducing costs [32].

Information is always accessible on the blockchain as only one of the thousands of nodes needs to be available to access it. Due to thousands of nodes existing on a blockchain, it is very likely a local node is accessible at or near a user. This is helpful for users with limited bandwidth who are located near a textile facility in a developing country.

The central feature of blockchain technology is an immutable ledger [30]. Immutable means that the contents of the payload of each block cannot be changed after it is committed to the chain. This is because each block hash is computed based on the payload of the block and the hash of the previous block as shown in Fig. 1. If we want to tamper with block i, we will need to recompute the hash of block i. That will require us to recompute the hash of every and all subsequent blocks as changing one hash will invalidate all subsequent hashes. Now, because the ledger is distributed, we will need to gain control and

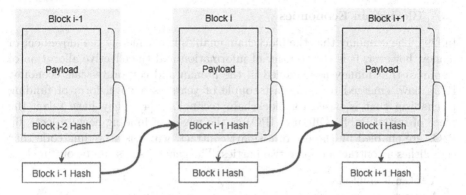

Fig. 1. Conceptual illustration of the blockchain.

change the hashes of at least 51% of the entire network. The sheer amount of required effort renders it practically impossible. One way to look at blockchain is through comparing it to the new application layer for Internet protocols because blockchain can enable both immediate and long-term economic transactions. The Ethereum blockchain [16], for example, is an open-source, public, blockchain-based distributed computing platform and operating system designed to allow smart contract functionality. A smart contract specifies the conditions for a transaction to occur [28].

1.2 Blockchain in Textiles

There are many benefits of blockchain. Yet, there is little to no adoption of blockchain technology in the textiles supply chain domain. Blockchain technology presents many features and characteristics that can be useful in textile industry aspects such as compliance, transparency, tracking, tracing, error reduction, payment processing, and many others [31]. IBM has revealed its intention to lead an "industry-wide collaboration" to create a supply chain and trading ecosystem built on IBM blockchain technology. It will use the Hyperledger Fabric, which provides a foundation for developing blockchain solutions with a modular architecture, pluggable implementations, and so-called container technology. There are numerous organizations, processes, systems, and transactions involved from field to fabric. Located at the intersection of agriculture, finance, and technology, the Seam with the help of IBM, is in a unique position to introduce blockchain technology to cotton-affiliated companies around the world. In conjunction with IBM, the Seam wishes to create a supply chain and trading ecosystem built on IBM blockchain using the hyperledger fabric. This new technology will be transformational for the cotton industry. There are numerous organizations, processes, systems, and transactions involved from field to fabric. The Seam and IBM launched the first cotton industry blockchain consortium.

1.3   Blockchain Economies

In [29], The economy that the blockchain enables is not merely the movement of money, however, it is the transfer of information and the effective allocation of resources that money has enabled in the human and corporate-scale economy. ICOs have emerged over the last couple of years as a novel form of funding mechanism that is based on blockchain technology [4]. They have taken the place of Initial Public Offering (IPO) as the means of funding new projects [6]. ICOs are enabled by the use of a smart contract, which is a binding code that establishes a contract between two parties. The general steps can be outlined as:

– A token is minted
– A smart contract is created
– The investor sends one type of cryptocurrency to the contract
– The investor would receive a set amount of the newly minted token

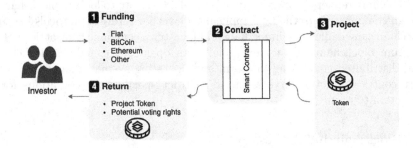

Fig. 2. Conceptual illustration of the ICO project cycle.

This cycle can be illustrated in Fig. 2. The important aspect to note in this model is that the tokens are not required to carry any voting rights in the actual underlying process of the project. Social media plays a big role in the success of the project due to level awareness [4].

2   Garment Industry

Transparency is a requirement of the stockholder through the transfer power from the operating establishment. Transparency is also a requirement of the supply chain manager to make informed evaluations of the firms' products during its processing. In relation to supply chains, consumers and other stakeholders, such as nongovernmental organizations and governments, are increasingly demanding transparency from companies [9,11]. Supply chain transparency can make this more effective and help overcome some of the problems (technical, financial, etc.) Studies have also demonstrated that customers are more willing to purchase products from transparent companies [3,12]. The author argues that transparency improves comprehensibility and comparability, however, it is far from certain if in practice this is enough to motivate consumers to pressure the company to make changes [12]. The transparency of the supply chain required conveying complex information along complex supply chains is limited to considerations related to transparency in supply chains through dual token blockchain. First is related to the management and the second is of the insert to the investors [34]. The Apparel market is one of the largest growing markets with an annual growth rate up to 6%, especially in developed countries such as China, India, and Indonesia. The total global market of apparel may reach a total of 1.5 billion for 2018 and expected to reach $1.8 billion in 2022. Figure 3 shows the expected change of the value of the global apparel market in the period 2018–2022 [21]. The apparel manufacturing market covers all clothing except leather, footwear, and knitted items as well as other technical, household, and made-up products. The global manufacturing market value annual growth is 4.4% and is expected to reach $992 billion in 2021. The apparel manufacturing chain is characterized by its globality in every component of the supply chain such as the raw material, accessories, production side, transportation, and retail. The production of chain or Latin America will export several markets of the globe. Figure 2 illustrates the global apparent trade flow in 2016. The USA imports 78% of apparel items from Asia while Asia counter exports all over the globe [10].

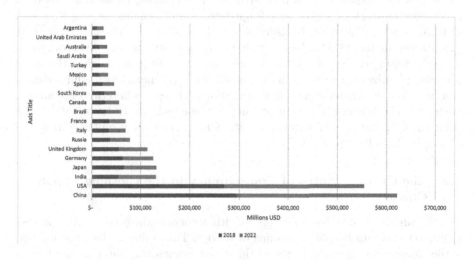

Fig. 3. Top 20 global apparel market in 2018–2022.

The above analysis indicates the complication and large data generated during the manufacturing of each item until it reaches the consumer [17].

2.1 Supply Chain Transparency

The term "transparency" is often used loosely in discourse around sustainability in commodity supply chains [14]. Some view transparency as having the potential to help overturn deep asymmetries in how different actors access information. Transparency is therefore often interpreted as inherently positive, and of central importance for efforts to create a more emancipator environmental politics and support bottom-up civil society action [24]. The transparency of blockchain consists of several items that depend on the interest of the inquirer to products' internal supply chain transparency, the profit firms' practices, and external stakeholder's supply chain transparency. In the case of the apparel industry, the higher competition is believed to reduce the transparency of the companies. The investigations of high transparency encourage all the players in the market: consumers, investors, stakeholders, government, financial, NGO, environmental organizations, managers, etc. [2]. The data requirements for the external data and internal data are transposable by defining supply chain transparency in the clothing. Though transparency is increasingly central to corporate sustainability and sustainable supply chains, the scholarly conversation about supply chain transparency is limited, as it defines supply chain transparency inconsistently and lacks an empirical basis [12]. The scholarly conversation about supply chain transparency is limited in two important ways. First, supply chain transparency is inconsistently defined, and individual scholars tend to focus solely on just one of the many dimensions of transparency. This leads to limited and often dualistic framings of supply chain transparency, with companies being claimed to be either transparent or nontransparent. The clothing industry is based on a complex network of global and fragmented supply chains leading to a lack of transparency. Therefore, transparency and supply chain traceability are core priorities to increase the fashion supply chain visibility and enable accountability [18] "Supply chain transparency" are unclear about how to define the term. For example, the transparency in the apparel industry means each administrator can reach the data from every single operation and express in terms of monetary value. For the investor, the transparency is the capability to know each of the companies' operation profit value, despite Nudie Jeans' focus on the dimensions of supply chain transparency [12].

2.2   The Current Status of Transparency in the Clothing Supply Chains

Textile supply chains have struggled with understanding the entire process required to produce/supply a product or service. This is due to the large and versatile supplier and demand in the world of fast fashion varieties that need quick response [20]. Moreover, the fashion is seasonable that add another pressure on the cloth supply chain to make it more dynamical. A key aspect of fashion supply chains is the lack of transparency caused by having multiple intermediary steps between the production of raw materials to the purchase of a finished product [18].

2.3   Defining Supply Chain Transparency in the Clothing

The supply chain in the clothing industry is made by connecting:

- Raw material sources
- Factories that use these raw materials and create final products
- Distribution network that delivers these clothes to consumers

This involves material, information, financial capital flow, the management of the flow of goods, services, and information involving the storage and movement of raw materials, building products, and full-fledged finished goods from one point to another (supply chain management). Supply chain management is the integration of key business processes from end users to original suppliers that provide products, services, and information that add value for customers and other stakeholders. In the apparel supply chain, this includes every organization starting from initial fiber suppliers to consumers purchasing apparel products for final consumption. Figure 4 gives the Apparel supply chain elements. The apparel supply chain management should take care of all the elements as illustrated in Fig. 5.

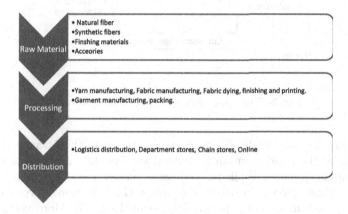

Fig. 4. Element of the apparel chain.

3   Capturing Operational Cost Using a Blockchain Token

Blockchain can be applied to many challenges of the Supply Chain industry such as complicated record keeping and tracking of products. Blockchain is a less corruptible and better-automated alternative to centralized databases [26]. In blockchains, records and data are secure, traceable, and auditable, and maintained on a peer-to-peer network [29]. The real-time tracking of a product in a supply chain with the help of blockchain reduces the overall cost of moving items in a supply chain. According to a survey of supply chain workers conducted by APQC and the Digital Supply Chain Institute (DSCI), more than one-third of people cited reduction of costs as the topmost benefit of application of blockchain in supply chain management. When blockchain is applied to speed up administrative processes in supply chains, the extra costs occurring in the system are

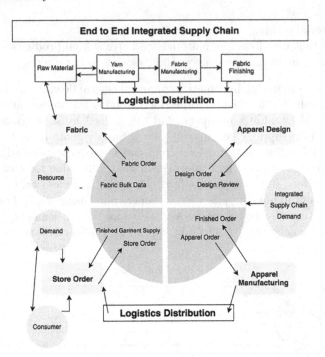

Fig. 5. The apparel supply chain management.

automatically reduced while still guaranteeing the security of transactions. The elimination of the middlemen and intermediaries in the supply chain saves the risks of frauds, product duplicity, and saves money too. Customers and suppliers can process payments within the supply chain by using cryptocurrencies rather than customers and suppliers relying on EDI [15]. Moreover, efficiency will be improved, and the risk of losing products will be reduced with accurate record keeping. Transparency in blockchain helps reduce delays and disputes while preventing goods from getting stuck in the supply chain. As each product can be tracked in real-time, the chances of misplacements are rare. Blockchain offers scalability through which any large database is accessible from multiple locations from around the world. It also provides higher standards of security and the ability to customize according to the data feed. Moreover, blockchain can be created privately too which will allow the data to be accessed explicitly between the parties who have permission for it [1,22]. The internal transparency of the blockchain should deal with the money values of each product taken into consideration:

– Raw material and accessory cost value
– Logistic cost value
– Inventory cost value
– Industrial cost value
– Waste cost value

– Overhead cost value
– Customer demands

Each of the above elements have a different impact on the total product value [5], as illustrated in Fig. 6.

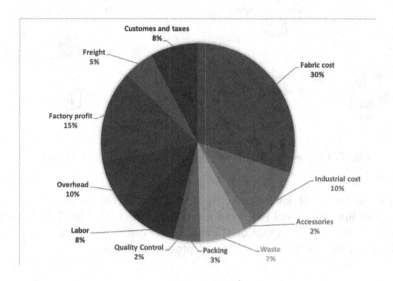

Fig. 6. The apparel elements cost breakdown.

4 Proposed Framework

To solve this issue, a dual token model is proposed as the basis of the system. This model is illustrated in Fig. 7. The framework takes into account that any real world is a bit more complicated and normally would address a problem that results in some actual asset. That asset needs to be represented by a digital non-fungible asset. The model has the following steps:

Funding. The first step is for the investor to send in the funding, thus activating the smart contract.
Contract. The contract is normally done through a passive code that is called a smart contract. The code performs an irreversible transaction based on certain input.
Project. This is the actual effort that will be funded out of the proceeds collected by the ICO.
Return. The return, in most cases, is the minted token, this could be a native token or a token based on an existing blockchain.
Operate. Each real-world project will have an operation that generates a digital asset.

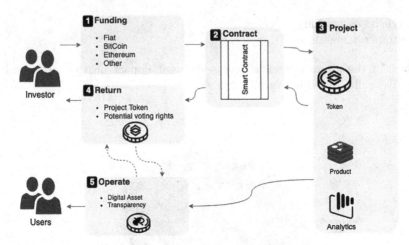

Fig. 7. Proposed ICO token architecture for blockchain projects.

As shown in the breakdown above, the added part in the proposed model is to focus on adding the actual produced asset from the start. The digital asset is a non-fungible token that cannot be traded like the utility or funding token, rather it is designed to represent the operation process accurately.

4.1 Manufacturing Contract

In the proposed work frame, a manufacturing smart contract must be created to represent either the inception of the non-fungible token or a manufacturing process that operates on it. The smart contract simply accepts an amount of the fungible token and generates or process the non fungible token. The contract can also accept a list of existing non-fungible tokens to represent a manufacturing process that consumes existing tokens to create a new one. The following are the proposed two types of manufacturing smart contracts:

Inception Smart Contract: (ISC) This contract accepts fungible-tokens and sends back non fungible tokens to the calling address. It generates the non-fungible tokens based on the specifications of the contract.

Manufacturing Smart Contract: (MSC) This contract accepts fungible tokens and a variable list of non-fungible tokens and sends back a new non-fungible token representing the result of the process according to the contract specifications.

5   Evaluation

To evaluate the difference in both models, we need to consider the underlying manufacturing processes. We have to consider the framework outlined in the U.S. Securities and Exchange Commission on ICOs:

The federal securities laws require all offers and sales of securities, including those involving a digital asset, to either be registered under its provisions or to qualify for an exemption from registration. The registration provisions require persons to disclose certain information to investors, and that information must be complete and not materially misleading [7].

As illustrated in Fig. 8, the proposed model separates the financial aspect from the actual manufacturing aspect, allowing both to be operated separately while interacting to capture the actual process. This is critical as the asset is non-fungible and does not represent a liquid asset intrinsically. Entangling both in one token limits the ability of the blockchain architecture to track a real-world asset. In the garment use case presented, it separates the actual garment produced from the financial token that represents the funding and status of the network. Through contrasting the single token framework with the proposed dual token framework, we can observe the benefits in Table 1. The financial token will operate just like the current ICO framework, allowing both the trading of the token and associating it with the manufacturing phases. The second token is the non-fungible token which tracks the actual production material from initial creation to the final sale and ownership by the end consumer. Similar to the minting of the financial token, the generation of the non-fungible token occurs during the manufacturing. For that to happen, the entity creating or processing the non-fungible token will link it to the creation or processing wallet address. The unique wallet address allows full transparency and tracking of the manufacturing process.

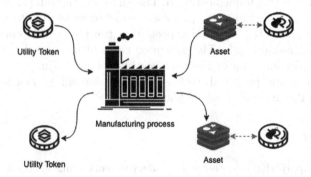

Fig. 8. Conceptual illustration of the manufacturing process.

Another evaluation is whether we can separate the financial (external) and manufacturing (internal) aspects in practical cases. The current single token ICO framework does not allow a clear path to ac hive costing transparency. In the proposed dual token framework, we can utilize the *ISC* and *MSC* so that a full manufacturing process can be mapped and modeled into a blockchain powered system, which provides insights into the internal and external costing of the

Table 1. Token system evaluation matrix.

Feature	Single token	Dual token
Allow anonymous project founding	Yes	Yes
Allow project token	Yes	Yes
Allow token trading	Yes	Yes
Allow manufacturing process modeling	No	Yes
Provide transparency into internal process	No	Yes
Allow generation of non-fungible asset	No	Yes
Provide separation between financial and manufacturing	No	Yes

produced end results. Since each manufactured asset is represented by a non-fungible token that has to be at least produced by utilizing a fungible token, the internal costing of the production can be tracked and mapped to the current cost.

6 Conclusion

Over the last few years, the introduction of blockchain technology has brought forth a new set of challenges to understand the acute nature of blockchain token economics and how to best model the underlying business needs. Many ICOs have focused on a single token that facilitated the initial project funding but complicated the actual implementation. This shortcoming could explain the large failure rate of such projects. The proposed model provides an alternative framework that separates the financial aspect from the real-world process allowing both to exist simultaneously. The presented garment use case demonstrates the real-world implementation of the proposed model successfully. Future work is needed to apply the proposed work on another domain as well as to provide simulation of the internal financial transactions.

References

1. Aabed: Supply chain in the readymade garments industry (zara case study), August 2017. http://www.journal.faa-design.com/pdf/7-4-abed.pdf
2. Agrawal, T.K., Koehl, L., Campagne, C.: A secured tag for implementation of traceability in textile and clothing supply chain. Int. J. Adv. Manufact. Technol. **99**(9–12), 2563–2577 (2018)
3. Bhaduri, G., Ha-Brookshire, J.E.: Do transparent business practices pay? exploration of transparency and consumer purchase intention. Clothing Text. Res. J. **29**(2), 135–149 (2011)
4. Chanson, M., Risius, M., Wortmann, F.: Initial Coin Offerings (ICOs): An Introduction to the Novel Funding Mechanism Based on Blockchain Technology (2018)
5. Choudhary, A.S.: Cost analysis in garment industry. Int. J. Recent Adv. Multi. Res. **2**(09), 0702–0704 (2015)

6. Collomb, A., De Filippi, P., Sok, K.: From IPOs to ICOs: the impact of blockchain technology on financial regulation (2018)
7. Commision, U.S.A.E.: Framework for "Investment Contract" Analysis of Digital Assets (2019). https://www.sec.gov/corpfin/framework-investment-contract-analysis-digital-assets. Accessed 11 Apr 2019
8. Crosby, M., Pattanayak, P., Verma, S., Kalyanaraman, V.: Blockchain technology: beyond bitcoin. Appl. Innov. **2**, 6–10 (2016)
9. Doorey, D.J.: The transparent supply chain: from resistance to implementation at nike and levi-strauss. J. Bus. Ethics **103**(4), 587–603 (2011)
10. Duan, J., Patel, M.: Blockchain in global trade. In: Chen, S., Wang, H., Zhang, L.-J. (eds.) ICBC 2018. LNCS, vol. 10974, pp. 293–296. Springer, Cham (2018). https://doi.org/10.1007/978-3-319-94478-4_23
11. Dubbink, W.: Transparency gained, morality lost: a critique of the administrative conceptualization of CSR, illustrated by dutch policy. Bus. Soc. Rev.-Boston New York **112**(2), 287 (2007)
12. Egels-Zandén, N., Hulthén, K., Wulff, G.: Trade-offs in supply chain transparency: the case of Nudie Jeans Co. J. Clean. Prod. **107**, 95–104 (2015)
13. ElMessiry, M., ElMessiry, A.: Blockchain framework for textile supply chain management. In: Chen, S., Wang, H., Zhang, L.-J. (eds.) ICBC 2018. LNCS, vol. 10974, pp. 213–227. Springer, Cham (2018). https://doi.org/10.1007/978-3-319-94478-4_15
14. Gardner, T.A., et al.: Transparency and sustainability in global commodity supply chains. World Dev. (2018)
15. He, S., Xing, C., Zhang, L.-J.: A business-oriented schema for blockchain network operation. In: Chen, S., Wang, H., Zhang, L.-J. (eds.) ICBC 2018. LNCS, vol. 10974, pp. 277–284. Springer, Cham (2018). https://doi.org/10.1007/978-3-319-94478-4_21
16. Hukkinen, T., Mattila, J., Smolander, K., Seppala, T., Goodden, T.: Skimping on gas-reducing ethereum transaction costs in a blockchain electricity market application. In: Proceedings of the 52nd Hawaii International Conference on System Sciences (2019)
17. IAF (2016). https://www.iafnet.com/industry/industry-statistics/
18. Jordan, A., Rasmussen, L.B.: The role of blockchain technology for transparency in the fashion supply chain (2018)
19. Liebau, D., Schueffel, P.: Crypto-currencies and ICOs: are they scams? An empirical study. An Empirical Study (2019). Accessed 23 Jan 2019
20. Linden, A.R.: An analysis of the fast fashion industry (2016)
21. Lu: Statistics: Global apparel market 2018–2022, January 2018. https://shenglufashion.com/2018/02/18/statistics-global-apparel-market-2018-2022/
22. Media, C.: In pursuit of transparency: the case for leveraging supply chain management platforms, August 2016. http://www.journal.faa-design.com/pdf/7-4-abed.pdf
23. Michael, J., Cohn, A., Butcher, J.R.: Blockchain technology. J. (2018)
24. Mol, A.P.: The future of transparency: power, pitfalls and promises. Global Environ. Polit. **10**(3), 132–143 (2010)
25. Polyakova, Y.: Estonian state's approach to cryptocurrency
26. Pratap: How is blockchain disrupting the supply chain industry, August 2018? https://hackernoon.com/how-is-blockchain-disrupting-the-supply-chain-industry-f3a1c599daef

27. Rogaway, P., Shrimpton, T.: Cryptographic hash-function basics: definitions, implications, and separations for preimage resistance, second-preimage resistance, and collision resistance. In: Roy, B., Meier, W. (eds.) FSE 2004. LNCS, vol. 3017, pp. 371–388. Springer, Heidelberg (2004). https://doi.org/10.1007/978-3-540-25937-4_24

28. Sadouskaya, K., et al.: Adoption of blockchain technologyin supply chain and logistics (2017)

29. Swan, M.: Blockchain: Blueprint for a New Economy. O'Reilly Media, Inc., Sebastopol (2015)

30. Tapscott, D., Tapscott, A.: Blockchain Revolution: How the Technology Behind Bitcoin Is Changing Money, Business, and the World. Penguin (2016)

31. Tapscott, D., Tapscott, A.: How blockchain will change organizations. MIT Sloan Manag. Rev. **58**(2), 10 (2017)

32. Wang, J., Li, L., He, Q., Yu, X., Liu, Z.: Research on the application of block chain in supply chain finance. DEStech Trans. Comput. Sci. Eng. (ICEITI) (2017)

33. Wright, A., De Filippi, P.: Decentralized blockchain technology and the rise of lex cryptographia (2015)

34. Zhang, Q., Novotny, P., Baset, S., Dillenberger, D., Barger, A., Manevich, Y.: LedgerGuard: improving blockchain ledger dependability. In: Chen, S., Wang, H., Zhang, L.-J. (eds.) ICBC 2018. LNCS, vol. 10974, pp. 251–258. Springer, Cham (2018). https://doi.org/10.1007/978-3-319-94478-4_18

Performance Benchmarking and Optimization for Blockchain Systems: A Survey

Rui Wang[1,2], Kejiang Ye[1(✉)], and Cheng-Zhong Xu[3]

[1] Shenzhen Institutes of Advanced Technology,
Chinese Academy of Sciences, Shenzhen 518055, China
{rui.wang2,kj.ye}@siat.ac.cn
[2] University of Chinese Academy of Sciences, Beijing 100049, China
[3] Faculty of Science and Technology,
University of Macau, Taipa, Macau, China
czxu@um.edu.mo

Abstract. Blockchain is a decentralized infrastructure widely used in emerging digital cryptocurrencies. With the fast development of blockchain technology, there are many new achievements in industry and academia. As a decentralized, shared and encrypted distributed ledger technology, blockchain has three distinctive features: decentralization, traceability, and non-tampering. Therefore, the blockchain technology has been used to implement transaction autonomy, save regulatory costs, and improve security. Its birth was even considered to be the fourth industrial revolution. However, the blockchain is still at an early stage of development, and has not been widely applied in practices. One of the main reason is the low performance issue. In order to better understand the state-of-art of the blockchain, we first introduce the architecture and consensus protocols of the current mainstream blockchain systems, then analyze some open source blockchain benchmarking tools, and summarize some blockchain systems optimization methods. Finally, we propose some suggestions for future development of blockchain systems.

Keywords: Blockchain · Protocol · Benchmark · Performance analysis · Performance optimization

1 Introduction

Blockchain, a kind of accounting technology that is jointly maintained by multiple parties, uses cryptography to ensure security during transmission and access process, and can achieve consistent data storage which is difficult to be tampered with. It is also known as distributed ledger technology. Blockchain was originally proposed by Nakamoto in 2008 [1]. Bitcoin is the most famous application of blockchain technology, but it is also the most controversial one, because Bitcoin has established a multi-billion dollars scale anonymous market which is not regulated by governments.

Currently, many applications are based on the trust in a centralized organization. The privacy and property security depend on third-party entities that may be cracked, tampered with, or stolen. Blockchain technology can establish a distributed and

© Springer Nature Switzerland AG 2019
J. Joshi et al. (Eds.): ICBC 2019, LNCS 11521, pp. 171–185, 2019.
https://doi.org/10.1007/978-3-030-23404-1_12

consistent representation of all past and current online behaviors and assets, and can be verified at any time after recording [2]. In the blockchain system, each party shares information and reaches an agreement with pre-defined rules. In order to prevent the consensus information from being tampered with, the system stores the data in units of blocks. The blocks form a chain data structure according to the chronological order and cryptographic algorithms. The record node is selected by the consensus mechanism, and the node determines the latest block. Other nodes participate in the verification, storage and maintenance of the latest block data. Once the data is confirmed, it is difficult to be deleted and changed, and only the authorization query operation can be performed.

With the recent development of blockchain technology, people begin to explore the feasibility of replacing existing distributed databases with blockchains. But the performance of blockchain should be well studied before replacing the existing technology. In this paper, we summarize and analyze the main factors affecting the performance of blockchain. We first introduce the architecture and consensus protocols of the current mainstream blockchain systems, then analyze some open source blockchain benchmarking tools, and summarize some blockchain systems optimization methods. Finally, we propose some suggestions for future developmentofblockchainsystems.

The rest of this paper is structured as follows. In Sect. 2, we describe the architecture of blockchain. In Sect. 3, we introduce the consensus protocols for blockchain. In Sect. 4, we introduce several open source performance benchmark tools for blockchain. In Sect. 5, we introduce some mainstream optimization methods for blockchain. Finally, we conclude the paper and give some views for the future development of blockchain systems in Sect. 6.

2   Architecture

There are many different implementations of blockchain systems, but there are some common components in terms of architecture. Figure 1 shows a reference architecture of blockchain systems. According to the white paper published by the CAICT [20], the architecture can be divided into 9 parts.

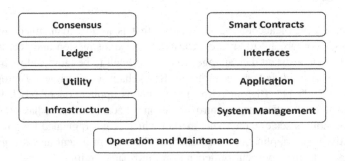

Fig. 1. Reference architecture of blockchain

The **Infrastructure layer** provides physical resources and drivers for the upper layer and is the basic part of the blockchain system. **The Utility layer** enables the recording, verification and dissemination of information in the blockchain system network. **The Ledger layer** is responsible for the information storage of the blockchain system, including collecting transaction data, generating data blocks, verifying the validity of the local data, and adding the verified blocks to the chain. **The Consensus layer** mainly includes the consensus algorithms and the consensus mechanisms, which enables highly distributed nodes to efficiently reach consensus on the validity of block data in the decentralized blockchain network. **The Smart Contract layer** contains scripts, algorithms, and smart contracts. The smart contract can automatically trigger execution when the constraints are satisfied, otherwise the contract can be automatically cancelled. **The System Management layer** is responsible for managing other parts of the blockchain architecture, including two functions: authority management and node management. **The Interface layer** is mainly used to complete the encapsulation of functional modules, and at the same time provide a relatively simple call method for the Application layer. **The application layer** of blockchain encapsulates various application scenarios and cases. The main function is to call the interface of the intelligent contract layer and deploy the blockchain applications such as Ethereum, EOS, and QTUM. **The Operation and Maintenance layer** is responsible for the daily operation and maintenance of the blockchain systems, including the log library, monitoring library, management library, and extension library. Under the unified architecture, blockchain platforms can be different according to their own needs and purposes. These differences can be reflected in the storage module, data model, data structure, development language, consensus protocol, etc. The performance of these blockchain systems can also be different.

3 Protocols

The consensus mechanism is the core part of blockchain system and is used to guarantee the blockchain security. The consensus mechanism mathematically allows thousands of nodes distributed around the world to agree on the creation of blocks. The consensus mechanism also includes an incentive mechanism to promote the efficient operation of blockchain system, which is the basis for building trust in blockchain. Different consensus mechanisms can also have different effects on the performance of blockchain. Table 1 gives a comparison of several mainstream consensus algorithms.

Table 1. Comparison of consensus algorithms

Consensus	Advantages	Disadvantages
PoW	• Safety and stability • Open and entirely decentralized	• Low performance • High power consumption
PoS	• Low power consumption • Open and entirely decentralized	• Complex implementation • Low security
PBFT	• High performance • Consensus finality • Excellent security	• Weak decentralized • Low fault tolerance

3.1 Proof of Work

Proof of Work (PoW) refers to a proof to confirm that a certain amount of work has been done. The PoW system (or protocol, function) is an economic response to denial of service attacks and other service abuse. It requires the attacker to perform a certain amount of operations, which means that it takes a certain amount of time. This concept was first proposed by Cynthia Dwork and Moni Naor in a paper published in 1993 [3]. The term PoW was actually proposed in 1999 by Markus Jakobsson and Ari Juels [4].

Bitcoin uses the PoW consensus. When generating blocks [24], the system allows all nodes to calculate a random number fairly. The node that first finds the random number is the producer of this block, and obtains the corresponding "Block Rewards". Since the function is a hash function, the way to calculate a random number is mathematically exhaustive. Due to the setting of the Merkel tree's root, the verification process of the solution of the hash function can also be implemented quickly. As a result, Bitcoin's PoW consensus threshold is low as no centralization authority is allowed, everyone can participate, and each participant does not need to be authenticated. At the same time, Satoshi Nakamoto solved the "SybilAttack" problem of the no threshold distributed system through the consensus of PoW. Attacks on the system require more than 50% of the computing power, and the system's security is strong. The advantages of the PoW consensus can be summarized as: the algorithm is simple and easy to implement, and the nodes are free to enter, and the degree of decentralization is high; Destroying the system requires a huge investment and the system is extremely safe [25]; The disadvantages of the PoW consensus can be summarized as: in order to ensure the degree of decentralization, the confirmation time of the block is difficult to shorten; No consensus finality, a checkpoint mechanism is needed to make up for the finality, but as the number of confirmations increases, the difficulty of reaching consensus increases exponentially. Due to these two aspects, in order to ensure safety, a transaction can be confirmed on the whole network after 6 new blocks are generated in Bitcoin system. Arthur Gervais et al. introduced a novel quantitative framework [7] to analyze the blockchain based on PoW and found that the existing PoWblockchain can achieve 60 transactions per second throughput while maintaining the security of the blockchain. Yonatan Sompolinsky et al. proposed a SPECTRE [8] protocol based on PoW. SPECTRE can run at a high speed of block creation, so it can quickly confirm transactions and is safe even under high throughput and fast confirmation time.

3.2 Proof of Stake

Proof of Stake (PoS), first proposed in PpCoin [5], is mainly used to solve the problem of resource waste in PoW [26, 27]. It is more intuitive to understand from the implementation algorithm formula of PoS. The formula is:

$$hash(block\_header) < target \times coinage \qquad (1)$$

$$coinage = number\ of\ coins \times remaining\ usage\ time\ of\ coins \qquad (2)$$

The calculation of the coinage is obtained by the number of coins multiplying the remaining usage time of coins, which means that the more coins you have, the easier it is to get the answer. Therefore, PoS solves the problem of resource waste in PoW. At the same time, PoS avoids deflation. The PoW-based cryptocurrency may lead to deflation due to various reasons such as user loss. The PoS-based cryptocurrency increases the currency at a certain annual interest rate, which can effectively avoid the occurrence of deflation and maintains stability. After Bitcoin, many new coins adopt the PoSconsensus. Many old coins also gradually replaced PoW with PoS.

However, the cryptocurrency of PoSconsensuscan only be issued through IPO, which leads to "a few people" (usually developers) getting a lot of cryptocurrency with very low cost. In the face of interests, it is difficult to guarantee that they will not sell in large quantities. And the cryptocurrency of PoSconsensus is not safe enough. In order to solve this problem, many blockchain platforms adopt the dual consensus of PoW + PoS, they use PoWconsensus to mine, and use PoS to maintain the network's stability. Or using the DPoSconsensusto enhance trust through community elections.

Aggelos Kiayias et al. proposed a PoS-based consensus "Ouroboros" [9]. Ouroboros is a chain-based PoS solution that randomly elects a node to produce a block. The probability of being selected is related to the share it has. The key is how to guarantee "randomness". The traditional PoS solution starts with the existing data on the chain, such as using the hash value of the previous block, and the timestamp of the previous block as the source of the random number, but these bring additional security risks. Since the information of the block itself is written by the node, and then the subsequent nodes are elected according to the block information, there is a risk of circular argumentation. Ouroboros introduced the concepts of "Coin-Tossing" and "VSS" to solve this problem. Ouroboros is the first PoS consensus whose security was mathematically verified. It not only gives the idea of PoS, but also presents a way to demonstrate this idea which can be extended to the proof of other consensus algorithms.

3.3   Practical Byzantine Fault Tolerance

PBFT is an abbreviation of Practical Byzantine Fault Tolerance. The algorithm was proposed by Miguel Castro and Barbara Liskov in 1999 [6]. The authors believe that the Byzantine fault-tolerant algorithm will become more important as more and more malicious attacks and software errors occur, and the failed nodes will behave arbitrarily. The early Byzantine fault-tolerant algorithm assumes the system is synchronized and the performance is low. The algorithm described in [6] is practical because it works in an asynchronous environment and improves response performance by more than an order of magnitude. PBFT consensus has high performance, but its fault tolerance rate is low. And due to the problem of node scalability, it is more suitable for closed node system. As each transcript node needs to synchronize with the consensus of other nodes in P2P, the performance of PBFT algorithm will decline rapidly with the increase of nodes, but it can have good performance in the case of fewer nodes and the probability of bifurcation is very low. Therefore, traditional consensus algorithms such as PBFT, PAXOS [39], RAFT [40] are preferred for permissioned chains and private chains which do not require a monetary system. PBFT can also be applied to the public chains if it can be combined with nodes like DPoS [38], and the Byzantine fault tolerance problem can be solved in an untrusted network [28]. The TPS (Transactions per Second) should also be much larger than the PoW.

Algorand is a cryptocurrency solution presented by Silvio Micali [10]. This scheme uses cryptography lottery algorithm to achieve the large-scale expansion of Byzantine consensus algorithm and can be applied to the public chain cryptocurrency system. Compared with traditional cryptocurrency consensus algorithms such as PoW and PoS, Algorand is more secure, almost non-forking and more efficient (each round of consensus is reached within 1 min). Algorand contains two main algorithms: (i) the cryptography lottery algorithm, which is used to ensure that the consensus committee members participating in the consensus each time are close to completely random; (ii) the BA* algorithm, which is run by consensus committee members to produce the blocks that should be packaged at that time. The BA* algorithm is divided into three stages: block generation, GC and BBA*. The stopping time of the algorithm is uncertain, but it is guaranteed to end in finite steps with high probability. Algorand adopts the VRF function and randomly determines the block generation and voter role, based on the balance proportion of the account. According to the simulated data, the TPS of bitcoin increased by 125 times after the PoW consensus was replaced by the Algorand consensus. Compared with DPoS + BFT, Algorand is more secure [29]. As long as more than 2/3 of the nodesare honest nodes, Algorand can guarantee the security of system.

4   Benchmarks

Blockchain benchmarks are needed to compare the performance of different blockchainsystems. Currently, there are two open source projects named Blockbench [11] and HyperledgerCaliper [12] that are very popular. Blockbench supportsEthereum [30], Parity [31], Quorum [32], Hyperledger [13], whileHyperledgerCaliper currently only supports Hyperledger's project, including: Hyperlegder Burrow, HyperledgerComposer, HyperledgerFabric, HyperledgerIroha, HyperledgerSawtooth. Table 2 compares the advantages and disadvantages between Blockbench and Caliper.

Table 2. Comparison between Blockbench and Caliper

	Advantages	Disadvantages
Blockbench	• Supports ethereum, hyperledger, parity and quorum • Supports to measure throughput, latency, scalability and fault tolerance • Easy to integrate private chains	• Constant workload • Unable to monitor resource utilization
Caliper	• User defined test module • Supports to measure throughput, latency, resource utilization • Easy to integrate private chains • Easy to configure	• Only for Hyperledger • Unable to analyze scalability and fault tolerance

4.1 Blockbench

TTA Dinh et al. developed a benchmarking framework, Blockbench, which is the first benchmark to examine and compare the performance of private blockchains. Since the performance of public blockchain has been widely studied, Blockbench focuses on the privateblockchain. The author abstracts the blockchain into four layers, i.e. consensus layer, data model layer, execution layer and application layer.

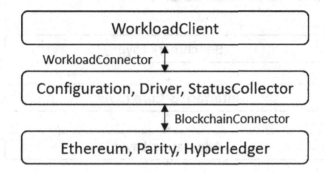

Fig. 2. Architecture of Blockbench

Blockbench evaluated the performance of back-end systems in four dimensionalities: throughput, latency, scalability, and fault tolerance (see Fig. 2). Blockbench has designed five macro benchmark workloads (i.e. key-value storage, OLTP (Smallbank), EtherId, Doubler, and WavesPresale) and four micro benchmark workloads (i.e. DoNothing, Analytics, IOHeavy, and CPUHeavy). Through these workloads, Blockbench compared three blockchain systems (i.e. Ethereum, Parity and Hyperledger) and drew two main conclusions: (i) the performance of blockchain system is limited, which is far lower than the most advanced database system (such as H-store); (ii) In the benchmark test, Hyperledger's performance is much better than Ethereum and Parity. But when Hyperledger has more than 16 nodes, it is no longer scalable.

4.2 Hyperledger Caliper

The Hyperledger community provides a tool called "Hyperledger Caliper" to test the performance of blockchain systems. The Caliper project was first launched by Huaweiin May 2017. Hyperledger Caliper is a blockchain benchmarking tool that allows to continuously track the performance characteristics of different blockchain systems. It allows users to test different blockchain solutions with predefined use cases, and get a set of performance test results. Currently supported blockchain solutions include: Hyperledger Burrow, Hyperledger Composer, Hyperledger Fabric, HyperledgerIroha, and HyperledgerSawtooth. Currently supported performance indicators include: Success rate, Transaction/Read throughput, Transaction/Read latency (minimum, maximum, average, and percentile), Resource consumption (CPU, Memory, Network IO, etc.).

Hyperledger caliper's architecture includes Adaptation Layer, Interface & Core Layer and Application Layer (see Fig. 3). The adaptive layer integrates the existing blockchain system into the caliper framework. The adapter uses the blockchain's SDK or RESful API to implement the "Caliper Blockchain NBIs". The interface & Core layer implements core functions and provides north bound interfaces for up-applications including: Blockchain operating interfaces, Resource Monitor, Performance Analyzer, and Report Generator. The application layer provides the tests implemented for typical blockchain scenarios.

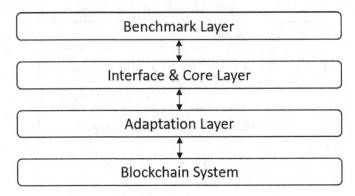

Fig. 3. Architecture of Hyperledger Caliper

Hyperledger Caliper's test cases are located in the "benchmark/" directory, written by the tester, and are configured into "test.rounds[.callback]" in the configuration file specified by "-c". Each test case contains a.js file (such as main.js, query.js) that defines the specific functions and two configuration files (config.json and fabric.json). "config. json" is a benchmark configuration file, which defines the parameters of the benchmark test, such as test rounds, workloads, etc.; "Fabric.json" is a blockchain configuration file that specifies the necessary information to interact with the SUT (system under test), i.e. the configuration of the blockchain network, such as the number of peers, the number of clients, and so on. These two configuration files are very important. Caliper is tested according to the settings of these two configuration files. We can also modify these two configuration files to simulate different test environments. If users want to write a new caliper benchmark, they need to write a smart contract for the system and write a test stream by using caliper NBI. Caliper provides a default benchmarking engine that is pluggable and configurable, making it easy to integrate new tests.

5   Optimization

Blockchain systems are subject to the famous "impossible triangle" of security, decentralization and scalability. In order to achieve the goal of decentralization, all nodes of the whole network jointly maintain data and jointly verify transactions. And the PoW consensus mechanism requires nodes to make worthless calculations to compete for accounting rights, which leads to a lot of redundant storage and calculation, but these are necessary for security. Therefore, how to improve the performance of blockchain systems has become an important issue. Currently, the mainstream methods to improve the performance and scalability of blockchain system are Sharding, Directed Acyclic Structure (DAG), Scalable consensus, Side-chain, On-chain and system optimization.

5.1 Sharding

Sharding is a traditional database technology that divides large data into smaller pieces that are smaller, faster, and easier to manage, and places the pieces on different servers for performance improvement and availability. Specific to the blockchain, the block is fragmented, each node only needs to verify the transactions in its own shard, there is no need to verify the transactions outside the shard, and it can be processed in parallel with other nodes on the network. A lot of verification work is completed in parallel with other nodes on the network. This will greatly reduce the redundancy calculation performed by the nodes, greatly improve the transaction processing speed of the public chain, and reduce the transaction cost [33].

Currently, there are three mainstream sharding strategies, which are divided into network sharding, transaction sharding, and state sharding. The most important challenge of sharding is to create shards. Developers need to develop a mechanism to determine which nodes can remain in the shard in a secure manner, thus avoiding attacks by people who control a large number of specific shards. The best way to defeat an attacker is to create randomness. By exploiting randomness, the network can randomly extracts nodes to form fragments. Such a random sampling approach prevents malicious nodes from overfilling individual fragments. The key to state sharding is to separate the entire storage so that different shards store different parts. Therefore, each node is only responsible for hosting its own fragmented data, rather than storing the complete blockchain state. If two popular accounts are handled by different shards, it may require frequent cross-fragmentation and state exchanges. Ensuring that cross-fragmentation communication does not exceed the performance gains of state sharding remains a problem worth studying. Restricting users to cross-fragmentation is a viable option, but it may limit the availability of the platform. State sharding can also cause data availability problems. The solution to this problem is to maintain an archive or perform a node backup, which helps the system to repair and recover those data that are not available.

Sharding also faces some problems in practice, such as defense against sybil attacks, how to create shards, how to assign nodes and tasks to shards, and how to determine the size of shards (the fewer the number of nodes in the shard, the faster the consensus will be reached, but if the number of nodes in the shard is too small, the security of the shard cannot be guaranteed), how to implement cross-shard trading (because cross-shard transactions require a lock protocol, the costs are high, and when the number of cross-shard transactions increases, it affects the throughput and profits of the entire network). Zilliqa [34, 35] is the first project to implement fragmentation technology, using network sharding and the consensus mechanism of PoW + PBFT. Zilliqa used 1400 nodes and 6 shards in the test and got a throughput of 2800 TPS.

5.2   Directed Acyclic Graph

The second method is to design the blockchain as a Directed Acyclic Graph (DAG) [21–23]. The Nxt community proposes to use DAG topology to store blocks and solve the problem of blockchain efficiency. In DAG, transaction packaging can be performed in parallel on different branch chains to improve the performance. In 2015, the concept of DAG-Chain [37] was proposed, and for the first time, the DAG network was upgraded from the block packaging dimension to the transaction-based level. After the transaction is initiated, the transaction will be broadcasted directly to the whole network, skipping the stage of packing the block, and the efficiency is theoretically improved. Table 3 gives a comparison of DAG-based blockchain and traditional blockchain.

Table 3. Comparison of DAG-based blockchain and traditional blockchain.

	Traditional blockchain	DAG-based blockchain
Element	Block	Transaction
Efficiency	Low	High
Scalability	Weak	Strong
Perpetrate	Hard	Harder
Transmission data	Few	Much
Shadow chain attack	Hard	Easy
Smart contract	Easy to develop	Difficult to develop

The DAG's verification method relies on the verification of the previous transaction by the latter transaction. This verification method enables the DAG to write many transactions asynchronously and concurrently, and finally forms a topology tree structure, which greatly improves the scalability. DAG also has some shortcomings: the transaction duration is uncontrollable, the amount of data transmitted by the network is greatly increased, the shadow chain attack, and the development of smart contracts is difficult.

5.3   Scalable Consensus Protocols

Another way to improve blockchain performance and scalability is to adopt a new scalable consensus protocol. The disadvantage of PoWconsensus is that mining causes to a large amount waste of resources, and the time for reaching consensus is relatively long, which is not suitable for commercial applications. PoSconsensus is an upgrade to PoW consensus. It reduces the difficulty of mining according to the proportion and time of each node in tokens, so as to increase the speed of finding random numbers. This shortens the time for reaching consensus to some extent, but still requires mining, which does not solve the pain point of commercial application in nature. DPoS (Delegated Proof of Stake) is a consensus algorithm based on voting elections. The holders select several representative nodes to operate the network, and use professional network servers to ensure the security and performance of the blockchain network.

PBFT Byzantine fault-tolerant algorithm has high performance, finality and good security, but the degree of decentralization is weak, the node system is closed, and the fault-tolerant rate is low. Ripple [36] consensus protocol completes the transaction in two stages: The first stage is to reach the consensus of the transaction set, and the second stage is to propose the newly generated blocks and finally form the consensual blocks. It achieves a faster consensus speed and ultimate stability by trusting each other within the subnetwork, but it can easily result in bifurcation, weak security, and very centralized. A large part of the accounting nodes are actually controlled by Ripple itself. From the above protocols, it can be seen that to improve the extensibility and performance of blockchain systems by changing the protocol is bound to lead to the weakening of the degree of decentralization.

Therefore, under the premise of achieving consistency, balancing efficiency, scalability and resources is the pain point of the consensus mechanism. Thus, the design of the best consensus mechanism also should consider local conditions. Trying to combine different consensus mechanisms is a new approach. By forming new consensus mechanisms (such as PoW + PoS, PoS + PBFT), we can foster their strengths and avoid the weaknesses.

5.4 Side-Chain

The concept of side-chain is to realize value transferring between main chain and side chain through bidirectional anchoring. The purpose of side-chain is to expand the function and performance of main chain. The essence of side-chain is to lock a part of bitcoin (or Ethereum) on the main chain first, and operate currency on the side chain, and then settle on the main chain after the end of the operation cycle. To solve the trust problem between blockchains, the transaction data verification between blockchains can be easily verified by notary mechanism or block header. In addition, the hash time lock can guarantee the atomicity of transactions, and all sub-transactions will either succeed or fail. Single custodian, alliance custodian and intelligent contract custodian can manage the locked assets when assets are transferred across the chains. Bitcoin's lightning network can also be considered A side-chain, as it allows users A and B not to trade directly on the main chain, but to trade frequently on the "side-chain" and then synchronize the final transaction results to the main chain. The code and data in the side-chain technology are independent, and do not increase the burden of the main chain in the transaction. It is a natural fragmentation mechanism. The side-chain increases the flexibility of the blockchain and can expand the application range and innovation dimension of the blockchain technology. Side-chain also has some disadvantages: the complexity of the side-chain is high and the creation of the side-chain requires enough miners, otherwise the safety cannot be guaranteed.

Plasma [14] is required for building side chains in Ethereum. Plasma consists of five core parts: (i) An incentive layer that can cost-effectively continue to calculate contracts; (ii) A tree-like arrangement of sub-chains that maximizes the low-cost efficiency and the net-settlement of transactions; (iii) A Map-Reduce computing framework that builds fraudulent proofs of state transitions in nested chains to be compatible with tree structures while reframing the state transitions to be highly scalable; (iv) A consensus mechanism based on the main chain; (v) A bitmap-UTXO commitment structure that ensures the correct state transition of the off-chain (main chain) trans-action while minimizing the cost of large-scale exits. Take Ethereum as an example, if the main chain of Ethereum itself is the root and trunk of a tree, then the side chain based on Plasma is the branch. These branches can handle most of these transactions, saving more space on the main chain and increasing processing speed. Each of the Plasma side chains is dominated by the main chain. Through smart contracts (see Fig. 4), these main chains control the participating nodes of the side chain, confirm activities and reach consensus. Therefore, this framework enables large-scale, secure and unified automated program execution. Plasma also has some problems: Plasma can only be used for asset trading; the main chain needs to be monitored all the time to ensure the assets are safe.

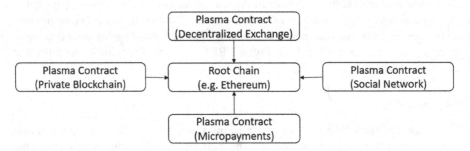

Fig. 4. Plasma is a series of smart contracts that allows multiple blockchains to be used in a single root blockchain.

5.5 On-Chain

Shehar Bano et al. introduced some ways to improve the scalability of blockchains through On-chain [15]. **Multiple Blocks per Leader**: Bitcoin-NG [17] shares the bitcoin trust model but decouples leader elections from transaction serialization. Unlike Bitcoin (the Bitcoin leader node can only propose one block to append the blockchain), Bitcoin-NG divides the time into epoch, and the leader node can unilaterally add more transactions to the blockchain during its epoch, until the new leader node is selected. **Collective Leaders**: This approach uses multiple leaders to quickly decide whether a block should be added to the blockchain. ByzCoin [18] replaces Bitcoin's probabilistic transactional consistency guarantee (with strong consistency) by extending Bitcoin-NG to achieve high transaction throughput. This has the advantage that the customer-submitted transactions are added to the blockchain and the blockchain is still non-forked, as all leaders immediately agree on block's validity. **Parallel Blockchain Extension**: In this approach, multiple leaders grow different parts of the blockchain in parallel (e.g., a transaction graph). Bitcoin has a linear process of growing blockchains: the miners try to solve the problem and the miners who find the answer add the next block. The framework proposed by Boyen, Carr, and Haines [19] parallelizes this process by abandoning the concepts of "blocks" and "chains" (supporting cross-validation of transactions, rather than linearity, can be understood as "block diagrams"). Each transaction confirms two transactions (its parents) and contains some payload (for example, cryptocurrency) and proof of work.

5.6   System Optimization

For Hyperledger Fabric, CPU resources are underutilized during the VSCC verification phase. The potential optimization is to process multiple transactions in the VSCC verification phase. Since the encryption operation is CPU intensive, some routine operations can be avoided by maintaining a deserialized identifier cache and its MSP information. Process transactions within and across channels can be improved to better utilize additional CPU power. CouchDB supports batch read/write operations without additional transaction semantics. Using bulk operations will reduce lock duration and improve performance. Using a database such as GoLevelDB and CouchDB without a snapshot isolation level results in locking the entire database during the approval and ledger update phases. Parth Thakkar et al. introduced three simple optimizations [16]:

- Adding a cache to the MSP (Membership Service Provider).
- Parallelizing VSCC (Validation System Chaincode) verification block.
- Batching read/write during MVCC (Multi-Version Concurrency Control) verification and submission.

By optimizing the combination, the overall performance of a single channel environment is increased by a factor of 16 (from 140 TPS to 2250 TPS).

6   Conclusion

In terms of architecture, there is a trend to integrate of public and consortium-blockchains. Consortiumblockchainis becoming more and more mature, while the development of private blockchainfaces some limitations. The consortiumblockchain is one of the most important ways to implement the blockchain, but it is not anonymous and has low scalability. Therefore, a hybrid architecture model of the public blockchain and the consortium blockchain is the future trend.

In terms of performance, there is an increasing demand for cross-chain and high performance. In order to improve the throughput of the blockchain systems, various high-performance solutions have been proposed. In terms of consensus, the consensus mechanism evolved from a single one to a mixed one. In terms of smart contracts, pluggability, ease of use, and security have become the focus of development. The richness of smart contract applications depends on the ability of the smart contract itself and its blockchain to support smart contract applications, while the development and execution efficiency of smart contracts depends on the development language and execution of the virtual machines. In the current ecosystem, the development language of smart contracts is not standardized. In order to adapt to smart contracts, it is necessary to create new contract languages or to add more formal specifications and verifications to existing languages. Smart contracts will enable fast startup times and high execution efficiency in a lightweight execution environment.

Although we are still in the early stages of blockchain development, we hope that in the future, we will be able to build a relatively decentralized, more collaborative, and more equitably distributed world through the blockchain technology.

Acknowledgment. This work is supported by China National Basic Research Program (973 Program, No. 2015CB352400), National Natural Science Foundation of China (No. 61572487, 61572488), Equipment Pre-Research Foundation (No. 61400020403), Shenzhen Basic Research Program (No. JCYJ20180302145731531), and Shenzhen Discipline Construction Project for Urban Computing and Data Intelligence.

References

1. Nakamoto, S.: Bitcoin: a peer-to-peer electronic cash system.https://bitcoin.org/bitcoin.pdf. Accessed 5 May 2019
2. Fisher, J., Sanchez, M.H.: Authentication and verification of digital data utilizing blockchain technology. U.S. Patent Application No. 15/083, 238 (2016)
3. Dwork, C., Naor, M.: Pricing via processing or combatting junk mail. In: Brickell, Ernest F. (ed.) CRYPTO 1992. LNCS, vol. 740, pp. 139–147. Springer, Heidelberg (1993). https://doi.org/10.1007/3-540-48071-4_10
4. Jakobsson, M., Juels, A.: Proofs of work and bread pudding protocols(extended abstract). In: Preneel, B. (ed.) Secure Information Networks. ITIFIP, vol. 23, pp. 258–272. Springer, Boston, MA (1999). https://doi.org/10.1007/978-0-387-35568-9_18
5. King, S., Nadal, S.: Ppcoin: Peer-to-Peer Crypto-Currency with Proof-of-Stake, vol.19. self-published paper (2012)
6. Castro, M., Liskov, B.: Practical Byzantine fault tolerance. OSDI **99**, 173–186 (1999)
7. Gervais, A., et al.: On the security and performance of proof of work blockchains. In: Proceedings of the 2016 ACM SIGSAC Conference on Computer and Communications security, pp. 3–16. ACM (2016)
8. Sompolinsky, Y., Lewenberg, Y., Zohar, A.: SPECTRE: a fast and scalable cryptocurrency protocol. IACR Cryptology ePrint Archive, pp. 1159 (2016)
9. Kiayias, A., Russell, A., David, B., Oliynykov, R.: Ouroboros: a provably secure proof-of-stake blockchain protocol. In: Katz, J., Shacham, H. (eds.) CRYPTO 2017. LNCS, vol. 10401, pp. 357–388. Springer, Cham (2017). https://doi.org/10.1007/978-3-319-63688-7_12
10. Gilad, Y., et al.: Algorand: Scaling byzantine agreements for cryptocurrencies. In: Proceedings of the 26th Symposium on Operating Systems Principles, pp. 51–68. ACM (2017)
11. Dinh, T.T.A., et al.: Blockbench: a framework for analyzing private blockchains. In: Proceedings of the 2017 ACM International Conference on Management of Data, pp. 1085–1100. ACM (2017)
12. Hyperledger Caliper Homepage. https://hyperledger.github.io/caliper/. Accessed 5 May 2019
13. Hyperledger Homepage. https://www.hyperledger.org/. Accessed 5 May 2019
14. Poon, J., Buterin, V.: Plasma: scalable autonomous smart contracts, pp. 1–47. White paper (2017)
15. Bano, S., Al-Bassam, M., Danezis, G.: The road to scalable blockchain designs. USENIX Secur. **42**(4), 31–36 (2017)

16. Thakkar, P., Nathan, S., Viswanathan, B.: Performance benchmarking and optimizing hyperledger fabric blockchain platform. In: 2018 IEEE 26th International Symposium on Modeling, Analysis, and Simulation of Computer and Telecommunication Systems (MASCOTS), pp. 264–276. IEEE (2018)
17. Eyal, I., et al.: Bitcoin-NG: A scalable blockchain protocol. In: 13th USENIX Symposium on Networked Systems Design and Implementation (NSDI), pp. 45–59 (2016)
18. Kogias, E.K., et al. Enhancing bitcoin security and performance with strong consistency via collective signing. In: 25th USENIX Security Symposium, USENIX Security 2016, pp. 279–296 (2016)
19. Boyen, X., Christopher, C., Haines, T.: Blockchain-free cryptocurrencies. A rational framework for truly decentralised fast transactions. IACR Cryptology ePrint Archive, pp. 871 (2016)
20. Blockchain Whitepaper. http://www.caict.ac.cn/kxyj/qwfb/bps/. Accessed 5 May 2019
21. IOTA Homepage. https://www.iota.org/. Accessed 5 May 2019
22. Churyumov, A.: Byteball: A decentralized system for storage and transfer of value. https://byteball.org/Byteball.Pdf(2016)
23. Baird, L.: The swirldshashgraph consensus algorithm: fair, fast, byzantine fault tolerance. Swirlds Tech Reports SWIRLDS-TR-2016-01, Technical Report (2016)
24. Wiki, Bitcoin. Block size limit controversy. https://en.bitcoin.it/wiki/Block_size_limit_controversy. Accessed 5 May 2019
25. Croman, K., et al.: On scaling decentralized blockchains. In: Clark, J., Meiklejohn, S., Ryan, Peter Y.A., Wallach, D., Brenner, M., Rohloff, K. (eds.) FC 2016. LNCS, vol. 9604, pp. 106–125. Springer, Heidelberg (2016). https://doi.org/10.1007/978-3-662-53357-4_8
26. Bentov, I., Gabizon, A., Mizrahi, A.: Cryptocurrencies without proof of work. In: Clark, J., Meiklejohn, S., Ryan, Peter Y.A., Wallach, D., Brenner, M., Rohloff, K. (eds.) FC 2016. LNCS, vol. 9604, pp. 142–157. Springer, Heidelberg (2016). https://doi.org/10.1007/978-3-662-53357-4_10
27. Bentov, I., et al.: Proof of activity: extending Bitcoin's proof of work via proof of stake. IACR Cryptology ePrint Archive, pp. 452 (2014)
28. Abd-El-Malek, M., et al.: Fault-scalable Byzantine fault-tolerant services. ACM SIGOPS Oper. Syst. Rev. 39(5), 59–74 (2005)
29. Pass, R., Shi, E.: Hybrid consensus: efficient consensus in the permissionless model. In: 31st International Symposium on Distributed Computing, DISC 2017. Schloss Dagstuhl-Leibniz-Zentrum fuer Informatik (2017)
30. Ethereum blockchain app platform. https://www.ethereum.org/. Accessed 5 May 2019
31. Parity. https://www.parity.io/. Accessed 5 May 2019
32. Chase, J.P.M.: A Permissioned Implementation of Ethereum (2018). https://github.com/jpmorganchase/quorum. Accessed 5 May 2019
33. Luu, L., et al.: A secure sharding protocol for open blockchains. In: Proceedings of the 2016 ACM SIGSAC Conference on Computer and Communications Security (CCS), pp. 17–30. ACM (2016)
34. Zilliqa. https://zilliqa.com/. Accessed 5 May 2019
35. ZILLIQA Team: The ZILLIQA Technical Whitepaper (2017)
36. Ripple. https://ripple.com/. Accessed 5 May 2019
37. Lerner, S.D.: Dagcoin: a cryptocurrency without blocks (2015). http://bitslog.wordpress.com/2015/09/11/dagcoin
38. Larimer, D.: Delegated proof-of-stake (DPoS). Bitshare whitepaper (2014)
39. Lamport, L.: Paxos made simple. ACM Sigact News 32(4), 18–25 (2001)
40. Ongaro, D., Ousterhout, J.: In search of an understandable consensus algorithm. In: 2014 USENIX Annual Technical Conference, USENIXATC 2014, pp. 305–319 (2014)

Developing a Vehicle Networking Platform Based on Blockchain Technology

Siu-Yeung Cho[1(✉)], Ningyuan Chen[1], and Xiuping Hua[2]

[1] Faculty of Science and Engineering, University of Nottingham Ningbo China,
Ningbo, China
david.cho@nottingham.edu.cn
[2] Nottingham University Business School China,
University of Nottingham Ningbo China, Ningbo, China

Abstract. Blockchain technology has been developing very rapidly through the entire world and is widely seen as one of the most disruptive forces in modern businesses. The applications of blockchain technology to the finance, insurance and automobile industries create extra values in innovation and motivation to the business. This paper is to describe the research and development work called *iCarChain* which is based on vehicle networking and blockchain technology, through distributed ledger, consensus mechanism, smart contract and other underlying architectures, using open and transparent value acquisition and an artificial intelligence based allocation algorithm to achieve value realization of data on vehicle and driving behavior. Each user (vehicle owner or driver) is referred to install an intelligent OBD device. The device captures the real-time data from vehicles to produce value identification. With such technology, the values of data acquisition and transparent can be transferred through the token carriers called *iCarToken* which is an incentive unit launched for users to contribute their behavior value, which is generated by blockchain and smart contract, and is gained through the value of contribution behavior.

Keywords: Blockchain technology · Vehicle networking · Driving behaviour · Artificial neural networks

1 Introduction

At present, the size of the car market in China is the first in the world, and the vehicle network industry is in the growth stage [1]. The potential market scale is huge. It is expected that in 2018, the market size of China's vehicle network industry will reach 310 billion yuan, and the market size will reach 401.4 billion yuan in 2021, and the annual average growth rate will be about 15.43% (Fig. 1). At the same time, the number of Chinese netizens also ranks first in the world. With the rapid popularization of smartphones, Chinese consumers have formed the habit of using the mobile Internet. It is expected that in 2018, the user size of the Internet industry in China will reach 15.37 million, and the user will reach 40.97 million users in 2021, with an annual growth rate of about 34.87% [2].

© Springer Nature Switzerland AG 2019
J. Joshi et al. (Eds.): ICBC 2019, LNCS 11521, pp. 186–201, 2019.
https://doi.org/10.1007/978-3-030-23404-1_13

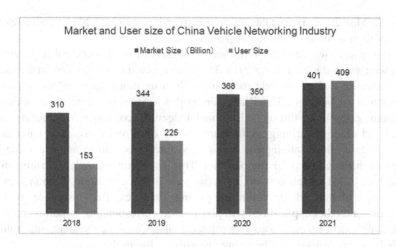

Fig. 1. Market and user size prediction of China's vehicle networking industry

Blockchain, as a general underlying distributed ledger technology that enables a variety of parties to co-create a permanent, unchangeable and transparent record of exchange and processing without relying on a central authority, accelerates penetrations from digital money to other fields and integrates with our real life. The application of future blockchain will be promoted by two camps. On the one hand, the IT camp starts from information sharing, establishes credit at low cost and gradually covers digital assets and other fields. On the other hand, the encrypted currency camp, starting from the currency, has gradually advanced to the asset and storage management, and spread to the application of credit collection and general information sharing, and the development ecology of the blockchain is gradually developing and enriching.

The application of blockchain in the field of vehicle networking began before 2015. So far, there have been a number of enterprises and institutions in the country and abroad that put into the application of the blockchain in the vehicle network, including reputable companies such as Alibaba, Tencent, Jingdong, IBM, Toyota and so on, and reputable research institutions such as Massachusetts Institute of Technology, Tsinghua University and so on. At the same time, start-ups are also emerging. These enterprises and organizations are exploring or initially implementing the application of blockchain in the field of vehicle networking [3].

With the improvement of the ecosystem, the vehicle networking will provide more diversified services and permeate into the Peer-to-Peer and the backup of car market, and cross-border cooperation and service innovation are becoming increasingly prominent. For example, Visa and DocuSign jointly launched a blockchain car rental project [4]. In October 2015, Visa launched a concept oriented demonstration project with DocuSign, a digital trading management company, using blockchain technology to record and keep car rental data to promote the digitalization of the car rental process. The project creates digital fingerprints for customers on the blockchain, registers on the chain, records transactions through distributed accounts, and updates the content of car rental agreements in real time, simplifying the tedious steps in the traditional car rental process. In May 2017, Toyota entered into partnership with MIT Media Lab to explore the application of blockchain in autopilot as well [5].

In this paper, we describe a research and development work called *iCarChain* project which was started at early 2018. This is an application of blockchain technology to the insurance and automobile industries will bring more values in innovation and motivation to the business. This iCarChain project is based on vehicle networking and blockchain technology, through distributed ledgering, consensus mechanism, smart contract and other underlying architectures, using open and transparent value acquisition and an artificial intelligence based allocation algorithm to achieve value realization of vehicle data and driving behavior. This iCarChain platform is mainly built on a blockchain based vehicle networking ecosystem. In this ecosystem, insurance and fee control applications, vehicle insurance pricing strategies, P2P insurance, used car transactions and other applications will play as their corresponding important roles. We expect that with the continuous extensions in iCarChain Eco-system, the value of iCarChain and its tokens will be rising and sustainable in the future.

2   Background of Blockchain Technology

2.1   Principle of Blockchain

A blockchain is essentially a distributed database of records or public ledger of all transactions or digital events that have been executed and shared among participating parties [6–8]. Each transaction in the public ledger is verified by consensus of a majority of the participants in the system. Once entered, information can never be erased. The blockchain contains a certain and verifiable record of every single transaction ever made. Blockchain technology is one of the core technologies that can promote the economic and financial transformation, displace trust-based intermediaries and disrupt traditional business models in various industries [9, 10]. It is stated as following the steam engine, electric power, information and Internet technology, and the most potential trigger of the fifth round of the wave of subversive industrial revolution.

The blockchain has two main parts: block and chain. The essence of it is to string up blocks, and then data are partitioned into continuous blocks, stored in computers. For example, the boxes in Fig. 2 below represent the names of cities in every country in each box.

Fig. 2. An example of the blockchain representing the names of cities

In addition, there is also a part called the hash value (hash) in each box, which is composed of a series of characters (such as "1hi515AHA5H"), whose values are determined by the inside information of each box. Because the production of the hash value is more complex in technology, it is easy to use the city name initials instead of the hash values of the track, such as the three cities of New York, Los Angeles and Chicago in the block of USA, then the hash value is "NYLAC" (as shown in Fig. 3), and each continuous blockchain contains the hash value of the previous block, temporarily, they are called "Prev Hash". This is a bit like a pointer to C language, linking blocks together. If someone wants to tamper with the block of USA, such as adding a city Boston, the new hash value of the block will become "NYLACB", but the "front hash value" stored in the next block UK is still "NYLAC", so it is not matched, and this chain is broken. The introduction of hash value is to prevent anyone from tampering to any block.

Fig. 3. An example of blockchain shows with the hash value.

The data of the blockchain are not only stored on a single computer. Those data are stored on those computers which are all accessible in the blockchain networks, and the data on each computer is the same. Every time you join the blockchain network, your computer will download all the blocks. If someone tamper with his version, the network will judge whether it is credible or not, and its strategy is to trust most people's version. In the blockchain network, except for data, all programs running on computers are the same. All computers execute the program together. This is different from most of the applications we see in our daily life, such as micro-blog, all of the data and processing programs are focused on micro-blog's servers, and the main functions of mobile APP, PC applications, web and other terminals are only used to interact with processing servers. But in blockchain network, it is centralized, and it relies on the computers of all the access blockchain network to execute their programs together. This means that every block in the blockchain network will stop to execute if every computer is shut down.

2.2 Merits in Blockchain

The original design of Blockchain was first presented in Nakamoto (2008), and at present Bitcoin is the most popular example that is intrinsically tied to blockchain technology [11]. It is also the most controversial one since too much hype is attached to it in spite of its limited business application; at the same time it helps to enable a multibillion-dollar global market of anonymous transactions without any governmental control [12, 13]. Hence it has to create and capture more value and deal with a number of regulatory issues involving national governments and financial institutions.

Although Blockchain has a humble origin as the primary infrastructure for the transfer of value in cryptocurrencies, Blockchain technology itself is non-controversial and has emerged as an attractive means for organizations to chronologically capture and store transactional data in an immutable fashion [14]. It has been successfully applied to both financial and non-financial world applications across the world. Some studies regard blockchain as a disruptive technology that will pave the way for novel business models centered on distributed consensus, while others state that much of the growth in the digital economy will be driven by the emergence of Decentralized Autonomous Organizations [14–16]. Marc Andreessen, the doyen of Silicon Valley's capitalists, listed the blockchain distributed consensus model as the most important invention since the Internet itself. Johann Palychata from BNP Paribas wrote in the Quintessence magazine that bitcoin's blockchain, the software that allows the digital currency to function should be considered as an invention like the steam or combustion engine that has the potential to transform the world of finance and beyond [17].

Current digital economy is based on the reliance on a certain trusted authority. All of our online transactions rely on trusting someone to tell us the truth—it can be an email service provider telling us that our email has been delivered; it can be a certification authority telling us that a certain digital certificate is trustworthy; or it can be a social network such as Facebook telling us that our posts regarding our life events have been shared only with our friends or it can be a bank telling us that our money has been delivered reliably to our dear ones in a remote country. The fact is that we live our lives precariously in the digital world by relying on a third entity for the security and privacy of our digital assets. The fact remains that these third party sources can be hacked, manipulated or compromised.

This is where the blockchain technology comes handy. It has the potential to revolutionize the digital world by enabling **a distributed consensus** where each and every online transaction, past and present, involving digital assets can be verified at any time in the future. It does this without compromising the privacy of the digital assets and parties involved. The advantages of Blockchain technology outweigh the regulatory issues and technical challenges. One key emerging use case of blockchain technology involves "*smart contracts*". Smart contracts are basically computer programs that can automatically execute the terms of a contract. When a preconfigured condition in a smart contract among participating entities is met then the parties involved in a contractual agreement can be automatically made payments as per the contract in a transparent manner.

3   Technical Aspects of the Proposed Platform

This paper addresses to propose a brand new Blockchain based intelligent platform for vehicular network or so-called Internet of Car (IoC), namely **iCarChain**. This iCarChain project focuses on developing an intelligent vehicular network based on blockchain technologies for smart city which allows the development of the distributed network of large-scale vehicles in a more efficient and effective way. Within the iCarChain, all the car data reflect the conditions of cars as well as the behavior of drivers which can be stored in the blockchain. They are not able to be erased or changed, and the evaluation of vehicles' conditions and drivers' behaviors are decentralized via an artificial intelligence methodology. Our goal is to build a decentralized Eco-system to benefit all the stakeholders in the car business. Different stakeholders ultimately benefit from our iCarChain platform as below:

- Every user is able to own their records of driving habits and car conditions.
- Every user is able to get incentives to reflect on their driving behaviors.
- Every car is able to be valued more openly and realistically.
- Every user as a driver is able to contribute to the community within the Eco-system.

Every other stakeholder in the community is able to build their own decentralized business applications within the Eco-system in a rather simple way.

3.1 Eco-System

iCarChain project aims at developing a decentralized, traceable, digitized and valued ecosystem for vehicular financing businesses, including, insurance, mortgage, vehicular trading and vehicular maintenance. A variety of types of digital assets related to the car can be registered, discovered, downloaded, transferred, distributed and consumed on iCarChain platform. Furthermore, token (called iCarToken) is introduced as incentive carrier for every stakeholder who contributes to the ecosystem. In the long term, as iCarChain further grows and expands in size, we expect that a mutually beneficial balance will be reached between owners/drivers and vehicular financing business holders in the first place of vehicular business industry to build and sustain a truly decentralized and distributed vehicular data distribution model. It will be the ultimate solution for vehicular data to be unshackled and valued from centralized platforms as well as for users to consume their vehicles at ease with fewer technological restrictions and more affordable expenses.

As indicated by Fig. 4, the Ecosystem built on iCarChain is to describe the roles and functions of each party involved in the business, and how this decentralized platform will facilitate the distribution of vehicular data incentivized by token economy (as shown in Fig. 4 as iCarChain 1.0). In the meanwhile, the ecosystem also presents how upstreaming industries like car insurance agencies and car mortgage institution will participate in the platform to develop the associated decentralized applications (as iCarChain 2.0). As one of the most inclusive ecosystem of vehicular financing business in history, iCarChain involves and incentivize everybody and every organization who can contributed to it.

- **Users**: Anyone who installs the intelligent device provided by us in his/her car to contribute their car data to the decentralized platform.
- **Platform**: The platform on which all iCarChain related businesses are built on.
- **iCarChain (private/consortium chain)**: It is a union chain to conduct data processing, public data ledgering and data transferring. It is accompanied with an open ledger system that authorized other stakeholders like car insurance agencies to access the data.

- **iCarToken (public chain)**: It is token issued on a public chain as incentive for the ecosystem and for users to contribute for their data as well as for their transaction of different financing products.

iCarChain Eco-system

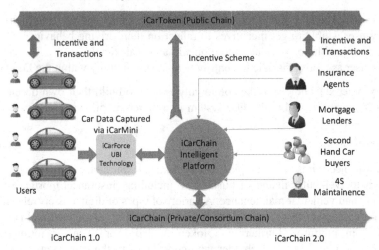

Fig. 4. The Eco-system of the proposed iCarChain platform

3.2   System Framework

The framework development of iCarChain platform will be in two stages:

- ICarChain 1.0

iCarChain 1.0 is to develop the framework of private blockchain for users based on the UTB technology that is made use of for the vehicle data collection. The data will then be cleaned and evaluated by the intelligent model for driving behavior scoring as well as deciding for the incentives to users. Those cleaned data with scores/incentives information are distributed to store via the blockchain.

The iCarChain 1.0 is built on a hierarchical architecture and is composed of three layers, which are from top to down as:

(1)   Exchange Layer;
(2)   Blockchain Layer;
(3)   Physical Data Modeling Layer

The framework is shown in Fig. 5 as below.

The major technological characteristics of these three layers are as below:

(1)   Exchange Layer:

The exchange layer supports exchange for users between iCarToken and other digital assets or the legal tender, and is an important bridge connecting different digital

Fig. 5. Architecture for iCarChain 1.0 framework.

assets. The value of iCarToken achieved is based on the incentive mechanism/scheme offered by the Blockchain layer to reward to users based on the driving behavior. The exchange layer also supports investors with iCarToken to participate in the market and offers trading with other digital assets provided by the exchange centers, such that allowing investors to gain from iCarToken exchange rate fluctuations.

(2) Blockchain Layer:

Based on the big data capturing daily over the automobile lifecycle, iCarChain platform has implemented blockchain layer in its system. In iCarChain 1.0, the blockchain layer is mainly to support the distributed data storage of the driving data and the evaluation results and incentives. The existing blockchain-based solutions have certain defects in practical application: in case of rapid data expansion, the length of a blockchain grows too fast, resulting in more time for consensus among all nodes and easily impairing the overall performance of the blockchain, which has become a pain point of bitcoin transactions. Therefore, the main chain of iCarChain platform will be implemented in a way that the records will be irreversible encrypted once a consensus has been reached between information in the platform and such information cannot be tempered and stored into a certain number of distributed nodes.

(3) Physical Data Modelling Layer:

The physical data modelling layer realizes the data capturing from vehicle UTB technology in which the iCarMini Intelligent Block is installed into each car for acquiring a variety of data points such as speed, engine starting time, engine stopping time, fuel level, and even trouble codes that are related to the car. iCarMini is a polled system, so data can only be returned as quickly as the time it takes to request it and return it. Moreover, a driver behavior model based on artificial neural network algorithm will be implemented into this layer in order to provide daily score of drivers for each vehicle. The score will be used to provide into the blockchain layer for issuing incentives via the decentralized incentive mechanism.

- ICarChain 2.0

iCarChain 2.0 is to develop for enhancing the framework of consortium blockchain for both users and other stakeholders on top of iCarChain 1.0. More advanced intelligent models for scoring to reward incentives to users will be developed. It is also the wallet that is more advanced for vehicle financing transactions in the future. The platform in version 2.0 will be allowed to build different decentralized APP (dAPP) for different application scenarios, such as vehicle insurance pricing strategies, P2P insurance, car transactions….etc.

The iCarChain2.0 is built on a hierarchical architecture of iCarChain 1.0 and is composed of four layers, which are from top to down as:

(1) Exchange Layer;
(2) App Layer
(3) Blockchain Layer;
(4) Physical Data Modeling Layer

The framework is shown in Fig. 6. The major technological characteristics of the Exchange layer, the Blockchain layer and the Physical Modeling layer are the same as the aforementioned in iCarChain 1.0, only the App Layer in iCarChain 2.0 is added as below.

Fig. 6. Architecture for iCarChain 2.0 framework.

(1) Exchange Layer: as the same in iCarChain 1.0
(2) App Layer:

The App Layer may consist of different kinds of decentralized applications with associated smart contracts to realize the business models of different application scenarios inside the iCarChain Eco-system. Different stakeholders in the community of Eco-system can contribute their APPs in order to benefit their own businesses. The examples of dAPP can be developed as below:

- UBI Car Insurance dAPP
- Vehicle financing dAPP
- P2P Car Rental dAPP
- Used-Car Transaction dAPP

With the continuous extension of the APP layer, increase of data volume, improvement of integrated validation and analysis capabilities, and rise in the value of application and business data, the value of iCarChain will also be rising.

(3) Blockchain Layer: as the same in iCarChain 1.0
(4) Physical Modeling Layer: as the same in iCarChain 1.0

3.3 Driving Behavior Modeling

Modeling human driving behavior and recognizing driver characteristics are used to relieve the driver's workload and improve the reliability and amenity of active vehicle safety systems, for example, collision detection and avoidance systems, and road departure warning systems. However, these active safety systems were designed based on an average of driver performance and rarely takes the individual driver's characteristics into consideration. Thus, even though average drivers can benefit from these systems, individual or special groups of drivers such as novices or the elderly might not be able to take advantage of them as effectively. If the characteristics of driver behavior can be accurately recognized and applied to dynamic vehicle systems, the vehicle might be personalized and therefore made intelligent. Recognizing driver characteristics is by itself not a simple task with the other requirements of active vehicle safety and comfort of vehicle adding to the complexity. Many active safety systems, such as the automatic braking system (ABS), lane departure warning system, acceleration slip regulation (ASR), and various human-friendly vehicle control systems like adaptive cruise control system, lane-keeping assistant system, have been invented over the years. Information about the driver's driving skill can be used to adapt vehicle control parameters to facilitate the specific driver's needs in terms of vehicle performance and active safety [18]. According to the different objectives set by the various tasks which can be regarded as these actions performed with the help of those functions such as steering, speed control, gear shifting, interpreting the road ahead, and navigation, driving skill can be defined in many ways [19, 20].

Human driving behavior is extremely complex and contains the human characteristics of nonlinearity, uncertainty, randomness, and so forth. Recently, a large number of articles about modeling driver behavior or recognizing driver model have been published [21] from the control point of view. Driver modeling is the simplification of the human driver with logical graphic and equation and so forth and can represent the basic characteristics of human driver like time delay and physical characteristics. Generally speaking, the goal of the driver model is to accurately imitate the driver while accomplishing some assigned tasks, which include two basic parts: longitudinal control (e.g., speed) and lateral control (e.g., steering angle).

In our blockchain based project, we build an artificial neural networks called Driver Neural Agent (DNA) for modeling driver behavior in order to evaluate the drivers' driving skills. Such evaluations can be used to allocate the incentives to the drivers for rewarding the contribution of their car data. The basic Driver Neural Agent (DNA) structure is as shown in Fig. 7 below.

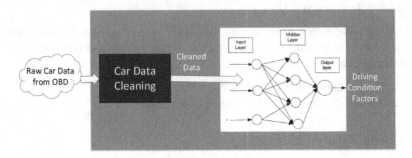

Fig. 7. The basic Driver Neural Agent (DNA) structure

In the proposed DNA model, the driver agent observes the car driving data from the On-Board Device (OBD) which is called iCarMini Intelligent Block and installed into the users' car. This iCarMini device is able to capture many different car data to reflect the condition of car shown in Fig. 8.

Car Data Capturing

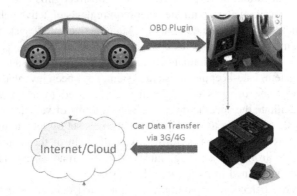

Fig. 8. The OBD device plugin to the car for car data capturing

In this project, we receive the raw data from the car via the Internet/Cloud every day and then we will do the pre-processing (such as data cleaning, data de-nosing ... etc.) to make all data are available for DNA modeling. After the pre-processing, the cleaned data are arranged with different daily attributes as shown in Table 1.

The selected attributes are acting as the input features of daily driving behavior for DNA modeling. The DNA model is basically applied by a classical Backpropagation (BP) neural network. As the term implies, BP is a propagation of error that requires an agent to have basic knowledge of the desired output action from the training data. A BP neural network calculates the error between the desired output and the actual BP output to propagate error back to each neuron in the network. Network weights between layers are updated by training until the error propagation becomes relatively small and weight values converge. The BP neural network follows learning rules associated with the gradient descent algorithm to gradually approximate driver behaviors from input data and target data from the training episodes. A BP neural network is composed of an input layer, hidden layer(s), and an output layer. Each layer has a certain number of neurons and each neuron has to be the same structure as in Fig. 9.

Table 1. Attributes for DNA modeling.

Over speed (f1)		Rapid acceleration (f2)		Rapid deceleration (f3)		Rapid turning (f4)			Tired condition (f5)		Weather condition (f6)
No. of times	Speed limit	No. of times	Current speed	No. of times	Current speed	No. of times	Current speed	Angle	Driving starting time	Driving ending time	Rain/snow

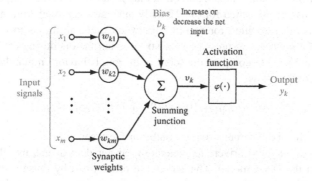

Fig. 9. A neuron structure of the BP neural network for this project.

A weighted sum of input and bias is calculated, and results are transformed by an activation function, where

$x_1.....x_m$: the input signals to such neuron, k;
$w_{k1}.....w_{km}$: the synaptic weights for such neuron;
b_k: bias for such neuron, k;
$\varphi(.)$: transfer function.
So the output y_k is:

$$y_k = \varphi \left(\sum_{m=1}^{M} x_m w_{km} + b_k \right)$$

(1)

A nonlinear sigmoid transfer function is used here. This function takes the value from the summation results and turns them into values between 0 and 1:

$$\varphi(z) = \frac{2}{1 + e^{-2z}} - 1 \tag{2}$$

The BP learning algorithm is divided into two phases: propagation and weight update. The propagation phase transfers training input forward through a neural network to generate the propagation's output activation. Then, BP error of output activation is transferred through a neural network using the target output to generate the gradient of all output and hidden neurons. In the weight update phase, output delta and input activation are multiplied to get the gradient of weight. Weights are brought in the opposite direction of the gradient by subtracting a ratio from the weight learning rate.

The agent receives the car condition information as the input layer of the neural network. Each input is weighted with an appropriate weight w. The sum of weighted inputs and bias becomes input to the transfer function in the hidden layer(s). The neurons of the last layer are the output of the transform function. In our model, the number of neurons at input, hidden and output layers are 12, 24 and 1 respectively. The 12 input neurons are presented for the 12 daily attributes captured from a car. The 24 hidden neurons are presented for mapping between input attributes to output factors and the 6 output neurons are presented for six different factors during driving in a day in which they are used to compute the score of driving behavior on that day, where the score can be computed as:

$$score = 25f_1 + 10f_2 + 10f_3 + 15f_4 + 35f_5 + 5f_6 \tag{3}$$

where $f_{1..6}$ are the six different driving condition factors.

Initially, we use 1000 drivers to generate their car data over a month as training dataset to train the DNA model. The scores are pre-defined by those training data by observations. After the model being trained, the scores can be generated to reflect the driver behaviors. Once the scores are confirmed and stored in the blockchain, those data feed to the model again to train up in every month. With this mechanism, we expect that the difficulty to achieve higher scores be increasing from time to time and hence the incentives are lesser to give from time to time. The implementation of our proposed DNA model are based on Python with Numpy import to develop and the codes will be opened source in GitHub.

4 System Performance and Discussion

We develop the application of this iCarChain project which is deployed in both Etherium blockchain network and Android platform. At the back-end of the system, both public chain and private chain have been setup in which the public chain is based on Etherium framework for token economy and the private chain is based on peer-to-peer transaction framework for car data ledgering. We have developed using 3 junction points as for data ledger at the moment and will be extended in future. The codes are written by Python and the sample codes are shown in Fig. 10. Data would be captured from each car in every 7 min after the engine was fired and the data would be processed every day during the mid-night period. The program is divided by two portions in which the first portion is for processing of car data. Data requesting would be executed to capture the raw data from the data API and then the raw data would be processed for driving behavior modeling as shown in Fig. 10a. The second portion is processed as blockchain for car data processing which is acting as a dictionary as shown in Fig. 10b. These dictionaries of each car in everyday would be processed as a list for the information to be stored in a block and a new lock would be generated with block height, timestamp, block information and previous hash value as shown in the code in Fig. 10c. The processing would be repeated in order to create the blockchain system for car data.

Meanwhile, driving behaviors are evaluated for every day and recorded into the private blockchain. Figure 11 shows screenshots of the system displaying the driving scores to reflect the driving behaviors every day at our developed platform. It is shown that the system would provide the scores for every driving route and sum up a score for the driving behavior every day. The score would be used to compute the incentive to reward back to the driver in order to reflect the driver's driving behavior. The incentive would be acted as the token called iCarToken (symbol as IIO) which would be deposited into the driver' wallet created by our system. Therefore, every car user has his own wallet to be bundled with the OBD device corresponding to the car data capture. The incentive reward mechanism would be integrated as a smart contract running under the Etherium blockchain network. The parameters for incentive reward is subjected to the score of driving behavior as well as the computational power of the OBD and the rate of incentive which is a variable calculated by the total number of tokens in the pool and the increasing number of users. The rate of incentive reward is decayed in every day if the total number of tokens in the pool decrease or the number of users increase.

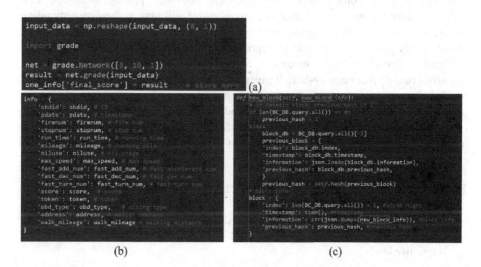

(a)

(b)

(c)

Fig. 10. Sample codes of car blockchain. (a) Data requesting and raw data process. (b) Blockchain for car data processing. (c) Block generation.

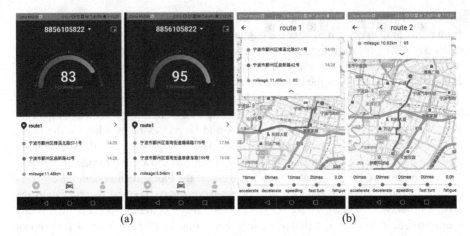

(a)   (b)

Fig. 11. Screenshots of the system displaying the driving scores to reflect the driving behaviors every day. (a) Average scores of driving behavior in every day; (b) Scores and driving behavior factors for every driving route.

5 Conclusion and Future Developments

This paper describes a novel blockchain application that is based on vehicle networking and blockchain technology, through distributed ledgering, consensus mechanism, smart contract and other underlying architectures, using open and transparent value acquisition and an artificial intelligence based allocation algorithm to achieve value realization of vehicle data and driving behavior. With this developed platform built, we are able to establish a blockchain based vehicle networking ecosystem. In this ecosystem, insurance and fee control applications, vehicle insurance pricing strategies, P2P insurance, used car transactions and other applications will play as their corresponding important roles. The development will be further extended to encourage, support, invest in this project's ecological enterprises and applications, and encourage global application developers and enterprises related to insurance, car rental and other industries based on our eco-system. It gives full play to the advantages of our improved blockchain system, improves the application system, and innovates to deal with industry pain points. It also promotes the steady expansion and vigorous development of the proposed ecosystem. The support of different industries related enterprises to access and use all kinds of applications under the ecosystem are encouraged.

References

1. https://www.statista.com/topics/1487/automotive-industry/
2. https://www.giiresearch.com/report/rinc298457-china-automotive-distribution-industry-automotive.html

3. Sharma, P.K., Moon, S.Y. Park, J.H.: Block-VN: a distributed blockchain based vehicular network architecture in smart city. J. Inf. Process. Syst. **13**(1), 184–195 (2017). (https://doi.org/10.3745/JIPS.03.0065)
4. https://www.rtinsights.com/blockchain-pilot-smart-contracts-docusign-visa/
5. http://corporatenews.pressroom.toyota.com/releases/toyota+research+institute+explores +blockchain+technology.htm
6. Crosby, M., Nachiappan, P.P., Verma, S., Kalyanaraman, V.: BlockChain technology: beyond bitcoin. Appl. Innov. Rev. **2**, 71 (2016)
7. Iansiti, M., Lakhani, K.R.: The truth about blockchain. Harvard Bus. Rev. **95**(1), 118–127 (2017)
8. Lewis, A.: A gentle introduction to blockchain technology. Gentle introduction reference papers™. Digital Currency Insights (2015)
9. Guo, Y., Liang, C.: Blockchain application and outlook in the banking industry. Finan. Innov. (2016). https://doi.org/10.1186/s40854-016-0034-9
10. Tapscott, D., Tapscott, A.: Blockchain Revolution: How the Technology Behind Bitcoin Is Changing Money, Business, and the World. Penguin, New York (2016)
11. Nakamoto, S.: Bitcoin: a peer-to-peer electronic cash system (2008). https://bitcoin.org/bitcoin.pdf
12. Papadopoulos, G.: Blockchain and digital payments: an institutionalist analysis of cryptocurrencies. In: Chuen, D.L.K. (ed.) Handbook of Digital Currency: Bitcoin, Innovation, Financial Instruments, and Big Data, pp. 153–172. Elsevier, London (2015)
13. Walker, M.: Blockchain and bitcoin: in search of a critique. LSE Bus. Rev. (2017). http://eprints.lse.ac.uk/85309/1/businessreview-2017-10-30-blockchain-and-bitcoin-in-search-of-a.pdf
14. Chong, A., Lim, E., Hua, X., Zheng, S., Tan, C.-W: Business on chain: a comparative study of five blockchain-inspired business models. J. Assoc. Inf. Syst. Forthcoming (2019)
15. Crosby, M., Pattanayak, P., Verma, S., Kalyanaraman, V.: Blockchain technology: beyond bitcoin. Appl. Innov. Rev. (2016). https://j2-capital.com/wp-content/uploads/2017/11/AIR-2016-Blockchain.pdf
16. Beck, R., Müller-Bloch, C., King, J.L.: Governance in the blockchain economy: a framework and research agenda. J. Assoc. Inf. Syst. **19**(10), 1020–1034 (2018)
17. https://www.asiaasset.com/news/BNPSS-gte_nim3_final_DM2202.aspx
18. Zhang, Y., Lin, W.C., Chin, Y.-K.S.: A pattern-recognition approach for driving skill characterization. IEEE Trans. Intell. Transp. Syst. **11**(4), 905–916 (2010)
19. Ers´eus, A.: Driver-vehicle interaction, identification, characterization and modeling of path tracking skill Ph.D. Thesis, Royal Institute of Technology (KTH), Stockholm, Sweden (2010)
20. George, J.A.: Understanding Driving: Applying Cognitive Psychology to a Complex Everyday Task. Psychology Press (2000)
21. Tokutake, H., Sugimoto, Y., Shirakata, T.: Real-time identification method of driver model with steering manipulation. Veh. Syst. Dyn. **51**(1), 109–121 (2013)

Decentralized Identity Authentication with Trust Distributed in Blockchain Backbone

Jiahe Wang$^{(\boxtimes)}$, Songjie Wei, and Haozhe Liu

School of Computer Science and Engineering,
Nanjing University of Science and Technology, Nanjing 210094, China
{jhwang, swei, 117106021958}@njust.edu.cn

Abstract. To overcome the difficulties in the traditional password-based identity authentication procedure with high security risk and complexity, and to avoid the privacy leaking problems arising from a series of new techniques such as using biometrics as key, this paper proposes a universal solution for decentralized identity authentication by block chain integrated with a trusted execution environment, through a separate hardware to establish a secure area, enabling identity anonymity and avoiding feature disclosure. Smart contract and consensus mechanism are adopted for building trusted identity nodes between decentralized nodes by constructing a traceable identity data structure in blockchain. We conduct formal theoretical and empirical evaluations to show that the proposed can realize user identity registration, cross-platform authentication, and guarantee security in the whole procedure with efficiency and reliability.

Keywords: Identity authentication · Blockchain · TEE · Privacy management

1 Introduction

With the rapid development of the Internet, people are increasingly dependent on the reliability of cyberspace. User behaviors expend from the offline social interactions to the online social network, resulting in more information exchange and interaction in Internet. However, it also faces security problems of potential threats such as entity identification, role authentication and access authorization to resources [1]. From a national governance perspective, recognition of network identity authentication and behavior traceability is instrumental to the construction of a modern national governance system. From a perspective of social development, establishing network of trusted identity is the premise and basis for people to enjoy various information services.

This paper designs and evaluates a universal solution to decentralized identity authentication intrusted execution environments, abbreviated as TEE. The trusted authentication procedure isolates an independent hardware environment on the end side to establish a security zone, and the hardware itself is difficult to break through. In addition, the security zone to the server is authenticated through blockchain, ensuring a credible secure channel between the trusted security zone to the remote server. The solution proposed constructs a traceable identity information data structure of

© Springer Nature Switzerland AG 2019
J. Joshi et al. (Eds.): ICBC 2019, LNCS 11521, pp. 202–210, 2019.
https://doi.org/10.1007/978-3-030-23404-1_14

blockchain through transparent and trusted rules in a peer-to-peer network environment, which has the advantages of decentralization, tamper resistance and high reliability. It effectively solves the problems of key management, creditability, security in identity authentication, and also realizes trust establishment between decentralized nodes, providing credibility and transparency for identity authentication.

2 Related Work

Trusted identity authentication technology, is the important guarantee for the construction of trusted network identity [2], designed to achieve the unification of online and offline identity. Presently, research on it falls into three categories, namely identity authentication based on identity secret, trust object and biometric identification [3]. According to the mode, it is also divided into static password, dynamic password and digital signature, etc. [4]. In order to achieve higher security to solve identity management difficulties of entities, identity authentication technology are constantly being innovated by scholars. Biometric identity recognition is widely used because of its uniqueness and non-replicability, Bailey et al. [5] proposed the identification and authentication technology of multi-modal biometric fusion, which greatly improved the recognition rate. Yafei et al. [6] proposed a fingerprint identification scheme for effectively protecting privacy through cloud systems in view of the lack of efficiency and privacy leakage of biometric data systems. Aiming at the security risks in the operating system layer-based identity authentication model, Jin [7] proposed a credential firmware-based identity authentication model, which can complete identity authentication before the OS starts and executes.

However, identity authentication is a process of establishing trust between entities. Existing technologies usually use the authoritative attributes of third parties to confirm user identity through user knowledge, ownership or biometrics, but the visibility and security of the third platform is also limited, thence trust between distributed authentication nodes and users is an urgent problem to be solved.

3 Technical Principle

3.1 Blockchain Technology

The backbone of the proposed system is an implementation of a decentralized identity authentication database, or blockchain. By constructing block application mode, we can make up for the shortcomings of traditional application mode, forming a complete solution based on blockchain technology, asymmetric encryption technology, identity authentication service and trusted hardware environment. The trusted identity authentication technology mainly utilizes the characteristics of one-way encryption, decentralization, non-tampering, distributed consensus of smart contract, according to distributed network protocol, distributed consensus algorithm and related framework technology [8], ultimately constructs a decentralized application program with distributed credibility.

3.2 Trusted Hardware Technology

The designed trusted execution environment or TEE, is a combined solution including multiple hardware, software and communication protocols, with five parts [9].

- *Offline physical hardware*, used to store and execute offline software and store private keys. It provides a user interactive interface as well as hardware equipment for data transfer with the networked hardware.
- *Offline software*, aiming to receive signature commands, sign transactions and send the signed transaction to the networked software.
- *Networked hardware*, which is a smartphone connected to offline hardware, with hardware devices for data transfer with offline hardware, mainly storing and executing networked software.
- *Networked software*, whose function is to send payment instructions to offline software, receive the signed transaction from the offline software, and broadcast it to the Bitcoin network.
- *Communication protocol*, representing the data exchange protocol for offline software and network software.

3.3 Technical Architecture

The architecture of the identity authentication proposed in this paper is as shown in Fig. 1. To be specific, the TEE hardware environment implements a security zone to ensure authentication between the client and blockchain server. Moreover, the trusted secure channel can recognize the storage and identity authentication capability based on blockchain, and fix the information and data security problems caused by the traditional centralized approach.

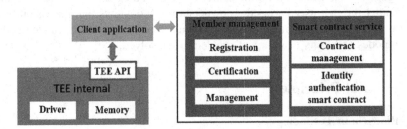

Fig. 1. Architecture of the distributed authentication system

4 Identity Authentication

4.1 System Architecture and Model

This section describes the model and system architecture of the decentralized authentication system and elaborates the authority authentication procedure with privacy protection. The authority identity authentication system of the solution is composed of a user (U_m) and a trusted hardware, an authentication server (S), and the blockchain network nodes, as shown in Fig. 2.

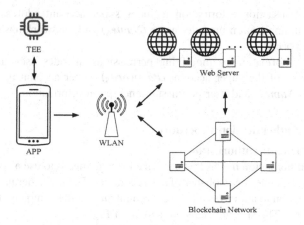

Fig. 2. Authentication procedures

1. User (U_m), providing user address (ID_m), public key $(PubKey_m)$ and signature information $(Signed_m)$.
2. Trusted hardware, outputting ID_m and $PubKey_m$, generating $Signed_m$.
3. Authentication server, using $PubKey_m$ to verify $Signed_m$ for authorization of logging in, and modifying the permissions of U_m.
4. Authentication nodes of blockchain, whose functions as follows:

One is initiating user identity registration and modifying permission transactions through smart contract. The other is verifying the initiated identity registration and modified permission transactions, and packaging multiple transactions into blocks and passing them into blockchain through a consensus mechanism.

4.2 Transaction Information

At the beginning of the smart contract phase, a contract creator defines the identity, permissions and capabilities of various roles, then saves them in the contract. The contents of the smart contract are also saved in blockchain. In addition, as a contract function, there is a judge of whether the caller of function conforms to the defined authority. In the contract function, after account is registered, it is required to enter a password, and the contract saves the hash of the password. When an user account calls a contract, the account needs to compare the entered password with the saved hash value. If the comparison is consistent, the function can continue as approved.

We call smart contract by sending transactions, and the transactions are mainly divided into registered transactions, authorized transactions, and modified rights transactions. The three transactions' information is depicted with details as follows.

- Registered transaction information includes address (ID_m) and user public key $(Pubkey_m)$.

- Authorized transaction information includes super account address $(SuperID_S)$, super account application provider name $(Name_S)$ and password hash of the super account $(Password_S)$.
- Transaction information of modifying permissions includes user address (ID_m), password hash of the super account $(Password_S)$, super account application provider name $(Name_S)$ and user permission encryption information.

4.3   Identity Authentication Procedure

4.3.1   Management Authorization

Management authorization means that a service manager needs to use a specific address to send an application to the publisher of smart contract. The publisher uses his account to issue a transaction to authorize the super account and set the company information of the super account. The specific steps are shown in Fig. 3.

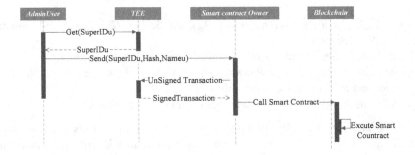

Fig. 3. Management authorization procedure

(a) The application provider obtains the public key through trusted hardware and uses the hash function to obtain the password hash value.

(b) The application service provider sends an application to the contract issuer to submit the super account address, password hash value and the third-party application information.

(c) The contract issuer sends a contract transaction to modify the information about the super account in the contract.

(d) The nodes execute the contract function, verify the sender's account belonging to publisher, and register the application where the super account is located.

4.3.2   User Registration and Permission Modification

For the first time, user registration is required. The specific registration procedure is shown as follows:

(a) Users get their own public key and other identity-related information through trusted hardware.

(b) A user sends a transaction message to blockchain and uses the smart contract to store the identity information.

Moreover, permission modification is the permission change of a user in the access application, and the authentication server needs to modify the user permission information saved in blockchain.

(a) The authentication server uses the super account address to send the modified permission transaction to blockchain nodes.
(b) The node executes the contract function, verifies the permission to send the transaction account, and modifies the contract status, finally subsequently modifies the account permissions.

4.3.3 Login Authentication

Login authentication refers that the user needs to confirm to the authentication server when logging into registered application, the specific steps are as shown in Fig 4.

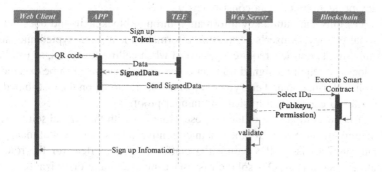

Fig. 4. Login authorization procedure

(a) Firstly, a user selects an application to log in, then the application will display a QR code for the user to scan. The QR code contains information such as a character string that needs to be signed by the user.
(b) When APP reads the information in the QR code, it sends a command to the trusted hardware to request the signature, and the trusted hardware returns the signature result.
(c) The APP obtains the signature result, then sends the relevant information to the authentication server. After receiving the signature information, the authentication server reads the user's public key and authority information from blockchain, through the public key to verify the signature.
(d) The web page is responds according to the permission information, and the user completes login.

5 Safety and Efficiency Analysis

- Preventing replay attacks

When sending a transaction of registering or modifying permissions, the nonce value of the transaction sent at the same address will increase in turn, and blockchain nodes will not accept transactions with repeated nonce value. If logging in, the random message will be signed each time, and the message will be recorded in the server. Sending duplicate signature information cannot be verified by the server.

- Preventing man-in-the-middle attacks

Two-way authentication is considered between blockchain-synchronized communication protocols, and all data propagated uses an asymmetric encryption algorithm. Even if an attacker can intercept the information, it cannot tamper with and decrypt the information itself.

- Privacy protection and data consistency

A user stores only the public key information through blockchain and does not reveal any personal privacy. A user's permission information is also encrypted and stored in blockchain. Smart contracts require a password when calling functions, so even a local call that does not require a signed transaction requires a password to be executed. The user's public information and encrypted information are stored on the distributed ledger of blockchain to ensure data trusted and tamper-proof.

Table 1 is the comparison of the proposed solution with the typical solutions in the area of identity management of blockchain currently. In terms of account management, Uport and ShoCard issue IDs within the platform or supporters for the role of the participating system [10]. Our solution is user-centric and any organization can issue IDs. As for scope of identity, ShoCard can only be used in the corresponding ecosystem. Ours is divided into on-chain and off-chain, through smart contract and trusted hardware, the identity on chain is bound to the public-private key pair off-chain, achieving the expansion of the ecosystem. About data storage, IDcard, Uport and ShoCard store all data in IPFS, and existing a risk of leakage. Our proposed solution stores privacy data in the terminal, and TEE ensures the security of information.

Table 1. Comparison of identity management based on blockchain

Comparison item	IDhub	Uport	ShoCard	Ours
ID issuer	×	√	√	×
User-centric	√	√	×	√
Identity in the ecosystem	√	√	×	√
Data storage hardware	×	×	×	√

- Time Efficiency

In order to complete the time consumption test on identity registration, login request and permission modification, we set up an authentication server and multiple blockchain nodes in the LAN. Both registration and permission modification procedure modify data on blockchain by sending a transaction and calling the smart contract.

Therefore, the test is performed to determine the time consumed for the nodes to package transactions into each block. The experimental result is shown in Fig. 5. The statistical result in the figures are time consumption of 100 transactions. Importantly, time consumption mainly depends on block generation efficiency of network, we chose GO-ETHEREUM to build an alliance chain for test, which takes between 10 s and 30 s, and the average time is about 20 s.

In addition, the time consumption of login request is mainly the time when the web page jumps after the QR code is successfully scanned. As can be seen from Fig. 5, time consumption that a web page successfully logs in fluctuates between 1 and 3 s, and the average time is about 2 s. All above test results are based on the fact that the network in the LAN is in a good condition. The whole system performs well during the experiment, and all procedures cost short time and could meet the security and feasibility of distributed authentication, possessing the ability of decentralized identity-based encryption authentication.

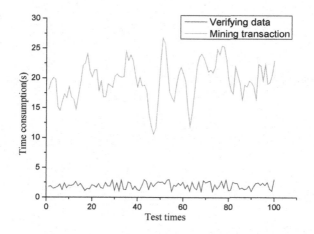

Fig. 5. Mining transaction and verifying data time consumption

Acknowledgments. This material is based upon work supported by the NSFC fund No. 61472189, CERNET Innovation Project No. NGII20180103, and Postgraduate Research & Practice Innovation Program of Jiangsu Province No. KYCX18_0484. Opinions expressed are those of the authors and do not necessarily reflect the views of the sponsors.

References

1. Nasir, A., Arshah, R.A.: Information security culture dimensions in information security policy compliance study: a review. Adv. Sci. Lett. **24**(2), 943–946 (2018)
2. Lind, J., Eyal, I., Kelbert, F., et al.: Teechain: scalable blockchain payments using trusted execution environments (2017). arXiv preprint arXiv:1707.05454
3. Ren-Ji, H., Xiao-Ping, W.U., Hong-Cheng, L.I.: Identity authentication scheme based on identity-based encryption. Chin. J. Netw. Inf. Secur. **2**(6), 32–37 (2016)

4. Zhang, L., Ning, H.Y., Du, Y.Y., et al.: A new identity authentication scheme of single sign on for multi-database. In: IEEE International Conference on Software Engineering and Service Science. IEEE (2017)
5. Bailey, K.O., Okolica, J.S., Peterson, G.L.: User identification and authentication using multi-modal behavioral biometrics. Comput. Secur. **43**, 77–89 (2014)
6. Yafei, T., Yunyong, Z., Ni, Z.: Cloud security certification technology based on fingerprint recognition. Telecommun. Sci. **31**(8), 2015211 (2015)
7. Jin, Z.: Research on remote identity authentication model based on trusted firmware. Netw. Secur. Technol. Appl. **2018**(09), 30–31
8. Marc, P.: Blockchain Technology: Principles and Applications. Social Science Electronic Publishing (2015)
9. Lu, D., Ma, J., Sun, C., et al.: Building a secure scheme for a trusted hardware sharing environment. IEEE Access **5**, 20260–20271 (2017)
10. Moyano, J.P., Ross, O.: KYC optimization using distributed ledger technology. Bus. Inf. Syst. Eng. **59**(6), 411–423 (2017)

Performance Evaluation of Hyperledger Fabric with Malicious Behavior

Shuo Wang[(✉)]

Tsinghua University, Beijing, China
wangs16@mails.tsinghua.edu.cn

Abstract. Hyperledger Fabric is a widely-used permissioned blockchain platform for enterprise consortium applications. It adopts Practical Byzantine Fault Tolerance (PBFT) algorithm as the consensus protocol in its version 0.6. Faulty replicas could intentionally delay messages, be not responsive and send inconsistent messages to different replicas. Faulty clients and replicas could also launch denial-of-service attack to make resources unavailable. The malicious behavior significantly undermines the system. However, the existing performance evaluation for Fabric is accomplished in a fault-free environment without malicious behaviors. In this paper, we analyze the impact of malicious behavior, design malicious behavior patterns and test the blockchain performance on Hyperledger Fabric.

Keywords: Hyperledger Fabric · PBFT · Consensus · Permissioned blockchain

1 Introduction

Blockchain is an open, distributed ledger that can record transactions between parties in a trustable and immutable way. The key contribution of blockchain is achieving consensus in a decentralized environment among replicas from different parties who cannot fully trust each other. With this advanced property, blockchain has been widely used as the underlying data structure and consensus mechanism of bitcoin [1], alternative cryptocurrencies (altcoins) and decentralized application platforms such as Ethereum [2] and Hyperledger [3].

Hyperledger Fabric is an enterprise-grade permissioned blockchain platform for distributed applications among company consortiums. As its latest version has not adopted a fault-tolerant consensus protocol, we now focus on its version 0.6 [4], which adopts PBFT [5] as the consensus protocol. There are some works on performance evaluation benchmark for Hyperledger Fabric. However, they evaluate in a non-faulty environment. For permissionless blockchains such as bitcoin and Ethereum, malicious behaviors and attacks happen frequently because their crytocurrencies and applications has great value in the real world. Attacks will also be targeted when more and more business applications are run in permissioned blockchain platforms.

© Springer Nature Switzerland AG 2019
J. Joshi et al. (Eds.): ICBC 2019, LNCS 11521, pp. 211–219, 2019.
https://doi.org/10.1007/978-3-030-23404-1_15

The attacks could come from malicious clients, which send faulty transactions and try to undermine the blockchain system. Peers could also conduct internal malicious behavior during the consensus process to diverge or break down the blockchain system. The complete analysis and experiments of the system performance with malicious behaviors are needed. In summary, we mainly have three contributions:

- We thoroughly analyze the impact of malicious behavior on the PBFT consensus mechanism.
- We design the malicious behavior patterns of the faulty replica and clients and test the performance on Hyperledger Fabric.
- Based on the analysis and experiments, we provide some sights on how to improve the system performance under attacks.

2 Related Work

2.1 Practical Byzantine Fault Tolerance

PBFT is a classic form of BFT state machine replication algorithm. The algorithm is designed to tolerate no more than f faulty replicas in an asynchronous network where $N = 3f + 1$ is the total number of replicas. It guarantees its safety by a three-phase consensus protocol: (1) **pre-prepare phase:** the primary receives request messages from clients and broadcasts pre-prepare messages. (2) **prepare phase:** when a backup replica receives and accepts the pre-prepare message, it then broadcasts the prepare message to other backups and also receives prepare messages from them. (3) **commit phase:** Once a replica collects $2f + 1$ prepare messages corresponding to its pre-prepare messages, it marks as prepared and multicasts commit messages. When it receives $2f + 1$ commit messages, it can conclude that all non-faulty replicas agree on the order of the requests across views. During each phase, if a replica does not receive enough messages to proceed to the next step before the timeout, it multicasts a view-change message. When the potential primary in the new view received $2f + 1$ view-change messages, it will multicast a new-view message to start a new view.

2.2 Hyperledger Fabric Architecture and Performance Evaluation

Hyperledger Fabric could run chaincode and support many programming languages. Fabric version 0.6 follows the traditional state-machine replication design and adopts the classic and native Practical Byzantine Fault Tolerance as consensus. Fabric then introduces a novel execute-order-validate paradigm in its version 1 [6]. The architecture and workflow of Fabric have some fundamental changes and Fabric version 1 introduces some new roles, such as endorsers, orderers and committers. Endorsers simulate transaction execution and provide writeset and readset. Orderers uses consensus to establish a total order of transactions and deliver blocks in sequence to committers, which update the world state.

There are some previous work on Hyperledger Fabric blockchain performance evaluation and benchmark frameworks. Blockbench [7] design different types of workloads to measure and understand performance at different layers on Fabric v0.6. Hyperledger Project also has an official benchmark tool Caliper [8], which provides metrics such as latency, throughput, and resource consumption on multiple Hyperledger blockchain frameworks including Fabric version 1, Sawtooth, Iroha and Burrow. Harish Sukhwani uses a Stochastic Petri Nets modeling formalism to model the workflow of Fabric and find critical steps which could be potential bottleneck for performance [9]. However, they did not consider the malicious behaviors and the consequences on blockchain performance. There are some other blockchain platforms with performance evaluation with malicious behavior. For example, in the Algorand blockchain [10], a particular attack strategy is proposed that the block proposer with the highest priority sends one kind of block to half of the replicas and another different block to the rest of replicas and evaluate the performance. Blockchains are designed to tolerate faults and there will be attacks targeted to them when they are practically used and involve real-world business.

3   Analysis of PBFT with Malicious Behaviors

Faulty replicas may intentionally delay messages, be not responsive, or multicast inconsistent messages to different groups of replicas. These behaviors undermine the system, especially when the faulty replica function as the primary, though view-change mechanism can restrict the malicious behaviors to some extent. Here, we analyze how the faulty replicas could undermine the network at their best efforts during each phase of PBFT consensus process and how their malicious behaviors could affect the performance.

When the primary is a non-faulty replica, since it only sends a unique type of request messages m, all the pre-prepare, prepare, and commit messages will correspond to this request. In this case, if faulty replicas send messages inconsistent with m, non-faulty replicas will simply ignore them. The faulty replicas can also delay messages or simply not reply them. The first pattern of malicious behavior is not to cooperate with the non-faulty primary and backups during the consensus process.

When the primary is a faulty replica, it can create different messages in each phase and send them arbitrarily. Each replica will receive particular messages specially designated by the primary. Other faulty replicas also know how these different messages are distributed and collude with the primary to send different messages to different groups of replicas.

As the faulty replicas want to keep the faulty primary's position to have a long-term impact on the system efficiency, the faulty replicas have to guarantee that no more than f replicas will send view-change message. Therefore, in the pre-prepare phase, the primary still has to send consistent pre-prepare messages to at least $f + 1$ non-faulty replicas. Likewise, at least $f + 1$ non-faulty replicas should be prepared and committed. In summary, in all phases, faulty replicas can decide which non-faulty replicas receive consistent messages (the number of those replicas is denoted as k).

Based on the analysis above, k cannot be less than $f + 1$ in any phase. In other word, $f + 1 \leq k \leq 2f + 1$. We denote the set of non-faulty replicas who receive enough consistent messages as set $\mathcal{N}_{pp}$, $\mathcal{N}_p$, $\mathcal{N}_c$ in pre-prepare, prepare, and commit phase respectively.

$$\mathcal{N}_c \subseteq \mathcal{N}_p \subseteq \mathcal{N}_{pp} \subset \mathcal{N} \tag{1}$$

The second pattern of malicious behavior is to keep some non-faulty replicas out of the normal consensus process.

When the primary is faulty, faulty replicas can delay the messages and make non-faulty replicas receive messages just before the timeout and it is called `delay attack`. Non-faulty backups rely on pre-prepare messages to trigger consensus process and have to wait for faulty replicas' messages to achieve a quorum. The third pattern of malicious behavior is to delay pre-prepare messages to trigger the consensus process late or delay prepare and commit messages to achieve a quorum late.

In the Fabric v0.6 implementation, the primary works in batch mode which means the primary creates a block with requests of batch size (500 by default) and multicasts pre-prepare message with the batch. Here, delaying pre-prepare messages means creating batches and sending pre-prepare messages at a low rate.

4   Denial-of-Service Attack

4.1   High-Rate Spam Transactions

In Fabric, malicious clients could flood the network with high-rate spam transactions by keep sending transactions to all peers. As malicious users may control many clients, they could also launch a distributed denial-of-service attack to exceed the capacity of blockchain.

When clients keep sending extremely high-rate transactions, message channels of peers are full of transaction messages and peers could not even receive critical consensus message. As a consequence, all peers are in frequent view-changes and could move forward.

4.2   Transactions with Infinite Loop

Clients could include an infinite loop in chaincode and send transactions to invoke the function with the infinite loop. When peers execute this kind of transactions, the execution will consume high usage of CPU. As a consequence, other normal transactions have limited CPU time to execute and the performance will severely degrade.

In Fabric version 1.0, the execute-order paradigm helps solve this problem. When the simulated execution time takes too much time, the endorsers stop execution and reply errors to clients. In this case, malicious clients cannot collect enough valid replies from endorsers and hence the malicious transactions will not undermine committers.

5   Performance Evaluation

5.1   Overall Experimental Setting

The experiments were performed on a cluster and each server has two 2.3GHz CPU, 4GB RAM, 100GB SSD and 1Gb/s Ethernet connections with Ubuntu 16.04. We employed the modules of sending requests and checking the block status from blockbench benchmark framework. To evaluate the consensus layer, we uses DoNothing workload in blockbench. The chaincode does nothing and simply returns so it would reflect more about the influence of malicious behavior in the consensus layer. For transactions with an infinite loop, we design a specific chaincode to execute infinitely with high CPU consumption. For non-faulty peers, we used the original code of Hyperledger Fabric. For faulty primary and backup peers, we modified the code to implement each mode of malicious behaviors.

5.2   Malicious Behavior in Consensus Layer

Design of Malicious Behavior Patterns. Here, we discussed multiple malicious behavior patterns. The quick dictionary for all conditions is summarized in Table 1. Case **N** is used to represent baseline comparison when there are no malicious behaviors.

A. We set the primary as a non-faulty replica. **A1.** The faulty backups do not reply to any message in any phases. **A2.** The faulty backups send arbitrary messages in the three phases.
B. We set the primary as a faulty replica but the faulty primary do not delay messages. We set $\mathcal{N}_c = \mathcal{N}_p = \mathcal{N}_{pp}$ where $|\mathcal{N}_c| = f + 1$. It means a set of $f + 1$ non-faulty replicas can receive consistent messages in all phases, while the rest of replicas will receive inconsistent messages from at least one phase.
C. We set the primary as a faulty replica and the faulty replicas conduct delay attacks. The primary and other faulty replicas could delay pre-prepare, prepare and commit messages before timeout. As we discussed in Sect. 4, the impact of delay attack is different when the faulty primary sends to part of the replicas and all of them.
C1. Faulty primary sends enough consistent messages to all replicas. In other words, $\mathcal{N}_c = \mathcal{N}_p = \mathcal{N}_{pp}$ where $|\mathcal{N}_c| = 2f + 1$. Delay attack has two modes.
C1-a. Faulty replicas delay messages in all three phases. After receiving the first prepare message from non-faulty replicas, faulty replicas wait for some time and then multicast prepare messages. After receiving the first commit messages, faulty replicas wait for some time and then multicast commit messages. After multicasting commit messages, the primary will wait for some time and then

create a batch and send pre-prepare message with it. The waiting time at each phase should be no more than timeout minus round-trip time so that non-faulty replicas could receive required messages in time. In all the experiments, the waiting time is set as 1 second which is the half of the view-change timeout.

C1-b. Faulty replicas delay prepare and commit messages as they do in **C1-a**. But the faulty primary creates batches and sends prepare messages normally. In other words, whenever the number of outstanding requests reaches the batch size or the batch timer reaches 0, the primary creates a batch for it. If clients send requests fast enough, the replicas may work on the consensus process for multiple blocks concurrently.

C2. Faulty primary sends enough consistent messages to part of the replicas. We set $\mathcal{N}_c = \mathcal{N}_p = \mathcal{N}_{pp}$ where $|\mathcal{N}_c| = f + 1$. For simplicity, faulty replicas do not send messages to the rest of non-faulty replicas. Delay attack also has two modes like **C1**.

C2-a. Faulty replicas delay messages in all three phases like **C1-a**.

C2-b. Faulty replicas delay only prepare and commit messages like **C1-b**.

Table 1. Malicious behavior patterns.

No faulty behavior			N	
Non-faulty primary	Not reply		**A1**	
	Arbitrary messages		**A2**	
Faulty primary	No delay attack		$\mathcal{N}_c = 2f + 1$	$\mathcal{N}_c = f + 1$
			N/A	**B**
	Delay attack	All phases	**C1-a**	**C2-a**
		Prepare & commit phase	**C1-b**	**C2-b**

Performance. The comparisons of throughput and latency metrics are shown in Figs. 1 and 2. Comparing with the baseline condition when there is no malicious behavior, the system achieved similar results on A1, A2, and B, because in all the four cases, there exist $2f + 1$ replicas working at their best efforts to achieve consensus. For C1-b, there are $2f + 1$ non-faulty replicas working and there is no delay for pre-prepare message. When the $2f + 1$ non-faulty replicas receive pre-prepare messages, they could work well without depending on the help of faulty replicas. Thus, the system can work properly with no obvious change in throughput and latency. For C1-a, there are also $2f + 1$ non-faulty replicas working. But the pre-prepare messages are delayed and are sent at a low fixed rate. In this case, the throughput is bounded by the rate of blocks and latency increases by the delay period of pre-prepare phase. Similarly, for C2-a and C2-b, the system delayed for each phase as there are only $f + 1$ non-faulty replicas working and they have to wait for faulty replicas' messages to achieve each step of consensus process, which leads to increased latency by the delay periods of all

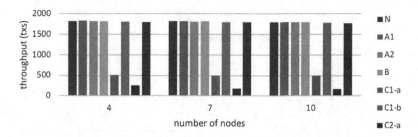

Fig. 1. Evaluation of throughput under multiple malicious behavior patterns.

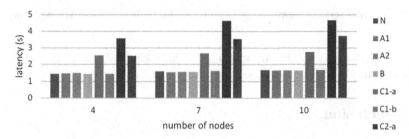

Fig. 2. Evaluation of latency under multiple malicious behavior patterns.

phases. For C2-b, as the system could work concurrently on consensus process of many blocks, the system efficiency can be guaranteed, although the time of committed the block will be delayed.

5.3   Attack of High-Rate Spam Transactions

For attacks of high-rate spam transactions in Fabric version 0.6, there are 10 peers and all of them are non-faulty. There are 5 clients and they try their best to utilize CPU and network bandwidth to send transactions to peers. The Fig. 3 shows the transactions committed per second with regard to time. During the first 58 s, the throughput is among 1200 transactions per second, which is much lower than the normal throughput, 1700 txs, shown in Fig. 1. At the 58th second, the throughput drops directly to zero. After checking the system log, the message channel of peers are full and peers reject any more message from each other, which causes all the peers to repeatedly send view-change.

5.4   Transactions with Infinite Loop

For attacks of Transactions with an infinite loop, specific chaincodes are written in go for both Fabric version 0.6 and version 1. The chaincodes for two versions are almost the same except some minor syntax. For both versions, there are 4 peers and all of them are non-faulty. The experiment result shows that in Fabric version 0.6 only two transactions could occupy all the CPU time. The normal transactions sent by clients are never executed or committed. In contrast, Fabric

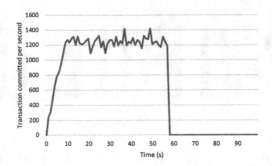

Fig. 3. Transaction committed per second under high-rate spam transactions.

version 1 performs well and are immune to these kinds of transactions because endorsers simply reject the transaction after seconds.

6   Conclusion

In this paper, we theoretically analyze the malicious behaviors in Hyperledger Fabric. We measure the blockchain performance under the designed faulty patterns. The results suggest that delay attack along with keeping some replicas out have a notable impact on the system performance. The malicious behaviors undermine the system most when the primary delay in all three phases and only sends enough consistent pre-prepare messages to $f + 1$ non-faulty replicas. For two kinds of denial-of-service attacks, Hyperledger Fabric version 0.6 fails in both cases and could not be available for normal clients. For Fabric version 1, the execute-order-validate paradigm helps resist attacks of transactions with an infinite loop. The result demonstrates the significance of performance analysis and evaluation under malicious behaviors. Future work would include other blockchain frameworks with different architectures and consensus protocols.

Acknowledgement. The work described in this paper was supported by the National Key Research and Development Program (2016YFB1000101).

References

1. Nakamoto, S.: Bitcoin: a peer-to-peer electronic cash system (2008)
2. Ethereum blockchain app platform. https://www.ethereum.org/
3. Hyperledger Fabric. https://www.hyperledger.org/projects/fabric/
4. Fabric version 0.6 source code. https://github.com/hyperledger/fabric/tree/v0.6
5. Castro, M., Liskov, B.: Practical Byzantine fault tolerance. In: Proceedings of the Third Symposium on Operating Systems Design and Implementation, pp. 173–186. USENIX Association (1999)
6. Androulaki, E., et al.: Hyperledger fabric: a distributed operating system for permissioned blockchains. In: Proceedings of the Thirteenth EuroSys Conference (2018)

7. Dinh, T., et al.: BLOCKBENCH: a framework for analyzing private blockchains. In: Proceedings of ACM International Conference on Management of Data, pp. 1085–1100. ACM (2017)
8. Hyperledger Caliper. https://www.hyperledger.org/projects/caliper
9. Sukhwani, H.: Performance modeling and analysis of Hyperledger Fabric (permissioned blockchain network)(2018)
10. Gilad, Y., et al.: Algorand: scaling byzantine agreements for cryptocurrencies. In: 26th Proceedings on Operating Systems Principles, pp. 51–68. ACM (2017)

Author Index

Printed in the United States
By Bookmasters